Also by Jason Vuic

*The Yugo: The Rise and Fall of the
Worst Car in History*

*The Sarajevo Olympics: A History of the
1984 Winter Games*

THE YUCKS!

TWO YEARS *IN* TAMPA
WITH THE
LOSINGEST TEAM
IN NFL HISTORY

JASON VUIC

Simon & Schuster
New York · London · Toronto · Sydney · New Delhi

SIMON & SCHUSTER
An Imprint of Simon & Schuster, Inc.
1230 Avenue of the Americas
New York, NY 10020

First Simon & Schuster hardcover edition August 2016

SIMON & SCHUSTER and colophon are trademarks of
Simon & Schuster, Inc.

For information about special discounts for bulk purchases, please contact
Simon & Schuster Special Sales at 1-866-506-1949
or business@simonandschuster.com.

The Simon & Schuster Speakers Bureau can bring authors to your
live event. For more information or to book an event, contact the
Simon & Schuster Speakers Bureau at 1-866-248-3049
or visit our website at www.simonspeakers.com.

Interior design by Paul J. Dippolito

Manufactured in the United States of America

10 9 8 7 6 5 4 3 2 1

Library of Congress Cataloging-in-Publication Data is available.

ISBN 978-1-4767-7226-4
ISBN 978-1-4767-7228-8 (ebook)

To Mila and Angel

Contents

Introduction   *1*

CHAPTER 1 The Promoter(s)   *11*

CHAPTER 2 The Suns of Beaches   *29*

CHAPTER 3 Ten Weeks of Two-a-Days   *55*

CHAPTER 4 The Aft Deck of the *Lusitania*   *85*

CHAPTER 5 Go for O!   *121*

CHAPTER 6 We Is the Champions!   *159*

*Epilogue: From the Yucks to the
Bucs and Back Again . . .*   *193*

Acknowledgments   *201*

Notes   *205*

Growing up, I was a huge Dallas Cowboys fan, but on Sundays we got Bucs games on TV. . . . Oh, I used to pray that lightning would come down and strike the tower so I could see the Cowboys. But it never did, so I had to watch the Bucs, "the Yucks" we called them, losing week after week.

—Warren Sapp, Hall of Fame defensive tackle,
Tampa Bay Buccaneers

THE
YUCKS!

Introduction

On Mount Olympus of futility, the [1976–77] Buccaneers are Zeus. . . . Take the 2008 Lions, the 1974–75 Capitals and the 1962 Mets and throw them into a bag. Then light it on fire. That's the Bucs.

          —James Irwin, *Washington Examiner*

About once a week, on NBC's famed *The Tonight Show,* comedian Johnny Carson played "Carnac the Magnificent," a turbaned and shawl-wearing mystic who answered questions, in sealed envelopes, by touching them to his forehead. The segment began when sidekick Ed McMahon introduced Carnac as "the Mystic from the East," and said with a grave voice, "I hold in my hand the envelopes. As a child of four can plainly see, these envelopes are hermetically sealed. They've been kept in a number two mayonnaise jar on Funk and Wagnall's porch since noon today." By this point, the audience, who knew the shtick, was laughing. "No one knows the answers to the questions inside these envelopes, but YOU, in your divine and mystical way, will ascertain the answers!" Carnac would nod and ask for silence. "The answer," he said, in one 1974 skit, "is bedbug. Bedbug." McMahon repeated the words while Carnac opened the envelope. He paused for effect. "Question: What would Republicans use to eavesdrop on a hooker?" The audience laughed. If they booed, Carnac threw them a curse: "May Dr. J slam-dunk your cat," he'd say, or "May your wife give mouth-to-mouth resuscitation to the Denver Nuggets."[1]

One recurring joke involved the Tampa Bay Buccaneers. In 1976, the National Football League's (NFL) newest expansion franchise lost every game, and by December 1977, it had lost twenty-six games in a row, an NFL record. Carson couldn't resist. Each night he told Bucs jokes in his monologue, and once, as the mystical Carnac, he provided this answer: "The *Titanic* and the Buccaneers." The question was "Name two disasters that were accompanied by band music." Referring to a well-known commercial in which the Pittsburgh Steelers tried, unsuccessfully, to destroy Samsonite luggage, Carson said the Bucs couldn't beat the bags. He began one show by saying, "What an opening! I haven't heard applause like that since the Tampa Bay Buccaneers sacked Fran Tarkenton in his hospital bed." Then, "I don't think the guys expected to win," he said. "I mean they trotted out on the field wearing leisure suits." Even David Brenner, Carson's substitute on *The Tonight Show*, opened with: "I can tell you're disappointed it's me tonight and not Johnny. It's like buying tickets to see the Oakland Raiders and having the Tampa Bay Buccaneers run out instead."

For a time, Carson was synonymous with the Bucs. In 1977, the *St. Petersburg Times* noted that Tampa Bay has "had no more caustic critic than Johnny Carson. Each defeat has brought new punch lines. Each shutout, a new chuckle."[2] Fans carried signs that read "Sack Johnny" and promised that someday, when the Bucs won, they'd scream so loudly that even he'd hear them in California. But Carson wasn't the only one. Everyone, and I mean everyone, goofed on the Bucs. Kids called them the "Yucks" and the "Sucks," and as the *New York Times* reported, Pam Pegg, a twenty-three-year-old teacher and Bucs cheerleader—a "swashbuckler"—had to change schools when students found out who she was.[3] Chuck Barris, the corny, absurdist host of TV's *The Gong Show,* who later claimed to be a CIA assassin, threatened to give contestants Tampa Bay tickets if they lost. Comedian Redd Foxx did a variety show skit in which he gave the team a halftime "pep talk," and Dwayne, the "Hey, Hey, Hey!" character from the TV show *What's Happening!!* developed a unique gambling system in which he unwisely picked the Bucs. (Rerun's uncle bet on the team and lost five hundred dollars.)

The low point, perhaps, was when Charles Nelson Reilly, the worst comedian in the history of, well, Earth, said: "My career has sunk so low I'm doing victory dinners for the Tampa Bay Buccaneers."[4] Victory dinners for the Tampa Bay Buccaneers. Dumb joke, but "that's how it worked," wrote one journalist. "The Bucs played. The Bucs lost. The nation laughed."[5] It laughed, in fact, through twenty-six straight games, nearly two full years of losing. The end came, mercifully, with an improbable 33–14 win in December 1977 at New Orleans. As Saints coach Hank Stram said before the game, "You know, sooner or later they're going to win one," and "you don't want it to be you."[6] Indeed, when the Saints lost to the Bucs, Saints owner John Mecom fired Stram, who said candidly, "We are all very ashamed of what happened. Ashamed for our people, our fans, the organization, everybody." This is the "worst experience of my coaching career." Said one Saints fan: "Eleven years I've supported this franchise! Eleven years! With all the money I've spent . . . I could have bought some land in Colombia and raised some pot."[7]

However, Bucs coach John McKay called it "the greatest victory in the history of the world," and was asked to appear—you guessed it—on *The Tonight Show*. Witty and acerbic as always and holding a five-foot-long cigar, McKay said no. "I'm not going all the way out there just to be on his show," he told reporters. "I was on the show once before and I was a star. Didn't you see me?"[8] Nevertheless, the Bucs' staff sent Carson a game ball, while the *St. Petersburg Times* organized a drive in which fans sent Carson thousands of "Bucs Sack Johnny" editions of the newspaper. A few days later, Carson, who'd been on vacation, opened with the Bucs. "Forget what's happening on the world scene," he said. "The big news is that the Tampa Bay Buccaneers finally won." The crowd roared its applause. "I understand that down there they had banners saying 'Sack Johnny' because of the jokes I've been making," but "I intend to continue." He then said that the Bucs had received a congratulatory note from President Richard Nixon (they hadn't—Nixon had left office and was living more or less in exile); that the Bucs had torn down the goalposts *during* the game; and that McKay hadn't really expected to win because he'd asked the team to "tie one for the Gipper." The jokes ended, finally, when Carson thanked McKay for the game ball, graciously, and said in the future, he'd be "behind the Buccaneers."

In the coming weeks, Carson referred to the Bucs just one more time, when Ed McMahon asked how Jimmy Carter was doing as president. "Well, let me put it this way," he said. "Tampa Bay won two more than he did." That was it; Carson's last Buccaneers joke. The next season the Bucs were 5-11, but had a better record than the Cincinnati Bengals, the San Francisco 49ers, and the Kansas City Chiefs. "That's when we realized," said Dick Crippen, the Bucs' former play-by-play announcer, "we weren't so unique anymore. We weren't so fun anymore. We were just bad."[9]

But really, how bad were the Bucs—I mean, the 0-26 1976–77 Bucs, the franchise with the longest losing streak in NFL history?[10] Let's do the math. In 1976, the Bucs were outscored 412 to 125. That's a per-game equivalent of 29 to 9. They were 28th in offense, 27th in defense, and were shut out 5 times. The team's first touchdown, ever, was a fumble return in week four. Its first passing touchdown was in week six, and even that was a "busted" running play in which running back Louis Carter was stopped on the goal line, but had the presence of mind to throw. The team's starting quarterback was Steve Spurrier. Yes . . . that Steve Spurrier, a career backup with the 49ers who had 7 touchdowns and 12 interceptions, and who was sacked 32 times. Louis Carter "led" the team in rushing; he had 521 yards and 1 touchdown. The Bucs' best receiver, Morris Owens, didn't play for the team until week three—he'd been cut by Miami and picked up on waivers—while the Bucs' two kickers were 8 for 18.

This was a terrible team, perhaps the worst team in the history of the NFL. In 2009, for example, the *Washington Examiner* offered this shameful tidbit: "On Mount Olympus of futility, the [1976–77] Buccaneers are Zeus. . . . Take the 2008 Lions, the 1974–75 Capitals and the 1962 Mets and throw them into a bag. Then light it on fire. That's the Bucs."[11] That same year, the nerds at SportSims.net, an online fantasy football company, hosted the "Stupor Bowl," in which history's worst teams played a "virtual" season of games. True to form, the 1976 Bucs went 4-12, the league's worst record, then lost 24–0 to the 1971 Buffalo Bills in the final. "I think this puts to bed any question about which team is the worst team of all time," said David Holt, a designer at SportSims.net.[12] But what did the Bucs think? What did John McKay think? Well, the Southern Cal legend once told the team: "If you play the best you can play, and they play their absolute worst, you'll still get blown off the field."[13] Err . . . thanks, coach.

Dubbed "Dial-a-Quote," by Philadelphia Eagles coach Dick Vermeil, McKay had a one-liner for everyone. "I loved his sense of humor," said Pat Toomay, a Bucs defensive end. "He was hilarious. . . . As long as it was directed out, it was a release. He disarmed a lot of people. But after a while, it started to turn in. Now and then, it got a little dark. During the week we didn't see him after the third game. He would stand farther and farther away at practice, symbolically disassociating himself."[14] McKay's most famous quote supposedly came after a reporter asked him, "What did you think about your team's execution?" To which he replied, "I'm in favor of it." Once, after a loss in college, McKay told his team there "were 700 million Chinese people who didn't even know the game was played." Unfortunately, "I got five letters from China asking 'What happened?'" The jokes were endless. "We didn't block real good, but we made up for it by not tackling," he said. "We've determined that we can't win at home and we can't win on the road. What we need is a neutral site." In 1983, toward the end of his career, McKay cut kicker Bill Capece during the season, telling reporters "Capece is kaput."[15] Doug Williams, the team's quarterback from 1978 to 1982, said "I don't think I've ever known anyone so direct. That cigar, that sucking on his teeth. People stayed out of John's way."[16]

Fans berated him. A common bumper sticker in Tampa read "Throw McKay in the Bay." Once, in the "Hot Line" section of a local newspaper, someone posted an ad: "Wanted—Coach and Football Team—Personnel with California Experience Not Wanted, Apply No. 1 Buc Place."[17] On another occasion, a disgruntled fan—shirtless, shoeless, and in shorts—ran into McKay's office to complain. "Things got so bad our family didn't go out for dinner," says Rich McKay, the son of John McKay and president of the Atlanta Falcons. "We just did the drive-through a lot. My mother even had to stop going to the grocery store. I went in undercover."[18] Rather than interact with the public, Steve Spurrier threw parties at his house. We "partied until the sun came up," says Barry Smith, a former receiver for the Bucs. "Then it was safe to go home."[19] The players believed, at least initially, that the Bucs had a chance. "I always felt we could win," said Richard "Batman" Wood, a linebacker who also played for McKay at USC. But then, "my first three years it was like, 'God, is it that hard to win?' . . . We had some outstanding people on that team. But it's a team game" and the team wasn't any good.[20]

Then there was Hugh . . . Hugh Culverhouse . . . Mr. C. . . . the Bucs' millionaire owner, a tax attorney from Jacksonville who was notoriously cheap. Culverhouse bought the team in 1974 for $16.2 million. He paid $4 million up front, and fans' season ticket payments were due two weeks before his payments were due. Good business, but as former Bears general manager Jerry Angelo put it, "Hugh was driven by the bottom line, not the goal line. . . . That was his philosophy and it permeated the organization."[21] Culverhouse gave each employee *one* season ticket. (Think about it . . . Who goes to a pro football game alone?)

According to one former player, a Bucs front office assistant qualified for welfare. The team's airplane was leased from the McCulloch Corporation, the chain saw people. There was a vending machine in the locker room that charged players for Cokes. Once, when a defensive back hurt his shoulder and trainers cut off his jersey to treat him, Culverhouse charged him for it. He billed roommates thirty-eight cents each for a seventy-five-cent phone call. In 1982, after quarterback Doug Williams had lifted the team from its 0-26 start and taken it to the playoffs three out of four years, he was the forty-second highest-paid quarterback in the league. There were twenty-eight teams. "Culverhouse was interested in one thing," wrote Williams, "and that was making money. I don't even think he cared about winning. I know he didn't care about his players. We were pieces of meat to him."[22]

A former boxer with a pockmarked face and a bulbous nose, Culverhouse proudly wore an orange Buccaneers blazer. The team's colors were orange, red, and white, with orange as the dominant color. Orange was supposed to represent Florida citrus, but the shade in question was ugly and, well, soft. Think walks on the beach at sunset, or Seals & Crofts singing "Summer breeze, makes me feel fine, blowing through the jasmine in my miiiiiiind." Fans called them the "Creamsicles." "The uniforms were already picked out by the time I got here," said John McKay. "I didn't give it too much thought until I saw our buses and said, 'My God, we're dressed just like that bus. That's not good.'"[23]

The crème de la crème, however, was "Bucco Bruce," the team's rakish, sexually indeterminate mascot who looked like a seventies Errol Flynn. Bruce was the brainchild of *Tampa*

Tribune cartoonist Lamar Sparkman, who seems to have felt very passionately that the Village People needed a pirate. He "was a curious chap who looked like Captain Hook's wayward brother," joked one journalist, "the one nobody in the Hook family talks about. Bruce is a long-haired, whimsical waif who wears an earring and a floppy hat topped by an ostrich plume. Sort of a Hedda Hopper/Barbara Stanwyck/Queen Mum look."[24] Oh, and did I mention he was winking? Well, he was.

However, Bucco Bruce was one thing; losing game after game after game was another. Because losing teams, even more than winning teams, reveal the intricate and at times strained relationship between cities, franchises, journalists, players, coaches, owners, and fans. If winning cures all ills, as they say, losing exacerbates them. Losing is personal. "I called out to God again and again," wrote Bucs offensive coordinator and devout Christian Joe Gibbs, who coached for the team in 1978. "'Why? What's going on here? Why is this happening? I believe you brought me to Tampa Bay—but for *this*?'"[25] Apparently, the team was so bad, losing so difficult, that Gibbs had questioned his faith. Gibbs could leave—he actually did, after just a single season in Tampa—but it was the fans who stayed.

With an average attendance in 1976 of just over 44,000, their numbers grew to nearly 53,000 in 1977, and to over 63,000 in 1978. Perhaps counterintuitively, the Bucs had lost twenty-six straight games, but somehow had gained fans. Clad in the ugliest of orange, some wearing "Go for O!" T-shirts or holding up signs at the ten-yard line that read "The Bucs Stop Here," they booed, threw trash at, mocked, teased, ridiculed, and—this is the crazy thing—actually embraced the Yucks. Why? Well, fans would say it's . . . uh, complicated: loyalty, community, masochism, boredom, a feeling that one day, someday, the Bucs would win. It's an attitude that's served them well. After all, the Bucs have had *twenty-seven* losing seasons in forty years. Needless to say, they all started with the Yucks.

Chapter One

The Promoter(s)

People always say: "Hey! You're the guy who brought the Bucs to Tampa!" And I say: "No. I helped bring a team to Tampa. I had nothing to do with the Bucs."

—Leonard Levy, Tampa booster

Bill Marcum was a promoter—not your smooth-talking, back-slapping, sell-anything-to-anyone type of promoter—but a promoter nonetheless. His product was football, professional football. The thirty-three-year-old's plan, in early 1967, was to bring his hometown something it had never seen before: a preseason exhibition game featuring two teams from the National Football League (NFL).[1] This was before the Bucs, before Tampa even had a stadium. A 46,000-seat, two-grandstand structure had been approved by local officials and was slated to open in November 1967, with a game between the University of Tennessee Volunteers and the University of Tampa Spartans.

In the meantime, the stadium's chief administrator, a local agency known as the Tampa Sports Authority (TSA), was looking for occupants. "The TSA was trying to justify the four million dollars it had spent to build that thing," remembers Marcum, a tallish University of Florida grad and former tennis star from Fort Myers, "so it focused on college games as a way of recouping its money." The University of Tampa would play home games there, but then the TSA hoped that Florida, Florida State, Miami, and Florida A&M would also play in Tampa at least once a year. The TSA had never even considered the NFL. "That was the bottom of the list," says Marcum. "That was literally the last thing in their minds when they built the stadium in the first place."[2]

But Marcum thought, "Why not?" Tampa was football crazy, and it was common in the 1960s for NFL squads to play preseason games, called "exhibition games," in even the smallest of cities. The rival American Football League (AFL) did it, too. There were games in Princeton, Ithaca, Bridgeport, New Haven, Norfolk, Rochester, Richmond, Raleigh, Morgantown, Tulsa, Wichita, Shreveport, Mobile, Memphis, Birmingham, and San Antonio, among others. Joe Namath's first pro touchdown was a 60-yard completion to Hall of Fame receiver Don Maynard in a 1965 preseason game in Allentown, Pennsylvania.[3] The games were almost always charity events, hosted by Boys Clubs or Rotary Clubs, and backed by Chambers of Commerce.

Marcum belonged to the Tampa chapter of the Junior Chamber of Commerce, the "Jaycees," and in 1966 he'd organized a Jaycee national tennis tournament at Tampa's University of South Florida. He'd done it for charity, for the fun of it; but then, in 1967, it occurred to Marcum that once Tampa finished its stadium, the Jaycees could bring an exhibition game to Tampa, too. So he bought an *NFL Handbook*, looked up the names and numbers of the league's general managers, and started calling.

His first call was to the Washington Redskins, which despite being a mediocre-to-bad team in 1966 was the most popular pro team in the South. The owner of the Redskins was George Preston Marshall, an infamous racist who created a Redskins radio and TV network that spanned Dixie and stretched as far south as Miami. In fact, in the years prior to 1966, when the Dolphins entered the AFL and Falcons the NFL, the Redskins were the only professional football team south of the Mason-Dixon Line. The price was sixty thousand dollars—thirty for Washington and thirty for the other team Marcum found, the Atlanta Falcons.

Sixty thousand dollars, "big bucks then," wrote *Tampa Tribune* sports editor Tom McEwen, a friend of Marcum's and early expansion supporter, but "chicken feed now."[4] To pay for the game, Marcum, who made maybe $12,000 a year as a sales engineer with General Cable, persuaded one hundred Jaycee members to sign personal guarantees of three hundred dollars each, with the rest, he hoped, coming through ticket sales. At Marcum's urging, the Jaycees called the game the Florida Suncoast NFL Classic, instead of the Tampa Classic, in order to attract fans from the surrounding communities of St. Petersburg, Bradenton, Clearwater, Lakeland, and Sarasota. Marcum told the club that Tampa alone couldn't support a game like this, but that the entire area could.

Indeed, as of 1967, the Tampa–St. Petersburg–Clearwater "metropolitan statistical area," a term used by the U.S. Census Bureau, was the thirty-first largest metropolitan statistical area in the United States. If you added Lakeland, Bradenton, and Sarasota, Tampa had a local population of more than one million people. The region, known colloquially as the "Suncoast," or simply the "Bay Area," was growing. Florida as a whole was growing as few American states or regions had ever grown before. Consider this: When Florida first entered the Union in 1822, there was no Miami. There was no Tampa, no St. Petersburg, and no Orlando, and everything south of St. Augustine was either forest or prairie land, or, of course, swamp. By 1900, in spite of a railroad boom and growth in the citrus, phosphate, timber, tobacco, fishing, and cattle industries, there were just 528,542 Floridians. Population-wise, the state was a tad bigger than Baltimore.[5]

It grew somewhat in the 1920s, but beginning in the 1950s, Florida boomed. Aided by cheap land and sunshine, a surging U.S. economy, an expanding interstate system, the GI Bill for veterans, and Social Security benefits for retirees, not to mention air-conditioning, the state's population grew 145 percent, to 6.7 million, between 1950 and 1970. It grew another 43.5 percent, to almost 10 million, by 1980. "In the half century after 1950," wrote Florida historian Gary R. Mormino, "the lure of retirement villages, beachfront condominiums, and trailer parks brought millions of new residents to the state, causing a chain reaction that resulted in new construction, landscaping, utilities, schools, highways, hospitals, and strip malls. To the question what does Florida do for a living? Modern history seemed to answer, Florida grows!"[6]

The unintended consequence was that no one was from there. By 2000, for example, more than half of Florida's residents had moved there since 1970.[7] And, in the five years preceding 1970, Florida had gained 1.4 million new inhabitants, including 189,446 New Yorkers, 83,347 Ohioans, 70,868 New Jerseyans, 67,813 Michiganders, and 60,715 Pennsylvanians. It also gained more than 184,000 foreign immigrants and 50,000 transcontinental "immigrants" from California.[8] Therefore,

The Promoter(s)

Bill Marcum was pitching his "Florida Suncoast NFL Classic" to a community, or, rather, a series of communities, in flux.

First, there was Tampa. A gritty industrial center at the confluence of upper Tampa Bay and the Hillsborough River, Tampa was founded in 1824 as a military fort during the decades-long conflict between the U.S. Army and Florida's Seminole Indian tribes known as the Seminole Wars. It survived as a fishing village until the 1880s, when a surveyor discovered phosphate deposits to the east of Tampa and the South Florida Railroad chose the city as its terminus. With lines running from Tampa to New York, the city then attracted Vicente Martinez Ybor (pronounced "E-bor"), a wealthy cigar manufacturer from Key West who moved his firm to an unincorporated plot of land immediately northeast of Tampa in 1886. This was "Ybor City." Other producers followed, including, among others, a young Cuban immigrant named Arturo Fuente, and by the early twentieth century, Tampa was the cigar capital of the world.

The Great Depression and the advent of mechanized cigar-rolling devastated Ybor City, but in 1939, the U.S. military established the Southeast Air Base in Tampa (a precursor to today's MacDill Air Force Base, home of the Pentagon's Central Command, whose area of responsibility includes Afghanistan and Iraq), and the city continued to grow. By 1950, it had 124,000 inhabitants, which more than doubled to 275,000 inhabitants by 1960. Yet, like other American cities, in the early postwar period Tampa experienced "white flight," the suburbanization of its white population to unincorporated planned communities in surrounding Hillsborough County. Despite the fact that in 1953 Tampa had annexed forty-four square miles of territory and more than 92,000 people, it had 611 fewer residents in 1970 than in 1960.[9]

Across the bay, and twenty-five miles by car southwest of Tampa, is St. Petersburg. Founded in 1888 when Russian aristocrat Peter Demens brought the Orange Belt Railway south from Longwood, Florida, to a mostly uninhabited stretch of the Pinellas Peninsula, St. Petersburg was a retirement mecca. Dubbed "Wrinkle City," "God's Waiting Room," or (even worse) "the place Mom and Pop go to die," St. Petersburg was one of the first retirement communities in the United States. For years, the city's symbol was a green park bench—for seniors to sit on—and by the late 1940s it had the largest shuffleboard club in the world.

In 1960, St. Petersburg had 181,298 inhabitants, whose median age was 47.1. Although in the 1960s civic leaders attempted to rejuvenate the downtown by removing green benches and redeveloping the waterfront district, by 1970 the city's 216,232 residents had actually grown older, to 48.1. In all, an astonishing 31 percent of St. Petersburg residents were sixty-five or older. Thus, with Tampa declining in population and St. Petersburg aging, the real growth was in the suburbs, in beachfront and inland communities in Pinellas County, such as Clearwater, in Bradenton and Sarasota to the south, and in unincorporated areas of north Tampa. "It was like the Wild West," says Betty Castor, a former Hillsborough County commissioner in charge of planning. "It didn't matter what it was—a house, a gas station, a condo—the thinking was, 'if you build it, they will come.'"[10]

And people did come, to three-bedroom, two-bath, ranch-style cinder-block-and-stucco homes in planned communities

The Promoter(s)

that appeared, seemingly, overnight. Typically, a developer would buy, say, fifty acres of land, a former farm or a citrus grove. Then he graded the land, gave it a made-up name such as "Seminole Hills," and divided the acreage into lots. At the edge of the property, preferably on a highway, the developer then built three model homes, with names like the "Colonial," the "Waldorf," or the "Rusticana." Then it was sell, sell, sell— often a hard sell, with television and radio spots as far away as New York, mailings, magazine ads, cold calls, "Win a Week in Florida" contests, and tours.

Some developments, built by corporations, were huge. In 1967, for example, the Deltona Corporation acquired more than 21,000 acres of uninhabited land forty miles north of Tampa in Spring Hill. In the blink of an eye, the company staked out more than 33,000 lots. It then sold 28,500 lots in three years.[11] Needless to say, the region's planned communities are too numerous to mention, but here's a tiny list: Carrollwood, Carrollwood Village, Winston Plaza Estates, Bay Ridge Estates, Lake Magdalene Arms, Four Oaks, Town N' Country Park, River Grove Park, Paradise Park, Westgate, East Bay, New Port, Tierra Verde, and Sun City Center. Now add thousands of apartments, built at twice the rate of houses, and nearly three hundred trailer parks in Pinellas alone.[12]

Although experts predicted that in fifty years, the one-hundred-mile region from Clearwater in the north to Punta Gorda in the south would be "Onecontinuouscity," the Bay Area's dozen or so communities proved stubbornly distinct.[13] For one, Tampa and St. Petersburg were rivals. They had been since the early 1900s, when a passionate *St. Petersburg Times* editor named W. L. Straub led an editorial campaign to "free" Pinellas from Hillsborough. (The two officially split in 1912.) Since then, they'd fought over *everything*, from railroad lines, military bases, and airports to bridges, highways, water treatment systems, pollution restrictions, state university campuses, even shrimp.

Tampa and St. Petersburg were so antagonistic that prior to the 1970s neither city actually embraced the term "Tampa Bay." The "Bay" was a body of water—a huge body of water—but it wasn't a locale. No one was *from* Tampa Bay. No one *lived in* Tampa Bay. And, if you asked residents if they were from there, they would have told you, invariably, "I am not fish!" "Of all the 1950s and '60s travel brochures in the Tampa Bay History Center," explains Travis Puterbaugh, the museum's former Curator of Collections and Research, "I cannot recall ever seeing any that explicitly referred to this area as Tampa Bay."[14]

Still, the Bay Area was a clearly identifiable region, a sprawling collection of Florida Gulf Coast communities whose capital, unofficially, was Tampa. Home to the region's only Fortune 500 company, the Jim Walter Corporation, a home builder; the Lykes Brothers meatpacking and citrus conglomerate; regional offices of GTE, Westinghouse, Honeywell, General Cable, and Metropolitan Life; Busch Gardens; the University of South Florida; the University of Tampa; and MacDill, it was Florida's busiest port. It also had a glistening new airport and, by 1968, a stadium.

"When we promoted that first game," says Marcum, "the stadium had just opened. It'd been open for less than a year. The Bay Area was booming, but it never occurred to me we'd get a team in Tampa. I mean our own team. I just wanted to sell tickets."[15] But, in promoting the Florida Suncoast NFL Classic, Marcum frequently stated, rather coyly, that "nothing impresses" the NFL more than "a good crowd."[16] He figured that at five dollars a ticket, roughly $34.00 in today's terms, he needed to sell nineteen thousand tickets to break even. By July, he'd sold twenty thousand tickets, and was told by the general managers of Washington and Atlanta that, as a rough estimate, he should multiply by two.

If that was the case, the Florida Suncoast NFL Classic would draw 40,000 people, the largest preseason crowd at a neutral site in the NFL that year. This was big news, bigger than anything Marcum had expected, and bigger than anything anyone in Tampa had expected, either. When the teams met on August 10, 1968, there were 41,651 fans in attendance. Wrote one journalist, the crowd "cared less about the caliber of play than about the reality that was unfolding. The NFL had anointed Tampa" and "never was such a meaningless preseason game so momentous to a community."[17]

The next day, local attorney Ed Rood, a former Florida Jaycee president and Tampa power broker, called Tom McEwen at work. Rood was interested in bringing an NFL franchise to Tampa, and asked McEwen for help forming the Suncoast Pro Football Committee, a nonprofit association tasked with winning a team. McEwen, a forty-five-year-old University of Florida grad, was more than a sports editor. He was a fixer, a doer, a civic-booster-cum-journalist who used his position at the *Tribune*, critics be damned, to put Tampa on the map. He was, in his own words, an "advocate," a cheerleader, a person who not only wrote about sports, but also "introduced the right people to each other."[18] In 1969, Tom McEwen introduced Ed Rood to Pete Rozelle.

———

An amiable, forty-two-year-old public relations expert and onetime general manager of the Los Angeles Rams, Rozelle had been NFL commissioner since 1960. His singular talent—if it could be called a talent—was getting the league's twelve disparate teams to buy into the concept of "League Think." By "League Think," Rozelle meant "unity of purpose," a plan by which NFL owners would share revenues and transform what had been "a feudal organization" of twelve distinct businesses "into a modern corporate combine."[19] The key was television. In 1961, Rozelle persuaded the league's owners to pool their television rights into a single, national package that quickly earned the NFL $4.65 million, or $320,000 per franchise, for the 1962 season.[20]

By 1964, CBS was paying the NFL $14.1 million a year, an amount, wrote one author, that was "ten times more than anyone in the league had made" under previous commissioner Bert Bell.[21] However, Rozelle wasn't finished. In 1966, he persuaded Congress to grant the NFL a coveted antitrust exemption, which allowed the NFL to merge with the AFL in a single, twenty-four-team league. As part of the merger, Rozelle promised two new expansion teams by 1968—the New Orleans Saints and the Cincinnati Bengals—and possibly two additional teams by 1970. The NFL had sixteen teams, the AFL ten teams, and they were slated to merge and begin playing each other in the fall of 1970.

The "new" NFL would have two thirteen-team conferences: the National Football Conference, made up of old NFL teams, and the American Football Conference, made up of ten AFL teams plus three. Rozelle's job was to persuade three NFL owners to switch. He'd been trying for months, and couldn't negotiate the league's new television contracts until both conferences were in place. "Bulwarked by half a century of tradition," wrote the *New York Times,* and "satisfied with the status quo," NFL owners feared that "any juggling could disrupt" traditional rivalries. "No one has dropped the ball yet," it continued, "but Pete is getting nervous."[22] Eventually, in May 1969, the Cleveland Browns, the Pittsburgh Steelers, and the Baltimore Colts agreed to join the AFC for a one-time compensation payment of $3 million each.

As for Rozelle, the commissioner told the two Tampans that expansion was possible, but because of "realignment issues" he would not give them a date. He did say, though, that to land a franchise, cities needed three things: 1) a market area big enough to support pro football, 2) a 50,000-seat stadium, and 3) proven interest, attendance-wise, in preseason exhibition football. Tampa had all of those things: a large population base, a stadium it could expand if it wanted to, and the fact that Marcum's Washington-Atlanta matchup had been the league's most-attended neutral-site exhibition game that year. What Tampa now needed was another game, or even a series of games, to show the league it was ready.

Therefore, shortly after Rood and McEwen met with Rozelle in New York, Bill Marcum contacted several professional teams, including the Miami Dolphins. The Dolphins were owned by Joe Robbie, an attorney from Minneapolis who told Marcum he could bring the Vikings to Tampa, in a matchup with the Dolphins, for $40,000 apiece. Marcum agreed, but then asked Robbie for a second, regular season, game as well. When Robbie offered a Dolphins matchup with either the Denver Broncos or the Boston Patriots, Marcum chose the Patriots, because

Boston owner Billy Sullivan was unhappy with the Patriots' stadium situation and was exploring a move to Tampa.

Although already committed to $160,000 in contracts, Marcum still hadn't told the Jaycees. He was about to, he says, but then Washington called and offered a third game with Detroit, which he accepted. "That's when I told the club what I'd done," explains Marcum. "But you know what? They balked. They'd stuck their necks out in '68," with the Redskins-Falcons game, "but now I had *three* games for $240K. For a nonprofit service organization, even a rich one, that was way too much money." Still, the Jaycees did sponsor the Redskins-Lions matchup of August 1969, but the two other matchups were on Marcum. "It's funny," he says, "I'd never planned on doing it, but there I was, a professional promoter."[23]

A divorced father of two, Marcum hadn't anticipated a career change. But, if the games sold well, he stood to make as much as $40,000 a contest, way more than he'd ever made in a year. Luckily, Marcum found a backer in Ed Rood, who covered the teams' appearance fees for 25 percent of the profits. Of course, the men wanted to make money, but in promoting pro football, as Jaycee members and boosters, they were helping the city grow. And with a new stadium opening in 1967 and three massive projects—including a state-of-the-art terminal at Tampa International Airport; a second, fourteen-mile span of the Sunshine Skyway Bridge connecting St. Petersburg and Bradenton; and a new deepwater port in south Tampa Bay known as Port Manatee—all slated to open in 1971, it seemed that no project was too big or too small, including professional football.

Therefore, in February 1969, Rood, Marcum, and McEwen

The Promoter(s)

hosted AFL commissioner Milt Woodard, who played golf with
Rood at Tampa's Palma Ceia Country Club, had lunch with the
mayors of Tampa and St. Petersburg, and toured Tampa Stadium. By now, Rood's Suncoast Pro Football Committee had
more than twenty members, including the Chamber of Commerce heads of Tampa, St. Petersburg, and Clearwater, the sports
editors of various radio and TV stations, and the publishers of
both the *Tampa Tribune* and the *St. Petersburg Times*. In 1970,
the committee vowed to underwrite, and thus guarantee the
sale of, thirty-five thousand season tickets if the Patriots moved
to Tampa. It also hired Woodard as a consultant, and convinced
Florida governor Claude Kirk to visit Sullivan in Boston.

The committee's goal was to land a pro franchise by either
relocating a preexisting team to Tampa, such as the Patriots,
or by winning a new team when the league voted to expand.
To that end, it flirted with Boston and Buffalo in 1970, then,
the following year, convinced Baltimore Colts owner Carroll
Rosenbloom to hold his 1972 preseason camp in Tampa while
playing three exhibition games at Tampa Stadium. At the time,
Rosenbloom was in a bitter dispute with Baltimore over im-
provements to Memorial Stadium, a cramped, aging facility that the Colts shared with the Orioles. Rosenbloom liked
Tampa, a lot, but in June 1972 managed to escape Maryland by
trading the Colts for the Rams.

The process was simple. The Rams' owner was Dan Reeves,
a football visionary who died of cancer in 1971 but who had
tasked his estate with selling the team. There were several suit-
ors, including Jacksonville attorney Hugh Culverhouse and Illinois heating and cooling magnate Robert Irsay. In June 1972,
Culverhouse bid $17.5 million, and was close to acquiring the

23

franchise when Rosenbloom and Irsay struck a deal.[24] Rosenbloom would give Irsay $4 million if he purchased the Rams—Irsay bid $19 million—and traded the Rams for the Colts. However, Culverhouse claimed that he and Rams general manager Bill Barnes had reached a verbal agreement, and in July 1972 he filed two different lawsuits against Rosenbloom, Rozelle, Irsay, the executors of the Reeves estate, the Rams, the Colts, and the NFL for contractual interference and violation of federal antitrust laws.[25]

Although unknown in football circles, Culverhouse was a formidable foe. Short, thickly built, with a round, misshapen nose, the fifty-three-year-old Culverhouse was "a pudgy Jimmy Durante."[26] He grew up poor in Birmingham, Alabama, during the Depression, the son of a train company engineer. In the late 1930s, Culverhouse attended the University of Alabama, where he was a member of the school's boxing team and a friend and sparring partner to future governor George Wallace. He graduated in 1941 with a business degree, served in the Army Air Corps during World War II, then returned to Alabama for a law degree in 1947.[27] From 1949 to 1956, Culverhouse was the assistant regional counsel for the Internal Revenue Service, Southeast Region, and was stationed in Jacksonville. His job was to research and prosecute tax evasion cases involving organized crime figures like Miami "bolita king" Howard Pinder. He was also a key investigator for the Kefauver Committee, the U.S. Senate's famed investigatory committee that targeted organized crime.[28]

However, in 1956, Culverhouse left the IRS to set up a Jacksonville firm specializing in tax law. Soon he had a branch office in Miami, where his clients included Richard M. Nixon and

The Promoter(s)

Nixon's close friend and associate C. G. "Bebe" Rebozo, as well as Ed Ball, the legendary Florida power broker who headed the DuPont estate. Case by case and hour by billable hour, Culverhouse became one of the richest men in Florida. "Hugh takes a piece of everything that crosses his desk," said one associate, "and more stuff crosses his desk than anyone I've ever seen."[29] In 1970, he paid $12 million for "Palmer Ranch," a massive, 12,500-acre stretch of Sarasota County, Florida, which he subdivided and seeded with homes. He also owned a bank, a department store, an insurance company, a mortgage company, and various commercial properties from Florida to Ohio.

His next project was the Rams, or, rather, suing the Rams (and the league) for $11 million. He probably wouldn't have won, but due to the league's 1966 antitrust exemption, wrote Culverhouse biographer Denis Crawford, any lawsuit claiming collusion by owners would have attracted "a suspicious congressional eye."[30] Thus, to placate Culverhouse, sometime in spring 1973, Rosenbloom approached the lawyer with a deal: if Culverhouse dropped the two lawsuits, he'd receive a monetary settlement, as well as one of two new franchises when the league voted to expand. Culverhouse accepted the deal, grudgingly, believing that whatever franchise he did receive would be in Tampa. But Tampa wasn't a lock. It faced stiff competition from Seattle and Memphis, while Phoenix was closing fast.

In fact, in September 1972, Bill Marcum and Leonard Levy, a Tampa printer and former head of the Tampa Sports Authority, joined officials from each of the three cities in petitioning Pete Rozelle. Tired of waiting, they wanted to know when the league would expand. Reluctantly, the commissioner agreed to a meeting in New York, in secret, but when word leaked to the press, he sent NFL executive director Jim Kensil instead. Speaking for the group, Memphis representative Mike Lynn asked Kensil if expansion was going to be discussed at the next owners' meeting. Kensil replied that he didn't know. The owners had to request it. "Well then, how many have to request it?" asked Marcum. To which Kensil replied, "One."

"We had no idea," insists Marcum. "If we'd read the damned NFL bylaws, we would have known that, but we hadn't. Any owner could bring up anything at a league meeting if he put it on the agenda maybe a week or two in advance."[31] Leonard Levy says this was "technically true," but that "getting the league to tell us anything was like cat-and-mouse. Rozelle would say, 'I don't make the agenda, the owners do.' Then we'd go to the owners and they'd say, 'We don't make the agenda, Rozelle does.'"[32]

The solution, the boosters realized, was to locate at least one pro-expansion owner, while pulling strings politically to force the commissioner's hand. Therefore, on the way home from New York, the two Tampans stopped in Washington, D.C., to visit Florida senator Ed Gurney, a member of the Senate Subcommittee on Anti-Trust and Monopoly who was pressuring the league to expand. Gurney felt that since Congress had granted the NFL an extremely valuable—and some would say legally questionable—antitrust exemption, it should have already added new teams. Therefore, Gurney wrote Rozelle a letter, reminding the commissioner that if expansion didn't happen, the league's antitrust exemption could be reexamined and possibly revoked.

Soon after, Bill Marcum visited Lamar Hunt, the Kansas City Chiefs' owner and oil tycoon, who had cofounded the

AFL. Hunt was in favor of expansion. In 1958, he had tried to buy an NFL expansion franchise himself, but was rebuffed, and a year later his offer to purchase the Chicago Cardinals and move them to Dallas was turned down. The oilman understood Tampa's plight, so he invited Marcum to a meeting at Dallas's downtown Petroleum Club, where he admitted, candidly, that the league owed Marcum an answer. Hunt would see to it that a simple yes-or-no vote was on the next owners' agenda.

The tactic worked, apparently, because in April 1973, at Hunt's request and Gurney's urging, league owners took up the issue and voted unanimously to expand. Under Rozelle's direction, the owners then formed a four-person "Expansion Committee" headed by Steelers vice president Dan Rooney, who in turn hired the Stanford Research Institute to produce a detailed study of twenty-four different cities that had expressed interest in landing a team.[33] The committee was to meet, examine potential sites, and name five finalist cities in February 1974. They were Memphis, Honolulu, Phoenix, Seattle, and Tampa.

The official announcement came on April 24, 1974, in Suite 404 of Manhattan's Drake Hotel. At exactly 5 p.m., Rozelle walked into the room. He took a chair in the front, which he turned around backward and straddled. He then leaned forward and said: "The National Football League has voted to expand to Tampa, Florida, and to at least one other city to be chosen later this year. The teams will be ready for the 1976 season. The franchises will cost $16 million. Are there any questions?" The room erupted. "Hallelujah," said Bill Marcum. "Hallelujah." Rozelle then shook hands with Leonard Levy and said, magnanimously, "Welcome to the NFL."[34]

Chapter Two

The Suns of Beaches

You're the second owner I've welcomed in three months,
Mr. Culverhouse. That's OK. I'm the fourth mayor Tam-
pa's had in eight months!

—Bill Poe, Tampa mayor

In April 1974, the month Bill Marcum and other Tampa boosters successfully convinced the NFL to award the city a franchise, the Bay Area was a mess. This was the era of Watergate,
the OPEC oil embargo, and the end of the war in Vietnam. Elvis
was alive, having recently performed his "Aloha from Hawaii
via Satellite" concert, but Jimi Hendrix and Janis Joplin were
dead. As a culture, America had veered away from the 1960s, a
period of promise and tumult if there ever was one, and into a
decade of decline. Racked by a stagnant economy brought on
by high oil prices, a stock market crash, and a recession, the
region that had wowed the NFL with its jaw-dropping growth
statistics quickly began to retract. Historians called it a "malaise," a "time of testing for Americans," in which many "came
to fear that the nation had lost its ability to master its problems."[1] Indeed, if you went to the theater in 1974, when tickets
cost $1.80, three of the year's most popular films were disaster
films—*The Towering Inferno, Earthquake,* and *Airport '75*—while

a surprise hit was the world-gone-mad Charles Bronson vigilante flick *Death Wish*.

Although Joni Mitchell's soft-rock album *Court and Spark* was the number-one album for 1974, somehow music had gotten harder, and angrier, and had formed, by this point, a stand-alone industry genre known as hard rock. In quick succession, America saw debut albums by Aerosmith (1973), Kiss (1974), Rush (1974), Bad Company (1974), Ted Nugent (1975), and AC/DC (1976), plus Pink Floyd's *Dark Side of the Moon* (1973) and Led Zeppelin's *Houses of the Holy* (1973). In fact, in May 1973, during a thirty-three-concert, thirty-city American tour, Led Zeppelin sold out Tampa Stadium, setting records for attendance (56,800) and gross receipts ($309,000) in what to that point was the largest single-act concert in American history. Although singer Robert Plant remarked that Tampa was the last place he'd ever expected to see a crowd of that size, for Bay Area boosters the 1973 Led Zeppelin concert was terrific news, more proof that residents there could support big-time entertainment, be it a rock show by a headliner or preseason exhibition football.[2]

Nevertheless, by spring 1974, almost all of the region's other economic indicators were bad—and getting worse. In St. Petersburg, for example, the value of construction permits, a measure of vitality in a growth-based economy, dropped 67 percent, from $127.5 million in 1973 to $41.6 million in 1974. In that same period, Tampa's permits dropped 52 percent, from $141.9 million to $68.5 million.[3] With construction down, the Bay Area depended that much more on tourism, but in 1974, the number of auto tourists, who made up 75 percent of all Florida tourists, declined 18 percent—24.3 percent in

Pinellas alone.[4] The resulting effect on the region's labor market was profound. Within a year, the area's unemployment rate jumped from 4.3 percent in March 1974 to a whopping 10.1 percent in 1975. The rate was so high, in fact, that the U.S. Labor Department officially designated Tampa–St. Petersburg–Clearwater as "an area of substantial unemployment," making it eligible for federal aid.[5] And, finally, a 1974 survey of consumer confidence found that Tampa residents had the "gloomiest" outlook in the nation, gloomier even than residents of Baltimore, Cleveland, or Detroit.[6]

With the economy down epically, the Bay Area's other, long-standing fissures began to show, including environmentally harmful land use due to lax building restrictions and codes, overcrowding, pollution, crime, and conflicts between local governments over water. With a population expected to total 3.5 million by 2000, the Bay Area already had air pollution levels that were as bad as Los Angeles.[7] The culprit in 1975 was TECO, the Tampa Electric Company, whose Big Bend power plant in Apollo Beach released more than 400 million pounds of sulfur dioxide, a poisonous by-product of using fossil fuels for energy production, into the air.[8] Next door to TECO in Gibsonton was TECO's sister polluter, the Gardinier phosphate processing plant, which gave the Bay Area its unsightliest feature: three 180-foot-high mountains of "mildly" radioactive phosphogypsum, a powdery waste product from the manufacture of fertilizer. Weighing perhaps 80 million tons each, and capped by holding ponds full of millions of gallons of sludge, the mountains towered over the bay "like environmental swords of Damocles," and reportedly leaked radium 226 into the water.[9]

Pollution by bad corporate actors was one thing; pollution by 1.5 million Bay Area residents who'd overrun the region's most basic sewage facilities was another. Each year, 22 billion gallons of sewage effluent, some of it treated, some of it untreated, flowed into Tampa Bay. Not only was the bay dirty in terms of liquid waste, but each year 24.9 million pounds of organic matter, including 10 million pounds of "suspended solids," sank to the bottom.[10] This led to algae blooms, which poisoned fish in periodic mass-kill episodes known as "red tides." In 1971, after one such episode, Bay Area marine patrol crews, assisted by prison laborers, collected 54 tons of decayed fish carcasses in two days.[11]

These were deplorable conditions, but in April 1974 the region finally received some good news: NFL owners had chosen Tampa for its twenty-seventh team. The response throughout the Bay Area was joy—joy mixed with relief. This is a "big league opportunity," wrote the *St. Petersburg Times*. "With so many population centers searching almost frantically for pollution-free industries and with many hobbled by a Watergate-era civic torpor, Tampa's winning bid for a National Football League team comes as both an economic and morale-boosting coup."[12] The question now was, who'd be the owner?

———

As of April 1974, there were fifteen potential candidates bidding for ownership, a group that included Hugh Culverhouse, Fort Lauderdale furniture magnate Harry Mangurian, and Philadelphia construction firm owner Tom McCloskey. Insiders believed Mangurian was the favorite. Since 1971, he'd maintained a potential-franchise ownership group called Suncoast

Pro Football, Ltd., whose members included various Bay Area business leaders as well as Bill Marcum. Mangurian hoped that, if awarded the franchise, he could use Marcum's promotional acumen to sell tickets. Marcum had already organized thirteen different games in Tampa, and had a computerized list of the names and addresses of every person who'd bought ticket packages from him, perhaps thirty thousand in all. As compensation, Mangurian promised Marcum 10 percent of the franchise.

Nevertheless, when league owners met in October 1974, they split almost evenly into a Mangurian group and a Culverhouse group, and chose as a compromise candidate Tom McCloskey.[13] Given the circumstances, the builder was a decent choice. During World War II, his father had owned a shipyard in Tampa, while his firm, McCloskey & Company, had built Tampa's First Financial Tower and its Bayshore Diplomat condominium. In addition, McCloskey had played football at the University of Pennsylvania, owned an NASL soccer franchise, and in 1968 had tried, unsuccessfully, to purchase the Philadelphia Eagles. The league liked him, as did most Tampa officials, but when McCloskey was awarded the franchise, Bill Marcum was distraught. After all, the 10 percent stake Mangurian had promised him was worth $1.6 million. Twenty years later, when Malcolm Glazer purchased the Bucs, that same 10 percent was worth $19.2 million.

The other loser was Hugh Culverhouse. The Jacksonville attorney believed that if and when a franchise was awarded, that franchise would be his. However, the owners believed that as part of the settlement Rosenbloom had brokered, they'd be giving Culverhouse *a* franchise, not specifically the *Tampa* franchise. So instead, in October 1974, the owners offered the attorney Seattle. The Washington State metropolis had been awarded a franchise in June and was slated to enter the NFL, along with Tampa, in 1976. Although no owner admitted it, it is possible the league was punishing Culverhouse for his earlier lawsuit with the Rams. But, if Culverhouse had had "dibs" on Tampa, legally, then he definitely would have sued. He didn't. Instead, he pitched Seattle to his wife, Joy, a native Southerner, but since she had no interest in moving from Jacksonville to the Pacific Northwest, Culverhouse declined.[14]

In the meantime, Tampa's expansion was a farce. McCloskey debuted as the new owner during a visit to the city in November 1974, but stumbled through a press conference in which he struggled to answer even the simplest of questions. At one point, he looked down from the press box and said, "I see you have real grass and not artificial turf down there."[15] It was odd, observers noted, that he didn't know that beforehand. "His heart wasn't in it," said Leonard Levy. "He was going through a divorce and couldn't buy the team while that was up in the air, and the capital he needed was tied up in the family business. Rumor was the McCloskey family wasn't entirely on board."[16] However, according to author David Harris, McCloskey's lack of preparation may have been the result of something else entirely. In his 1986 book, *The League: The Rise and Decline of the NFL*, Harris cites an anonymous source who claimed McCloskey had been a proxy candidate "thrown in place momentarily to conceal the deal Rosenbloom and Rozelle had cut with Culverhouse back in 1972."[17]

It's difficult to prove this claim, but in late November 1974 McCloskey backed out of the purchase and the franchise went to Culverhouse. The price was $16 million, plus $100,000 for a share of NFL Properties, and $100,000 for a share of NFL Films. Culverhouse put $4 million down, and promised to pay $2 million a year for six years at a nominal rate of interest. He brought on three co-owners: Marvin Warner, a fellow Alabama grad and financier from Cincinnati who grew up with Culverhouse in Birmingham; Hulsey Lokey, the chairman of Host International, an airport hotel and food conglomerate who had served with Culverhouse in the army; and John Jennings, a business acquaintance of Carroll Rosenbloom from Detroit. Culverhouse owned 51 percent, Warner, 48 percent, and Lokey and Jennings less than 1 percent each.

On December 7, 1974, Culverhouse held a brunch and press conference at CK's revolving restaurant at the top of Tampa's Host Airport Hotel. "Brunch with Hugh was a classy affair," wrote Tom McEwen. "Bloody Marys for the few who chose to partake, followed with assorted delectable hors d'oeuvres served by good-looking waitresses before the courtly Culverhouse took over the mike."[18] With confidence and panache, Culverhouse greeted the press, and at just the right moment had the rotating restaurant stopped so attendees could look at Tampa Stadium and its "fine, emerald green, well-tended grass."[19] He then took questions. No, he hadn't named the team and he didn't have a mascot. He hadn't decided if he'd hire a pro coach or a college coach, and he didn't have a GM. He had no idea how he'd stock the team, nor what division it would be in, but he wanted "a strong rivalry" with the Miami Dolphins. As to whether he'd met Bill Marcum, Culverhouse said yes, he'd met the promoter, and hoped there was a job for Marcum somewhere in the organization.[20]

The Yucks!

There was, as its director of marketing, and in January 1975, Marcum was the first person Culverhouse hired. His second hire was a "blue ribbon" advisory committee whose members included, among others, Leonard Levy, the publishers of both the *Tampa Tribune* and the *St. Petersburg Times,* and Dick Pope, the president of Cypress Gardens. In February, the committee met in a private room on the top floor of the downtown Exchange Building to select both a name and color scheme for the team. Dick Pope suggested that in honor of Florida's citrus industry, the team use orange as its dominant color. The committee agreed, then chose as its secondary colors teal and white. Apparently, no one in the room realized that orange, aqua, and white were the team colors of the Miami Dolphins. The NFL did, however, so when Culverhouse released the scheme to the press, he was told to change it. Luckily, Levy was a printer. He brought a color palette to the committee's next meeting and suggested orange, red, and white. The orange he proposed was soft, a tangerine color used by the Miami Floridians of the American Basketball Association. With some tinkering over the tint, the league announced the new colors in June 1975.

The next item was the team name. A local radio station, WFLA, sponsored a name-the-team contest, and more than six hundred names were submitted to the committee. They "ran from A to Z," said one member. Many were "in the bird and fish area, things like Barracudas and Sea Gulls. Several people have suggested Americans because the team is beginning operations in the Bicentennial year. And there were some interesting ones, too, like Godfathers, Aquanuts, Florida Fruits, and Tampa Suns of Beaches. No kidding. That's what it said."[21]

The committee's most popular submission was "Buccaneers," a name long associated in Tampa with José Gaspar, a legendary though fictitious pirate who was said to have raided Spanish Florida in the eighteenth century.

The word *buccaneer* is an English version of the French word *boucanier*, a hunter of cows and pigs on the island of Hispaniola (today Haiti and the Dominican Republic) who would cure meat on a wooden frame called a *boucan*. Many buccaneers became pirates and attacked ships traveling through the Gulf of Mexico from bases on the Florida coast. Each year, Tampa celebrated Gaspar as the "last of the Buccaneers" during its "Gasparilla Festival," a Mardi Gras–like celebration during which civic leaders in pirate costumes invaded the city by boat. For a Tampa-based team, the name *Buccaneers* "just seemed right," says Leonard Levy. "The committee looked at the submissions and chose Buccaneers because it had such strong connotations locally. But, what we also liked was that the name was alliterative. It was inclusive. You didn't say 'Tampa Bucs.' It wasn't just Tampa's team. It was the Bay Area's team. You said Tampa Bay Buccaneers."[22]

Now the hard part was designing the mascot. What did a buccaneer look like? A pirate? The team had to be careful here. The Oakland Raiders used a pirate-like logo, and Al Davis, the owner of the Raiders, would have sued. Therefore, when *Tampa Tribune* artist Lamar Sparkman submitted a skull and crossbones and also a hangman's noose, Bill Marcum nixed the ideas. A buccaneer was a French pirate, Marcum said, not Long John Silver, so he asked Sparkman for something classier, a character like d'Artagnan from *The Three Musketeers*. Sparkman came back with "Bucco Bruce," a classy, rakish rogue, a cross between a 1970s Bee Gee and a swashbuckler. Bruce had long, flowing hair, a pencil-thin mustache, and an earring. In his teeth was a blade, and on his head a floppy, plumed hat. Satisfied, Marcum brought the design to the advisory committee, which decided that instead of wearing an eye patch, Bruce would close one of his eyes in a sneer. However, in the revised drawing, the sneer looked like a wink, a "no-no" in the manly world of professional football. "The committee liked the design," recalls Marcum, "but several people thought it was soft. You know, the winking. But a woman in public relations thought it was sexy, so we kept it."[23]

———

Its colors and mascot in place, the Bucs now turned to hiring a staff. The general manager was first. By May 1975, Culverhouse had claimed to have interviewed at least fifty candidates, including a thirty-six-year-old Raiders personnel director named Ron Wolf. Wolf had started his career in the early 1960s as an office worker at *Pro Football Illustrated*, whose editor had heard that Oakland president Al Davis was looking for someone "who was good at remembering names."[24] That was Wolf, who had the bizarre ability to see a player's number and immediately recall who he was and where he went to school. It wasn't a photographic memory, he explained, but he did pass a name-that-player test administered by Davis over the telephone. In 1963, he moved to Oakland and became a Raider.

Wolf's "feel" was legendary. Each year he developed scouting reports for thousands of college seniors. He also ranked each NFL player at each position, and scouted the Canadian Football League (CFL). A notorious workaholic with few hobbies outside of football, Wolf spent so much time in the film room that coaches joked they had no idea who he was. John Madden described him as "a one-man full-time personnel staff . . . who knew every player everywhere."[25] Wolf was so good at finding talent, the Raiders refused to join any of the league's three scouting combines. On occasion, Wolf conducted trades, but his specialty was the draft. In 1974, the Raiders went 12-2 and won the AFC Western Division title. Incredibly, Wolf had picked twenty of the team's twenty-two starters, including Alabama quarterback Ken Stabler, a former second-round draft pick who won that year's Most Valuable Player award. The roster included nine Pro Bowl players and a rookie tight end named Dave Casper—another Wolf pick— who in 2002 was inducted in the Pro Football Hall of Fame.

For Culverhouse, Wolf was a no-brainer, and he hired him in April 1975. "I had a chance to hire a number of men with bigger names and more years of experience," he said, but "in five years, he'll be recognized as the top executive in the NFL."[26] Although the *Tampa Tribune* called Wolf "the NFL's youngest chief executive" and described him as the team's general manager, his official title was "Vice President of Operations." "As soon as Hugh Culverhouse decided on my title," wrote Wolf in his 1999 memoir, "I should have known I could be headed for trouble. Instead of naming me general manager with total control over football decisions," he made me "prove myself to him." He said, "You can work your way into being a general manager."[27] To Wolf that was fine. When he started, the Bucs had no coach, only three employees, and Wolf was the only football guy. But later, when Culverhouse hired University of Southern California (USC) legend John McKay as his coach, Wolf and McKay began butting heads over personnel. That was two years into the future.

In the meantime, Wolf began assembling a staff. One of his first hires was Tom Bass, a scout and coach with the Cincinnati Bengals whom Wolf named director of pro scouting. Bass was a hulking man with a penchant for poetry who had been a receivers coach with the San Diego Chargers before joining the Bengals in 1968, the team's inaugural year. Now with the Bucs, Bass scouted college and pro teams through the fall of 1975. He'd visit college teams during the week, see a game on Saturday, then fly to an NFL city for a game on Sunday. The reason for the crowded schedule was that Bass was scouting players for *two* drafts—the March 1976 expansion draft and the April 1976 NFL Draft.

First held in 1960, the expansion draft was how NFL owners stocked new teams. They'd "freeze" a certain number of players on each roster, say thirty out of forty, then let expansion teams choose from the rest. In 1975, owners agreed to freeze thirty players from their forty-three-man rosters, plus two more from their injured reserve lists, which meant Tampa and Seattle had some four hundred players to choose from. But there were other rules. Each time a team lost a man, it could protect a man, and the most any team could lose was three. "That was some draft," Bass says with a laugh, "and that was before free agency. You couldn't just shop around for a good player like teams today. You had the college draft and the expansion draft, and that was it."[28]

Technically, the NFL had free agency, but few players ever switched teams, because of the "Rozelle Rule." Implemented in 1963, the Rozelle Rule held that when a player's contract ended, he could sign with another team, but his new team had to compensate his previous team for the loss. However, here's the rub: if the two teams couldn't agree on compensation, Rozelle decided the terms himself. In 1968, for example, the commissioner ruled that the lowly New Orleans Saints owed the San Francisco 49ers not one, but two consecutive first-round draft picks for a receiver named Dave Parks. Although Parks had been to the Pro Bowl twice, in 1967 he'd had just 26 receptions for 313 yards. But Rozelle wasn't compensating the 49ers per se; he was punishing the Saints in order to limit free agency. The fewer free agents there were, the lower salaries would be. The effect was startling. Between 1963 and 1974, only thirty-four players actually played out their contracts and signed with other teams.[29] Everyone else stayed with the team that drafted them, or was traded.

In 1975, when Wolf and Bass came to the Bucs, the head of the NFL Players Association (NFLPA), the former Colts tight end John Mackey, was suing the league for antitrust. Mackey claimed that the Rozelle Rule violated the Sherman Antitrust Act by denying players fair-market value for their services. He won, but before even a single player could switch teams, in 1977 the NFLPA bargained away its free agency rights in exchange for a higher compensation package in its collective bargaining agreement with the NFL. This limited free agency until 1993, when owners finally allowed veterans to change teams in exchange for a salary cap. Thus, while the 1976 expansion Buccaneers had no free agents, the 1995 first-year Carolina Panthers had a league-high seventeen.[30] They included eleven starters, their best rusher, and their top three receivers, who led the team to an expansion-best 7-9 record.

Still, the Bucs could sign true free agents—players who'd
been waived by NFL teams, or cast off by the World Football
League (WFL) or the CFL, or who'd been bagging groceries
since college. So Bass looked at everyone. So did Wolf. In fact,
the Bucs' brain trust evaluated every player in the league, particularly guys at the low end who could contribute that first
year. Wolf himself believed that no matter how many players
the Bucs took in the expansion draft, only a few of them would
help the team. His focus, therefore, was on the college draft,
and the player he wanted was Lee Roy Selmon, a 6'2", 262-
pound defensive tackle from Oklahoma. The only problem
was, would he get him? The Bucs and Seahawks were scheduled to pick one-two in the 1976 college draft. To decide the
order, Culverhouse and Seahawks managing partner Herman
Sarkowski drew pieces of paper from a hat at a Steelers-Colts
playoff game in Pittsburgh in December 1975. Seattle got the
first pick in the expansion draft, while Tampa Bay got the first
pick in the college draft. "You couldn't compare the two," said
Bass. "The college draft was everything, and Lee Roy was the
best player we'd seen in a long, long time."[31]

An AP, UPI, American Football Coaches, Football Writers,
Walter Camp Foundation, *Sporting News*, and *Football News*
All-American, Selmon was also the 1975 Outland Award winner as the nation's best interior lineman. During the 1974 and
1975 seasons, he'd led Oklahoma to a 22-1 record and two
national championships. His senior year, he had 132 tackles, 88 unassisted, and 10 tackles for a loss. He ran a 4.8 forty.
He could stand, flat-footed, and dunk a basketball. Without a
doubt, Selmon was an instant starter, a superstar in the making. Yet his most defining characteristic wasn't his athleticism,

it was his humility. Lee Roy was incredibly kind. "In the four years I've known Lee Roy," said a coach at Oklahoma, "he's never raised his voice in anger, never questioned his coach, and never criticized anyone. Most coaches will tell you that if a player leaves school a better man, they're happy. Well, it's just the opposite here. I'm a better man for having known Lee Roy and his brothers."[32]

His brothers were Lucious and Dewey Selmon, who, like Lee Roy, were gifted football players who starred at Oklahoma. (All three were all-Americans. Lucious graduated in 1974 and played in the WFL, while Dewey and Lee Roy graduated in 1976.) They grew up the youngest of nine children on a farm near Eufaula, Oklahoma. They said "yes, ma'am" and "no, ma'am" and lived in a house with no running water. Their mother, Jessie, was a tough but loving woman who raised the boys to always be respectful. They were devout Baptists and ordered their lives through Bible readings, family discussions, and church. At one such discussion, the family decided if thirteen-year-old Lucious would play football. Jessie "wasn't too excited about letting Lucious play," said Eufaula coach Paul Bell. "She thought it was 'rasslin.'" However, once Jessie observed a player "calling witness," she approved.[33] Lucious, Dewey, and Lee Roy would play football. Years later, Oklahoma fans chanted: "Thank God for Mr. and Mrs. Selmon!"

Unfortunately for the Bucs, Wolf believed that apart from Lee Roy, the 1976 college draft was the worst in years. There were no first-round quarterbacks, he insisted, and though normally there were twenty-six to twenty-seven "quality" players available, he could find only eight.[34] Therefore, Wolf had to be extremely accurate in the first three rounds, where, traditionally, 80 percent of rookie starters and 75 percent of five-year starters were drafted.[35] Fortunately, NFL expansion rules permitted the Bucs two additional picks at the end of the second, third, fourth, and fifth rounds, which gave them seven picks in rounds one through three and twenty-five picks overall. (There were seventeen rounds.) Where the Bucs' quarterback would come from, Wolf had no idea. He did say, however, that if the quarterback didn't come through the college draft, he'd most certainly come through a trade.[36] Possible pickups included former Chicago starter and Florida State star Gary Huff, Rams backup Pat Haden, and two former University of Florida quarterbacks, the 49ers' Steve Spurrier and the Bengals' John Reaves.

———

A bigger issue was the coach. In January 1975, the New Orleans *Times-Picayune* reported that Notre Dame coach Ara Parseghian had accepted team stock and a ten-year, $1.5 million contract to commandeer the Bucs.[37] But Culverhouse had never met Parseghian, and in any case, his man was John McKay, the fifty-two-year-old USC coach who'd won four national championships and five Rose Bowls in fifteen years. McKay's record, at the time, was an astonishing 119-36-8, for a .755 win percentage, and his 1972 team was widely considered the greatest ever in college football. Twelve and zero and winner of the national championship, it had ten draft picks, five first-team all-Americans, and a junior superstar named Lynn Swann. As of 1975, McKay had won more AP national championships than Woody Hayes, Johnny Majors, Vince Dooley, Bo Schembechler, and Joe Paterno *combined*. "Without a doubt," said John Robinson, a McKay assistant and future coach of the Rams, he's "one of the best ever in football."[38]

The son of a mine superintendent from Everettsville, West Virginia, McKay grew up poor at the height of the Great Depression. When McKay was thirteen, his father died of pneumonia. "We went from living well to near poverty overnight," he wrote. "We never had to go without food but there sure weren't many cookies around the house."[39] To earn money, McKay bused tables and worked at the high school as a janitor, where he earned all-state honors as a running back his senior year. During World War II, he served as a tail gunner in the Army Air Corps and played football and basketball for the corps at Maxwell Field, Alabama.

In 1946, he attended Purdue University, where, as a twenty-three-year-old freshman, he started on defense and was teammates with Abe Gibron, a future Chicago Bears coach and Bucs assistant, and future Chiefs and Saints coach Hank Stram. McKay transferred to the University of Oregon the following year, where he platooned on offense and defense and played in the Cotton Bowl. In 1950 he was drafted by the New York Yankees of the All-America Football Conference but opted to stay at Oregon as an assistant coach. He married, started a family, and in 1959 accepted a position as running backs coach at USC. When head coach Don Clark resigned in 1960, McKay got the job. "I must be one of the luckiest guys in the world," he wrote in his 1974 autobiography. "There's nothing you can do to try to become a head coach. Just work hard and be in the right place at the right time."[40] For the 1960 and '61 seasons, McKay went 8-11-1 and was nearly fired. In 1962, though, he guided USC to a perfect 11-0 record and a 42–37 victory over

Wisconsin in the Rose Bowl. It was USC's first national championship since 1939.

As a coach, McKay was a lifelong proponent of the "I-formation," in which the fullback and tailback line up directly behind the quarterback. The play typically went left or right. The guard pulled, the fullback blocked, and the quarterback pitched the ball to the tailback, who ran parallel to the line before turning the play upfield. It appeared, at times, that the tailback was running toward the student section, so McKay dubbed the play "Student Body Right" or "Student Body Left." It was his trademark, and USC ran the play over and over, year after year, with what one analyst called "stultifying regularity."[41] In 1968, for example, USC running back O. J. Simpson rushed for a then-NCAA record 1,709 yards. Impressive yes, but Simpson carried the ball 355 times.

The offense worked, of course, because McKay had athletes—lots and lots of athletes. Southern California was (and is) a recruiting hotbed, and McKay, coaches joked, could sign a blue-chip recruit "just by walking out his office."[42] Indeed, more than a dozen USC all-Americans came from Los Angeles, including Mike Garrett, the 1965 Heisman winner, and Ron Yary, the number-one pick in the 1968 NFL draft.

To players, McKay was autocratic, sarcastic, and mean. He "wasn't a benevolent dictator," recalled star quarterback and current USC athletic director Pat Haden. "He was a dictator."[43] Nevertheless, McKay's coaching style was aloof. He often watched practice from a raised platform, or sat away from his players, alone and smoking a cigar, in a golf cart. To journalists, McKay was pathologically glib, an endless source of quips and witticisms that sometimes had an edge. "McKay is credited with saying some of the funniest things in the history of coach-speak," wrote USC historian Steven Travers, but "his commentary often came . . . with an icy stare and a heaping helping of ironic sarcasm."[44] McKay called it his defense mechanism. Once, when asked at a postgame press conference if tailback Ricky Bell should have run the ball forty times, McKay said: "Why not? It isn't heavy." He called Stanford the "Radcliffe of the West" and once said, "Emotion is overrated. My wife is emotional and she can't play worth a damn."[45]

McKay's favorite subject was the pros. He followed the NFL "habitually," wrote *Los Angeles Times* reporter Jeff Prugh, and prefaced many of his sentences with "Now if I were coaching a pro team, I'd . . ."[46] He said repeatedly that football was football, that winning in college required the same thing as winning in the pros. There's a "mystique about NFL football," he said, "that only pros could teach it." But "I've gone to the pro camps. They throw the ball, they catch the ball. I'm not amazed at what they do."[47] What did amaze McKay, however, was the money. Pro coaches made huge salaries. In 1974, his old UCLA rival, Tommy Prothro, signed a multiyear contract with the Chargers worth $100,000 per year. By contrast, McKay's salary at USC was $72,000 per year, and that was for two positions: athletic director and coach. Although on three occasions he'd been offered the Rams job—the final offer in 1970 was for $90,000 per year—McKay claimed the timing wasn't right.

Not so in 1975, when at the recommendation of Alabama coach Paul "Bear" Bryant, Culverhouse offered McKay a five-year contract at $150,000 per year, plus $750,000 in life insurance policies, $250,000 in Florida real estate with "a guarantee against depreciation," a $10,000-a-year expense account, and three cars.[48] McKay accepted the deal in September, and a formal announcement was made in October 1975. In December, he was formally introduced at Tampa's Downtown Holiday Inn as coach of the Buccaneers. He opened with a joke: "I heard a player say just the other day: 'No wonder we can't win. We've got a pro coach!'" Holding court for an hour, McKay discussed everything, from whom he'd pick first in the draft (a lineman, probably), to Archie Griffin's future as a pro (not good), to the qualities of John Robinson, the USC coach who replaced him (excellent). "John wasn't exactly what you'd call a talented football player," quipped McKay, who coached Robinson while at Oregon. "John was our pivot end. He'd pivot as the ball carrier went past him and say, 'There he goes!'"[49] The big question: who was in charge of player personnel—John McKay or Ron Wolf? Although Wolf had said repeatedly that the two men would work together, McKay told the crowd, rather ominously, "What's that song Frank Sinatra used to sing? I'll do it my way? Well, that's what we're going to do. We're going to do things my way."[50]

The first thing McKay did do was hire a staff. It included eight coaches, as well as a personal assistant from USC named Dick Beam. Beam did everything for McKay. He brought him food, scheduled his appointments, made his phone calls; he even picked up the coach in the morning. After practice and sometimes drinks at Malio's, a Tampa establishment, he brought him home. In fact, the staff liked to kid Beam that he was "McKay's valet." Joining Beam were three USC coaches— Willie Brown, Wayne Fontes, and Phil Krueger. Brown was the Bucs' receivers coach and had been the leading rusher on McKay's 1962 national championship team. He'd played three years in the NFL and returned to USC as a coach in 1967. Wayne Fontes was the Bucs' defensive backs coach and had worked at USC since 1972. Fontes had been a receiver at Michigan State and played briefly with the New York Titans of the AFL. McKay's final USC assistant was offensive backs coach Phil Krueger. Krueger had worked for McKay from 1966 to 1970 before moving as head coach to Utah State University. He left USU when McKay offered him the job.

McKay's other coaches included Jerry Frei, Abe Gibron, John Rauch, Dick Voris, and Dennis Fryzel. A guard in college, Frei was the team's offensive line coach and had been a teammate of Elroy "Crazylegs" Hirsch at the University of Wisconsin. Frei and McKay had both been assistants at Oregon, where Frei had been head coach from 1967 to 1971. The Bucs' defensive coordinator and defensive line coach was Abe Gibron, a former All-Pro lineman with the Browns who had played with McKay at Purdue. From 1972 to 1974, Gibron had been head coach of the Chicago Bears and in 1975 head coach of the Chicago Winds of the WFL. Dick Voris was the team's linebackers coach. A longtime NFL assistant, Voris's claim to fame was a dismal 1-29 record, from 1958 to 1960, as head coach of Virginia. (To be fair, though, it should be noted that Voris gave Don Shula his first-ever job in coaching.)[51] John Rauch was the team's offensive coordinator and quarterbacks coach. A quarterback himself at the University of Georgia, Rauch had been head coach of the Oakland Raiders, where in 1967 he was the AFL Coach of the Year.

McKay's final assistant was Dennis Fryzel, a former head coach at the University of Tampa who had lost his job when the school disbanded the football program in February 1975. The school blamed its decision on the Bucs, insisting it couldn't compete with a pro football franchise, and had projected a $400,000–$500,000 deficit the team's inaugural year.[52] Even so, by March 1976, the Bucs had sold only thirty-four thousand season tickets, less than half of the soon-to-be-expanded, 72,000-seat Tampa Stadium, because at $80, $100, and $120 for ten-game packages, the tickets were too expensive. Bill Marcum had told Culverhouse that, insisting that of twenty-eight NFL cities, Tampa was second to last, ahead of only New Orleans, in disposable income. But Culverhouse wouldn't listen. He said it was Marcum's job to sell tickets. Of course, it bothered Culverhouse that Tampa's expansion rival, the Seattle Seahawks, had sold 59,000 season tickets in *two weeks*.[53] But, with such high ticket prices, there was little Marcum could do. What he needed was a draw, a player with name recognition, if not a star, who could bring people to the gate. That was Steve Spurrier.

Born in Miami, Florida, but raised in Johnson City, Tennessee, Spurrier was a graduate of the University of Florida, where in 1966 he led the team to a 9-2 record and was awarded the Heisman Trophy. That year, Spurrier edged out Purdue quarterback Bob Griese to win the Heisman, and was the first southerner to be given the award since Louisiana State University's Billy Cannon in 1959. As one scout described him, he had "the arm of Sammy Baugh, the poise of Johnny Unitas, the leadership of Norm Van Brocklin, and the quickness of Joe Namath."[54] He was also confident, quick-witted, and arrogant, and chafed as a backup to John Brodie in San Francisco after being selected third by the 49ers in 1967. As a pro, Spurrier's primary role had been punter, though he went 13-12-1 as a backup for the Niners while once leading them to an upset victory over the Colts in 1969. When asked after the game if his Colts victory was the biggest thing he'd ever done in pro football, Spurrier responded, "it was the only thing."[55]

Seven years later, the thirty-one-year-old Florida legend was still sitting the bench in San Francisco. John Brodie had retired, but Spurrier was now backup quarterback to Norm Snead and San Francisco was looking to add Jim Plunkett, who was then with the Patriots. Spurrier was expendable. In February, Niners coach Monte Clarke contacted Ron Wolf, and in April the teams made a deal—two players from the expansion draft and a second-round draft choice for Spurrier.[56] It was Tampa Bay's first franchise trade. Spurrier was in Gainesville, on a golf course (of course), when he heard the news. "With all the rumors about Plunkett coming out of San Francisco," he said, "I was ready to go anywhere. But my first choice would have been Tampa. They have a fine organization" and took "some good players in the expansion draft. . . . I'm looking forward to it."[57]

Held in March 1976 at the NFL headquarters in New York, the expansion draft was a two-day, twenty-plus-hour affair. McKay, Wolf, and Bass worked in a private room in one wing of the headquarters, while the Seahawks staff was across the building in another. On Monday, March 29, at 11 a.m., the teams were given a list of which players were protected and which players were not. Then they had twenty-one hours to review the list and could ask the NFL for a player's contract information as needed. "That was important," says Bass. "You had to know how much players were making, because once you picked them, they were yours. You had to be careful, too, because teams used the draft to dump old or injured players or players with bad contracts. They weren't trying to help you. Most of the allocated players were players they couldn't use."[58]

Exhibit A was Doug Swift. In 1975, the twenty-seven-year-old Dolphins linebacker started thirteen games for the fourth-ranked defense in the league. The Bucs chose Swift but had no idea, apparently, that the brainy Amherst College grad was quitting football forever and going to medical school.[59] Don Shula did, which is why he'd added Swift to the list. Likewise, Chargers coach Tommy Prothro added Terry Owens to the list, though the veteran lineman had serious back problems and had asked to be waived. When neither the Bucs nor the Seahawks picked him up, Prothro let him go. Several teams allocated players who'd never been in the NFL—for example, WFL or CFL players whom they'd drafted at some point and whose rights they owned. This list included J. K. McKay, the USC receiver and son of Bucs coach John McKay, who played the 1975 season with the WFL's Southern California Sun, but whose rights were owned by the Browns. The Jets put McKay's WFL teammate Anthony Davis on the list, while the Patriots parted with an Ottawa Roughrider named Kerry Marbury. Drafted by the Seahawks, Marbury, a onetime West Virginia star, never played a down.

———

On Tuesday, March 30, the draft began. The teams had thirty minutes for each pick in rounds one through thirteen, then fifteen minutes per pick in the twenty-six rounds after that. When the dust settled, the Bucs had chosen twenty defensive players and nineteen offensive players, including, at most, fifteen serviceable veterans. On defense, the most notable picks were Pat Toomay, a defensive end with the Bills; safety Ken Stone of the Redskins; defensive end Council Rudolph of the Cardinals; linebacker Larry Ball of the Lions; safety Mark Cotney of the Oilers; and Colts nose guard Dave Pear.

On offense, the Bucs chose tight end Bob Moore and running back Louis Carter of the Raiders, tackle Mike Current of the Broncos, offensive lineman Howard Fest of the Bengals, tackle Dave Reavis of the Steelers, center Dan Ryczek of the Redskins, and Packers receiver Barry Smith. They also chose Anthony Davis, a Jets running back then in Canada, and J. K. McKay. (Two other picks—the Dolphins' Bruce Elia and the Rams' Willie McGee—were traded for Steve Spurrier.)

"I think we came out well," said McKay. "There were better players in the expansion draft than we thought possible."[60] What McKay didn't say was that all of these players were backups: backups, has-beens, overlooked first-year players, and also-rans. There was talent here, to be sure. The Bucs' Dave Pear became a Pro Bowler, the Seahawks' Dave Brown an All-Pro. But in 1976 the NFL's expansion plan was patently unfair. It was as if the league had said: We'll choose the first 768 players; then you, Tampa Bay and Seattle, choose from everyone else. As one journalist put it, it was "like some hallowed college fraternity. The elders would accept you as a pledge but not without the necessary hazing rituals to put you in your place."[61] For Bucs personnel director and Wolf assistant Ken Herock, "that's just how it was." The expansion draft "was the very bottom of the barrel. I mean, some survived it, but all you really had was the college draft."[62]

Dubbed "Operation Success" by Ron Wolf, the college draft took place on April 8–9, 1976, in New York City. The Bucs had twenty-five picks—one in the first round, three each in rounds two through five, and one each in rounds six through seventeen. However, Wolf used five of his picks in trades for veteran players, including a second-round pick for Spurrier, a third-round pick for Colts cornerback Mike Washington, a fourth- and a fifth-round pick for Rams linebacker Jim Peterson, and an eighth-round pick for Jets linebacker Steve Reese. With twenty picks in hand, Wolf went to work.

His first pick was Lee Roy Selmon. That, everyone knew. In the second round, Wolf chose Jimmy DuBose, a Florida fullback who finished sixth in the Heisman vote, as well as Lee Roy's brother Dewey, a defensive tackle. At 6'1", 257 pounds, Dewey was smaller than Lee Roy, but mean. In the third round, the Bucs took Steve Young, a 6'8", 270-pound tackle from Colorado. (His quote in the Bucs media guide: "I like breakfast. In fact, I like all my meals.") Other first-day picks included Steve Wilson, an offensive tackle from Georgia; Curtis Jordan, a defensive back from Texas Tech; and Parnell Dickinson, a rangy quarterback from Mississippi Valley State. These were productive picks.

Day two, however, featured eight picks that would never play for the team. One was future Houston Oiler and Pro Bowl kick returner Carl Roaches, whom the Bucs cut in practice, while another was Tennessee tight end and future Clemson coach Tommy West. West tried out, but was waived. "It has been fun," said Hugh Culverhouse. "And from my observation they were well prepared and handled the draft in a professional way. Ron, his staff, and the coaches worked well together. . . . If we can perform on the field comparably, we'll be in the Super Bowl. But, don't ask me when."[63]

Chapter Three

Ten Weeks of Two-a-Days

Football players don't like two-a-day practices, calisthenics, or coaches. They like ice cream and dances.

—John McKay, coach

Pat Toomay was Tampa Bay's second pick in the 1976 NFL expansion draft. A 6'5", 245-pound defensive end, Toomay had been sent to the Bucs as punishment. His crime was a bad one, the absolute worst thing—apart from gambling—that a player could possibly do. He'd written a book. Titled *The Crunch*, it was an inside look at life with the Dallas Cowboys, the team that had drafted Toomay in 1970. As a kid, Toomay had been raised on NFL Films and the booming voice of John Facenda, but when he got to Dallas, he said, "Things didn't jibe with that. Things were dissonant. So I wrote them down."

What Toomay described was a Cowboys franchise that wasn't quite "America's Team." Its management was greedy; far from being a principled genius, Coach Tom Landry was petty, thickheaded, and cruel. There were mangled knees, pulled muscles, ripped tendons, and sore backs, he wrote. One veteran had a cracked vertebra. Players lived in constant fear of being cut or injured. There were racial tensions, and more than one star, too old to perform or outplayed by a rival, was unceremoniously let go.

The Crunch and its revelations were tame by today's standards, but Dallas general manager Tex Schramm, a close friend of Rozelle's and member of the league's Competition Committee, considered it an act of treason. By the book's release in 1975, Toomay had left Dallas and was playing for Buffalo, where the Bills booster club had voted him defensive lineman of the year. In fact, it was in Buffalo that Toomay had a sack, a fumble recovery, and an interception return in the same game. Yet somehow, Toomay ended up in the draft. In retrospect, the onetime defensive end says he wasn't blackballed. "It was more subtle than that. I was exiled to Siberia."

Naturally, Toomay came to Tampa with a sense of dread. McKay was a college coach who'd hired college coaches, and there was a lot of "rah-rah" going on. Plus, McKay's comments about how coaching in the NFL was no different than coaching in college hadn't gone over well with other coaches and he had a target on his back. The worst thing, says Toomay, was playing for a new coach on a new team. "It's the legend of Bear Bryant," he insists. "Bryant coached at Texas A&M and took his players to Junction, Texas, where he tortured them until only a handful were left. Those were the guys he went with. They could lose every game, but they were his guys and had the qualities he wanted in a player. That's why veterans hate going with new coaches on new teams. They're going to put their stamp on things. You're gonna hit all the time, you're gonna practice twice a day, and you're gonna have one hellacious camp."[1]

As Toomay predicted, the Bucs' camp was incredibly long—

a full fifty-five days, from July 6 to August 29—with nearly ten weeks of two-a-days into September. It was, perhaps, the longest camp in the league. "Two-a-days just don't exist today," explains receiver Barry Smith. "Teams don't do them. But even in those days, ten weeks of two-a-days was unheard-of. Nobody did it. That's two practices a day, in pads, getting knocked on your ass. We were exhausted."[2]

Although Culverhouse had briefly considered a training camp location in Vero Beach, Florida, on the state's east coast, players practiced in Tampa at a brand-new facility next to the airport known as One Buccaneer Place. Built in spring 1976 for $500,000, it was a brutally ugly, stucco-faced box. The facility went up quickly, lacked a proper equipment room and weight room, and was incredibly small. Crammed into 16,500 square feet were showers, exercise and locker facilities, a training room, a classroom, a film room, offices for coaches and administrators (including Culverhouse), a ticket office, and a lounge. By comparison, the Bucs' current weight room, built in 2006, is 16,000 square feet, just 500 square feet smaller than the entirety of the first Buccaneer Place.[3] The facility "wasn't the greatest in the world," says former Bucs equipment manager Pat Marcuccillo. "In fact, the manager of the Falcons came for a visit once and was laughing at it. He asked me, 'Where's your equipment room, Pat?' And I said, 'You're standing in it!'"[4]

———

On July 6, 1976, there were 86 players in camp. By the end of the 1976 season, an astonishing 141 players had cycled through. "We had guys coming and going," says Tom Bass. "Here's the thing. . . . When you look at a player and see that

57

there's no way in the world you could win with this guy, then you're more apt to find somebody else. It wasn't like we were trying to replace Pro Bowl players. We were trying to replace guys who shouldn't have been in a uniform."[5] Like, for example, Biff Burrell, a former USC basketball player who never played a down in college but still tried out for the team. He and Pete Rome, a free agent from Miami University of Ohio, were the first players cut. "I did 'em a favor," said McKay, caustically. "One thought he could play, and after talking with them, the other decided he couldn't."[6]

Within a week, ten more had been cut, including Bubba Broussard, a Bears linebacker picked up in the expansion draft, and Mel Washington, an eleventh-round draft pick from Colorado State. Washington had been given no guarantees, but demanded Tampa pay for "the incomplete portion" of his education.[7] Wolf said no. Punter Randy Walker, a free agent waived by the Packers, simply up and quit. He "walked in and said he'd lost his desire to play football," quipped McKay. "I don't understand that. All he's been doing is eating steak and standing around."[8]

The process of getting cut was routine. After breakfast but before morning practice, the condemned player was approached by Dick Beam, the McKay assistant whom players called "the Turk." The Turk, in NFL parlance, is the angel of death, the person who utters the phrase: "Coach wants to see you. Bring your playbook." He wasn't very popular, Beam admitted, and most rookies and free agents avoided making eye contact with him. As a joke, rookie quarterback Parnell Dickinson covered his eyes whenever he saw Beam, but for a time, he truly avoided him.[9] That was nothing. At least Beam was nice about it. He knocked on doors. Other teams cut players in public, in front of other players, while at one point the 49ers' Turk was a teenage boy.[10]

Once summoned by Beam, each player met privately with McKay. He explained his decision and gave the player his opinion as to whether he'd be picked up by another team. According to McKay, he didn't cut players; they more or less "cut themselves."[11] From there, each player had a checklist: an exit physical, a visit to the equipment room, a visit to the accounting office, then a five-minute trip to the airport. As a final step, the Bucs sent a telegram to New York informing the NFL that the player had been waived. If anyone wanted him, teams had ten days to sign the player under the terms of his original contract. After that, he was an unrestricted free agent. The NFL sent the list of waived players to each team through a point-to-point teletype machine called the TWIX. McKay watched the TWIX religiously, but the problem, he explained, was that for each player he picked up he had to cut one, and then there was a learning curve.[12]

The turnover was amazing. Kicker Booth Lusteg spent a week with the team; quarterback Bill Bowerman, only a few days. "That first year we might as well have had a revolving door on the dressing room," said Bob Huckabee, the team's ticket manager. "I mean, they came in, practiced, packed their bags, and were gone."[13] Once, during camp, Ron Wolf asked equipment manager Pat Marcuccillo to pick up a player from Los Angeles at the airport. An hour later, however, Wolf informed Marcuccillo he'd changed his mind, and that he was to meet the player at the gate and give him a return ticket to L.A. As Marcuccillo put it, Wolf "cut him over Denver."[14]

By midseason, Tampa's roster included thirteen waived players, eight of whom were starters.[15] The biggest turnover, evaluation-wise, was at kicker. In May, special teams coach Dennis Fryzel held a tryout camp at Leto High School in Tampa. He'd received at least two hundred and fifty inquiries. "We've been inundated," he said. "The stream has been unending. Everybody knows somebody who can place-kick or punt."[16] There was a Canadian med student, a trash man, two professional soccer players, a pilot, and an exterminator. The pilot drove in from Orlando; he hung out at One Buc Place until Fryzel gave him a tryout. He even brought an old leather ball "that had been kicked," said Fryzel, "at least 90,000 times."[17]

The star of the tryout was Democratic state representative Don Hazelton of Boca Raton, a forty-seven-year-old chairman of the House Corrections Committee who wanted to be like George Blanda, the forty-eight-year-old Raiders kicker, who in August 1976 had finally retired. Hazelton had been a kicker in high school, and showed up in maroon shorts and an aqua T-shirt with the number two on it. He was ready. Since November, he'd been waking up at 5 a.m. to kick footballs on a Florida State practice field in Tallahassee. He was accurate from thirty yards in but from farther out wasn't very good. "I gave it my best," he said. "I wasn't the best kicker there, but I wasn't the worst."[18]

The title of worst kicker may have been up for grabs, but the title of best undoubtedly went to Derek Smethurst, a Tampa Bay Rowdies soccer forward and former Chelsea star known as "the Stork." Tall and gangly, Smethurst could kick. From thirty-two to forty yards out, he made twelve in a row; from forty-two to fifty yards out he made ten of fifteen; and from fifty-two-plus made ten of sixteen. In addition, he punted eight times for a 56.9 average, with an average hang time of 4.68 seconds. His first punt went sixty yards. Fryzel was impressed but wondered if, in a game situation, Smethurst could handle the pressure.[19] For now, the issue was moot. The Rowdies were in season, and Smethurst was playing soccer through September.

That left the free agent list and the waiver wire. By the last game of the preseason, the Bucs had brought in seven different kickers, but cut six of them, including Greg Enright, Tom Klaban, Rod Garcia, Booth Lusteg, Wolfgang Taylor, and Pete Rajecki. A German immigrant from the University of Georgia, Rajecki had scored Tampa's first-ever preseason points in a 26–3 loss to the Rams. A week later, though, he missed a point-after attempt versus the Packers. There was no rush, and the snap, reportedly, was perfect. When asked why he had missed, Rajecki told the press that McKay made him nervous. "That's unfortunate," McKay responded, "as I plan on attending all the games."[20]

All told, during the 1976 preseason, the Bucs cut at least sixty-three players, including six kickers, seven running backs, eight receivers, five tight ends, four quarterbacks, three punters, three offensive linemen, eight defensive linemen, nine linebackers, nine defensive backs, and a center.[21] While some made it with other clubs, for most being cut by the Bucs was the end of the road. Those who remained faced brutal practices in the stifling Florida heat. "That's what I remember," says Pat Toomay, "the heat. You'd come off the field and your shoes were full of sweat. They'd squish. You'd sweat through everything. And you couldn't stop sweating no matter what you did. We sat in vats of ice, in the showers, to cool down."[22]

In Tampa, afternoon temperatures in the summer reached at least 90 degrees. But with swamplike humidity at 60 to 80 percent, it felt more like 110 degrees—day after day after day. "I'm in the best shape of my life," said center Dan Ryczek at the time, but "I lost nine pounds I didn't have to lose. This is a different kind of heat down here. Don't let anyone tell you otherwise."[23]

In his 2000 memoir, veteran tackle Mike Current told the story of Ira Gordon, a free agent guard from San Diego who joined the team in July. Gordon was 6'2", 280 pounds, and spent his first practice in Tampa watching the offense in hopes of catching up. Even on the sidelines, the heat and humidity got to Gordon, who after fifteen minutes was down on one knee. After another fifteen minutes he was down on both knees, desperately in need of fluids. When McKay noticed, he told the corpulent lineman to get up, that kneeling wasn't permitted. That's when Gordon yanked off his helmet and yelled, " 'Get me some water. I'm a racehorse, not a fuckin' camel!' "[24]

A six-year veteran with sixty-two appearances in San Diego, Gordon had been selected by the Bucs in the expansion draft. He held out until late July 1976 and wanted more money, reportedly, than Lee Roy Selmon. But Gordon wasn't a starter. In fact, he'd been the 179th pick in the 1974 WFL draft. He'd spoken with the Redskins, briefly, but in 1976 no one wanted him—only the Bucs. Nevertheless, the mouthy Gordon promised to "whup" the Selmons, called Rams defensive end Merlin Olsen "*Marilyn* Olsen," and said he was the meanest player in the league. "I can handle any defensive lineman," he bragged. "I tell you, San Diego made a mistake in letting me go."[25] After weeks of negotiations, in which Gordon claimed the Bucs had gotten him "at a discount," he came to camp overweight and out of shape. "He was a common sight at the water tank," wrote one reporter, and liked to complain. Once, he had his knee X-rayed and said, "Coach, I got the X-ray, but I don't feel better."[26] Gordon's biggest gripe, however, involved two-a-days. "No one would say anything," he explained. "Here we were ready to start the regular season, and we're still doing two-a-days. It had never happened to me before. So I opened my mouth to no one in particular." When defensive coordinator Abe Gibron heard him, however, he yelled back, "Go and get yourself an eight to five then!"[27]

Clearly, McKay felt a demanding practice schedule was necessary. Players were out of shape, he said, and every roster spot, including quarterback, was open. From the team's opening practice on July 6 to a scrimmage with the Saints on July 24, the Bucs hit eighteen days in a row. There were thirty-five sessions. Soon everyone was hurt. Two weeks into practice, there were no healthy tight ends or receivers. Two different running backs were hurt. "It's worse out there than the Bataan Death March," said McKay, "but we'll go hard tomorrow." The injuries were to be expected, he believed. "Football players don't like two-a-day practices, calisthenics, or coaches. They like ice cream and dances."[28]

On July 24, 1976, the Bucs scrimmaged the Saints at Colonial High School in Orlando. In addition to various drills, each team's offense played the other team's defense on opposite ends of the field. There were one hundred plays total. Units ran five plays each before cycling out. On offense, Steve Spurrier was sharp, as was Carl Roaches, a speedy receiver and return man who scored on a bomb. Running back Manfred Moore, an expansion pick from San Francisco, ran five times for twenty-seven yards.

On defense, the Bucs' front four included three seasoned veterans: Pat Toomay, Dave Pear, and Council Rudolph, who stuffed Saints running backs and harassed Saints passers all day.[29] They were missing Lee Roy and Dewey Selmon, the team's first- and second-round draft picks, who were tied up with the annual college-pro "All-Star Football Game" in Chicago. An event that would be incomprehensible today, the game featured a team of college all-stars versus the previous year's Super Bowl champions—the Pittsburgh Steelers. They had no chance. As expected, the Steelers won lazily, 24–0, and held the collegians to just fifty-eight yards.[30] Lee Roy, however, was an animal. The Sooner grad helped hold the Steelers to three first-half field goals, and earlier, in practice, astounded coaches by breaking a blocking sled.

Lee Roy, of course, was an important part of the Bucs' "four-three" defense, which featured four down linemen and three linebackers. From left to right, the line included Council Rudolph, a 6'4", 255-pound defensive end formerly of the Cardinals; Dave Pear, a 6'2", 245-pound tackle and weight-lifting fanatic who'd spent a year with the Colts; and Selmon and Toomay. Talent-wise, Rudolph was a decent pass rusher of average ability—another team's backup. By contrast, Toomay and Pear were NFL-level starters, while Lee Roy was, well, Lee Roy—a future star. He simply needed time to develop. Dewey, an undersized nose tackle, was a backup.

Next was the Bucs' linebacking corps, the "three" in its

"four-three" defense, whose day-one starters included three NFL veterans who'd almost never started before: Jimmy Gunn, Cal Peterson, and Steve Reese. Backup Larry Ball had been a rookie on Don Shula's 1972 team, the one that went 17-0. By 1976, however, karma had caught up to Ball and sent him kicking and screaming to the Bucs. Slow, injury prone, and not very good at tackling, eleven different linebackers would eventually play for the Bucs during the season, but only two, Richard Wood and Mike Lemon, would be with the team at the start of season two. How bad were they? "In one game," said McKay, "our middle linebacker never made a tackle. I wouldn't have believed that was possible."[31]

At defensive back, the Bucs were relatively good, if players on an 0-14 team can be called good. The starters were corners Mike Washington and Joe Blahak, and safeties Mark Cotney and Ken Stone. Stone was an NFL journeyman but a respected, mostly backup defender. Blahak was a castoff; he played just two games for the Bucs before being cut. The real gems were Cotney and Washington. Both were second-year men—Cotney an expansion pick, Washington a Wolf trade—and played for the team into the 1980s.

For defensive coordinator, McKay chose Abe Gibron, the fifty-year-old former head coach of the Chicago Bears. The son of a Lebanese factory worker, Gibron grew up in Michigan City, Indiana, where he starred in high school and earned a scholarship to Purdue. Five-ten, 250 in his prime, Gibron was an elite blocker, a rotund man with quick feet who in the 1950s helped lead the Cleveland Browns to six championship games in a row. By all accounts, Gibron was the biggest character on the team and seemed to consume life. He had friends everywhere—from lowly equipment managers and janitors to politicians, team owners, and stars. He treated everyone the same. "I think Abe had three goals," said McKay. "First, to win football games. Second, to love and be loved by his family. And third, to feed the best food possible to every relative and friend seventeen times."[32] It was true: Gibron was an eater. No . . . Gibron was a gourmand. He ate the finest foods at the finest restaurants, and took his friends with him. "Abe and I would go to dinner," said Bob Asher, a former tackle with the Bears, and "every restaurant we'd pass a waiter would come out yelling 'Abe, try this! Abe, try this!' He ate two full meals on the way to our meal."[33]

While he was head coach of the Bears, Gibron's training tables were notoriously robust. Bob Markus, a longtime sports reporter with the *Chicago Tribune*, remembers steak, cutlets, chops, fruits and berries, and a variety of cheeses. There was a soul food night, a Greek night, and a party at the end of camp featuring three legs of lamb, a roast pig with an apple in its mouth, and a round of roast beef.[34] Although certainly well fed, the Bears went 11-30-1 under Gibron, and in 1974 he was fired. The next year, Gibron resurfaced as head coach of the Chicago Winds, a dying WFL franchise, and in 1976 he came to Tampa.

"Don't let the record fool you," said one journalist. "He was a victim of bad circumstances. His knowledge of the game is comparable to any coach."[35] So was his girth. By 1976, Gibron had a fifty-inch waistline and weighed 320 pounds. His neck was twenty inches—the same as Bears legend William "Refrigerator" Perry—while his shoe size was eleven triple-E.[36] "I tell you, though," says Buccaneer trainer John Lopez, "Abe's heart was bigger than he was. Everybody loved him . . . the players, the coaches, the staff. He liked to do things for people. He'd make a call, and whatever problem you had he took care of it. Abe had connections."[37] One time, he treated half the office to a Frank Sinatra concert. He bought a bed for a secretary; a suit for a ticket manager.

On the field, however, Gibron was surprisingly intense. He cursed, ran back and forth during line drills, and exhorted the team to be mean, especially Lee Roy. Said one former Buc, "Abe used to always tell Lee Roy that if he played meaner, they'd have to ban him from the game."[38] Gibron's favorite player was Dave Pear, a frenetic, überaggressive nose guard who'd been a backup with the Colts. Pear was small for the position, but ran a 4.6 forty and could bench-press five hundred pounds. "Allrightallrightallright!" he'd scream, having fought through a line of three-hundred-pound blockers to get to his man. "Allrightallrightallright!"

Reporter Ron Martz described Pear as "two hundred and fifty pounds of concentrated aggression, an impressive parcel of deltoids and latissimus dorsi."[39] Martz was right. Pear looked like Arnold Schwarzenegger in the Conan movies and loved to excite crowds by pumping his pythonlike arms into the air. Dave "didn't hold anything back," said John McKay, "but that's something you want in a defensive lineman. Pear was wild."[40] Bucs announcer Jack Harris remembers Pear as "one emotionally charged dude." He'd "run through a wall and then ask 'What do I do now? I'm on the other side.' "[41] In practice, Pear was so intense he fought with teammates or forgot what scheme he was in. "I was the one blocking him," said center Dan Ryczek. "I should know. He was crazy. He played every play like it was his last play . . . like his life depended on it. So not only did I have ten weeks of two-a-days, I had ten weeks of Dave Pear."[42]

Off the field, Pear was an eccentric. He ate vitamins by the handful, roomed alone during away games, and sometimes sat inside his cubicle to decompress. He was finding his "place in the universe," he said, and football was "a trip."[43] He had long flowing hair that poured from his helmet and onto his shoulders. Once, when Kansas City center Jack Rudnay called him a "hippie freak," Pear looked at him and laughed.[44] Without a doubt, Pear was the meanest, oddest, most aggressive player on the team. Gibron loved him. "If Abe could have adopted Dave," said Dewey Selmon, "he would have. I think Abe saw a lot of himself in Dave."[45]

On offense, Gibron's counterpart was offensive coordinator John Rauch. In college, Rauch had been a star quarterback at the University of Georgia, where he passed for a then–NCAA record 4,044 yards. In 1949, he was drafted number two by Detroit, but was traded to the New York Bulldogs for running back Doak Walker. Rauch played three years in the pros before taking a job as an assistant coach at the University of Florida. He coached at various colleges through the 1950s, then in 1963 joined Al Davis and the Oakland Raiders as a running backs coach. When, in 1966, Davis left the Raiders briefly to become AFL commissioner, Rauch became head coach. In 1967 he went 13-1 and was AFL Coach of the Year. He then went 12-2 in 1968, but clashed constantly with Davis, a notorious meddler who wanted more input on the field.[46]

In 1969, Rauch left the Raiders to become head coach of the Bills. His teams there went 4-10 and 3-10-1, and Rauch was accused of having misused O. J. Simpson, who had just 1,185 yards rushing in two years. In 1971, Rauch and Bills owner Ralph Wilson had a falling-out over Rauch's treatment of two veteran players. Rather than apologize, Rauch resigned. He resurfaced in 1973 as head coach of the Toronto Argonauts, a CFL team, then in 1975 was a running backs coach with the Atlanta Falcons.

As Tampa Bay's offensive coordinator, Rauch was tasked with implementing the team's offense and designing plays. Personally, Rauch preferred a horizontal passing attack similar to Oakland's—an early version of the "West Coast offense." Such an offense involved short, well-timed passes to multiple receivers, and represented a perfect fit for Steve Spurrier, a weak-armed quarterback who, at 6'1", 205 pounds, was in his tenth season as a pro. Yet McKay favored—no demanded—the "I." Soon tension developed between coordinator and quarterback on the one hand and the head coach on the other.

Caught between Spurrier and McKay was Tom McEwen, the *Tampa Tribune* editor who, without question, was the Bucs' number-one booster. A founding member of Ed Rood's Suncoast Pro Football Committee, McEwen adored McKay. The day the coach was hired, in fact, McEwen's column carried a headline that read: "John McKay Coup Judged: Terrific!" The two men were drinking buddies. They could be seen late after games in a booth at Malio's, where they were joined occasionally by George Steinbrenner. McKay even looked like McEwen, and the sly reporter had a story he liked to tell. "People used to confuse us all the time," he said. "I was driving on Westshore one time leaving One Buc Place and stopped at a light. Some guy pulled up beside me and did a double-take, like, 'Are you him?' I shot him a bird and drove off. I knew he'd think it was McKay."[47]

McEwen was also friends with Spurrier—good friends. He was the quarterback's biggest fan and in 1966 had lobbied journalists and some say swung the Heisman to Spurrier when the quarterback was at Florida. In 1982, he even persuaded John Bassett, the owner of the United States Football League team the Tampa Bay Bandits, to hire Spurrier as coach.[48] McKay was aware of the relationship, and liked to kid McEwen by saying *"Your* quarterback is late," or *"Your* quarterback is slow." *"My* quarterback?" McEwen would ask in mock surprise, but what McKay said was true.[49] "I told McEwen once that I was a Florida fan and that Spurrier had always been a hero of mine," said Bill Marcum, "and he said, 'mine, too.' "[50]

Then there was John, McKay's son, a receiver from USC. The press called him J. K. McKay, for John Kenneth, but the 5'10", 175-pound rookie preferred John. The younger McKay had been a star in college. In 1974, he had 34 catches for 550 yards and 8 touchdowns, and in January was the Rose Bowl MVP. He'd been drafted in the eighteenth round by the Cleveland Browns, but opted instead for the WFL's Southern California Suns, where in 1975 he and former USC quarterback Pat Haden played. McKay had good hands, but ran a 4.8 forty and probably shouldn't have been a pro.

Indeed, the Bucs' receiving corps was the offensive equivalent of its linebacking corps—it stunk. On opening day, only Barry Smith, a former Florida State star and expansion pick from the Packers, had any NFL experience. He'd played three years total for a run-heavy Green Bay offense and had caught just forty-one balls. That was it. The other receivers were Isaac

Hagins and Lee McGriff. A speed demon from the University of Minnesota, Hagins had been picked up off waivers. He wowed fans with two preseason kickoff returns for touchdowns, but had no receptions. McGriff was 5'9", 160, a former walk-on at Florida who had beaten the odds to become an all-SEC performer. As a pro, though, he didn't have a chance.

These were the receivers, but Spurrier focused his attention, and his angst, on McKay—actually, on both McKays. He argued with the father and wouldn't throw to the son. "Why don't you throw to the damned X?!" the coach would yell. "Why don't you throw to the damned X?!" As John Crittenden of the *Miami News* explained, the X was Johnny.[51] According to Lee McGriff, Spurrier would needle McKay by walking out onto the practice field with no shoes on, or by visiting the golf course during lunch. The practices were "unbelievably long," said McGriff. "But Steve, sometimes between practices, would go and hit golf balls. I promise you. I thought, 'This is unbelievable. We're all dying; we've been doing this forever, and this guy's out here hitting golf balls.' And that drove Coach McKay insane."[52]

Due to the Bucs' offense, the smash-mouth I-formation, the team's running back position was a revolving door. In all, the team used eight running backs during the 1976 season; they cut seven in the preseason and had two on injured reserve. Their best back, presumably, was the team's second-round draft pick from Florida, Jimmy DuBose. A 5'11", 215-pound fullback and the 1975 SEC Player of the Year, DuBose had averaged an NCAA-best 6.8 yards per carry. However, DuBose suffered a nagging ankle injury in the preseason and had just twenty attempts in fourteen games. The Bucs' most reliable backs were

Louis Carter, a second-year expansion pick from Oakland and former Maryland star, and free agent Ed Williams and trade pickup Essex Johnson, both formerly of the Bengals. Williams and Carter were backups—both had zero starts and fewer than one hundred career carries—while Johnson was a thirty-year-old former starter with bad knees. By contrast, the Bucs tight ends were surprisingly good and included a former Stanford star and Raider named Bob Moore. Between 1973 and 1975, Moore had started forty-two straight games for the Raiders, one of the best teams in football, but came to the Bucs when future Hall of Famer Dave Casper supplanted him at tight end.

The Bucs offensive line was, well, bad. A mixture of four first-year players and five veterans led by Mike Current and Howard Fest, it had as a unit more than 150 starts. The problem was that Fest and Current had almost all of them. A thirty-one-year-old tackle and nine-year veteran with Denver, Current had come to the Bucs through the expansion draft; so had Fest, a thirty-year-old guard and eight-year veteran with the Bengals. They were joined as starters by free agent guard Tom Alward of the WFL's Birmingham Vulcans; fourth-year center and Redskins veteran Dan Ryczek, a former thirteenth-round pick; and Steve Young, the 6'8" rookie at tackle, who was a project. Young was in the lineup due to a game three injury to Dave Reavis, a third-year tackle and expansion pick who'd been with the Steelers.

"It was a strange experience," said Reavis. Going from a two-time Super Bowl champion to an expansion team, "nobody seemed to know what was going on."[53] Dan Ryczek agreed. "He's right," he says. "He's absolutely right. We didn't. We had five guys on the line from five different systems. Then add backups and injuries and two months of two-a-days, and what do you get? Zero and fourteen."[54] In one famous story, McKay was lecturing the team when Fest fell asleep. "Gentlemen, losing starts with mistakes, losing starts with turnovers, losing starts with . . ." McKay looked at Fest. "Fest!" he yelled. "Where does losing start?" The startled lineman replied, "Right here in Tampa Bay, Coach."[55]

———

Actually, the losing started in Los Angeles, in the Bucs' first-ever preseason matchup with the Rams. Winner of three consecutive NFC West championships with a roster that included seven Pro Bowlers, the Rams had one of the best defenses in the league. But preseason is preseason; it's evaluation time, so both the Bucs and the Rams were planning to use at least seventy players. As McKay put it, he'd be "busier than a one-armed paper-hanger" trying to get players into the game.[56]

The team traveled by charter, in a plane, as mentioned earlier, that Culverhouse leased not from a commercial airline, but from the McCulloch Corporation. McKay knew the owner of McCulloch, explains Pat Toomay, "so it came to pass that we chartered McCulloch's rattletrap 707. In the vast enterprise of McCulloch International Airlines, it was the only plane in the fleet."[57] The McCulloch "rattletrap" sat on the tarmac in view of the practice field at One Buc Place. "They didn't cover it, either," says Tom Bass, "so it'd be a hundred degrees in Tampa, but three hundred on the plane. We'd sweat like pigs."[58] The seating chart was as follows: Hugh and Joy Culverhouse and members of the press and guests sat at the front of the plane. Next were coaches, officials, and trainers, then players, and

finally, McKay in the back. Equipment manager Pat Marcuccillo recalled how once somebody asked McKay why he sat
back there. "You see all those people in front of me?" he replied. "Have you ever seen a plane back into a mountain? If
this plane goes down, I want all those sons of a bitches to go
before I go."[59]

For McKay, the trip to Los Angeles was a homecoming.
He'd coached at USC since 1959 and still had family there, including a daughter, and a son-in-law named Tim Donnelly, the
actor who played "Chet" Kelly on the popular TV show *Emergency!* (Kelly brought the cast of *Emergency!* to the game.) "I
love L.A.," said McKay. "I think it's a great city. I got lots of
calls and notes from my friends and former associates. I just
hope that we play real well."[60]

Odds were they wouldn't. The spread was fourteen, and
no expansion team had ever won its first preseason game, not
even the Vikings, who opened in 1961 with a 38–13 loss to
Dallas, a team whose record the previous year had been 0-11-
1. But the Bucs had a secret weapon: the thirty-seven-year-old
kicker Gerry "Booth" Lusteg. A Connecticut grad and pro football journeyman who'd last played in the 1960s, Lusteg broke
into the league with Buffalo. At a tryout in 1966, the onetime
waiter, math instructor, and "off Broadway bit player" earned a
spot by beating out more than one hundred kickers when Bills
star Pete Gogolak famously jumped leagues and signed with
the Giants.[61]

Lusteg led the Bills in scoring, but after he missed a 19-yard
field goal in a game against the Chargers, an enraged Bills fan
punched Lusteg in the face. When someone asked Lusteg why
he hadn't reported the incident to the police, he responded,

"because I deserved it."[62] In July 1976, the Bucs signed Lusteg to compete with Pete Rajecki, a free agent from the WFL's
Charlotte Hornets who was the last kicker in camp. Lusteg
had only been in Tampa for four days when he flew with the
team to Los Angeles. The problem was that Lusteg wore black
flat-toed kicking shoes, while the Bucs' shoes were white, no
exceptions.

When word reached McKay that Lusteg planned to wear
the shoes, the coach told him he wouldn't be allowed in the
game. In a pinch, assistant equipment manager Frankie Pupello bought two cans of white spray paint and just hours before kickoff the eccentric kicker painted both of his shoes. He
then stood on the sidelines, saw no action whatsoever, and
was cut. His career in Tampa had lasted seven days. Nevertheless, Lusteg did ruin a Wilshire Hyatt House table after paint-
ing his shoes on it, and the bill, remembered Pupello, was four
hundred dollars.[63]

That evening of July 31, 1976, the Bucs played the Rams
in the Los Angeles Coliseum in front of 55,000 fans. Starting
at their own twenty-seven yard line, the Rams drove seventy-
three yards on eleven plays for a touchdown. The Bucs went
three and out, then the Rams went fifty-three yards on eight
plays for a field goal. They were led by All-Pro running back
Lawrence McCutcheon, who had nine rushes for sixty-five
yards. In two drives, the Rams had run the ball fourteen times.

"We didn't hustle," said McKay after the game, and "there's
no excuse for the way we tackled. Other people tackle Ram
runners. We didn't."[64] The Bucs' second drive netted a first
down—a six-yard swing pass from Steve Spurrier to running
back Manfred Moore. Unfortunately, on a third-and-three from

the Bucs' forty-eight, a Spurrier pass to McGriff fell incomplete. The teams traded punts until early in the second, when Rams quarterback James Harris went 6 for 6 on a seventeen-play, 80-yard drive. (The Rams actually gained 105 yards from scrimmage, but were penalized three times.) The score was 17–0. With 3:23 left in the second, the Bucs had given up 235 yards. They'd gained thirty-eight yards, had one first down, and punted three times.

Finally, at the end of the second quarter, the Bucs scored. It came on a Pete Rajecki field goal following an eighteen-play, 63-yard drive, Spurrier's best of the game. Although sacked twice and harried by Rams defenders, Spurrier managed to complete a 27-yard pass to J. K. McKay on third-and-sixteen. The quarterback then drove the team to the three-yard line, but failed to score on first-and-three and second-and-two, so the Bucs kicked a field goal as time expired. The Rams led 17–3.

In the second half, the Bucs were better, at least defensively. Led by Dave Pear and Pat Toomay, they limited Harris's backup, Ron Jaworski, to just 1 of 5 passing and the Rams to 98 yards. Still, the Buccaneer offense couldn't score. In the fourth, McKay replaced Spurrier with rookie backup Parnell Dickinson, who engineered a 79-yard drive to the one-yard line that ended in a fumble. Dickinson led three more drives, but was sacked twice and intercepted on a bad throw late in the quarter. The game ended with a final score of 26–3. However, it might as well have been 50–3. After all, the Bucs had been practicing for three and a half weeks, while their opponent, the Rams, had had the same lineup and had been Super Bowl contenders for three years. And, throughout the game, McKay belittled the team from the sidelines, calling them "UCLA rejects" and "chickens." "When are we going to send in our good players?" he yelled. "When are we going to send in our good players?"[65]

The next week, by the Tuesday after the opener, NFL rules required teams to have no more than sixty players. To comply, the Bucs cut thirteen, including Ted Jornov, a game one starter at linebacker, and placed four on injured reserve. Meanwhile, the scouting department continued to find players. By midnight of August 25, just three days before the Bucs' fifth preseason game, the league required teams to cut rosters to forty-nine players, forty-three by September 6. By then, teams who had stockpiled talent would have to release players—players Wolf hoped would help the team.[66] Therefore, to prepare, Bucs scouts saw dozens of games. Tom Bass, for example, attended a San Diego–Philadelphia matchup the night of the Rams game. He then went to a Seattle–San Francisco game on Sunday, and a Kansas City–Houston game on Monday night. The next week, when the Bucs were in Green Bay, Bass was in Cincinnati for a Bengals game versus the Bills.

Four and ten in 1975 and one of the worst teams in the league, Green Bay was almost as bad as the Bucs. But instead of taking a "win now" approach in the preseason, McKay used the game to evaluate players, including quarterback Parnell Dickinson, and to practice the "I." Led by Louis Carter, four different backs pounded the ball, maniacally, rushing 35 times for 108 yards, a measly 3.1-yard average. Although Tampa Bay did score a touchdown on a one-yard dive by Vince Kendrick, the first in team history, it had six three-and-outs, two interceptions, a fumble, and punted seven times. On defense, however, the Bucs were surprisingly stout, holding the Packers to a touchdown and a field goal through eleven different drives. The final score was Green Bay 10, Tampa Bay 6.

Through two games, the Bucs had improved mightily. They still couldn't run the ball, or even pass, but Dickinson had showed speed in flashes and the defense had hung tough. Luckily, their next game was a winnable matchup in Jacksonville with Atlanta, a team with a talented second-year quarterback named Steve Bartkowski. The 1975 NFL Rookie of the Year, Bartkowski led the Falcons into field goal range on the game's opening drive, but a penalty forced them to punt. They never recovered. On Tampa Bay's second possession, Spurrier hit Barry Smith for a forty-one-yard reception to set up a Mirro Roder field goal. The score at the end of the quarter was Tampa Bay 3, Atlanta 0. With that first field goal, said tight end Bob Moore, "we suddenly realized 'My God! We're playing better than they are.'"[67] Neither team scored in the second, but at the nine-minute mark in the third, Falcons running back Bubba Bean fumbled on a pitchout at the Atlanta five, which Dave Pear recovered. On first down, Kendrick rushed to the Bucs' one, then Spurrier, on a quarterback keeper, scored. The Bucs had a ten-point lead.

The Falcons responded with a field goal, making the score 10–3, but with three minutes left in the third, the Bucs unleashed a twelve-play, 70-yard drive ending in a touchdown. The score was Tampa Bay 17, Atlanta 3. No doubt embarrassed by the Bucs, Falcons coach Marion Campbell left his starters in into the fourth. Bartkowski, for example, went 5 for 8 for 60 yards in the stanza, but Atlanta didn't score. Although inept versus the Rams, the Bucs' secondary had been flawless against the Falcons, holding Bartkowski to just 15 of 30 passing and 153 yards. He had no touchdowns and was intercepted twice.

"I don't have any answers," said Bartkowski. "I do know that this was a very low point in my life, about the lowest I've ever had on a football field."[68]

The Bucs, on the other hand, were overjoyed. On offense, they'd run 73 plays to the Falcons' 59 and outgained Atlanta 284 to 215. In addition, they'd run the ball 50 times for 152 yards and burned over 36 minutes of clock. "We said before the game we had to keep the ball some," said McKay. "In our other games, Los Angeles and Green Bay had the ball all the time" but tonight "our blocking was better. . . . Oh well, another dynasty."[69] Ron Wolf couldn't resist. "Let's see," he said. "Correct me if I'm wrong, but I believe Seattle's record now is 0-3 and isn't ours 1-2?"[70] Believe it or not, the Bucs had won before eight other teams had won, so on Monday, they were ranked twentieth out of twenty-eight teams on the Dunkel Pro Index, a Sagarin-like statistical system that's still in use today. According to Dunkel, three weeks into the preseason, the league's best team was Pittsburgh, followed by Oakland, Los Angeles, and Miami.

The next week, Tampa Bay was set to play Miami at the newly expanded, 72,000-seat Tampa Stadium. Funded by $13 million in bonds and contributions from the city of Tampa and Hillsborough County, the expansion was finished by August 1976. Culverhouse had a thirty-year lease; he paid the TSA 10 percent of the gate but received a majority of all skybox revenue, a portion of parking and concessions, and most of the in-stadium advertising, including ads on the scoreboard. (Priced at more than a million dollars, the scoreboard was forty-two feet by thirty-two feet, took six people to operate, and generated $550,000 a year in advertisements.)[71] He also received 50 percent of gate receipts for any concert in Tampa Stadium that drew more than 50,000 people, and half of parking and concessions if Tampa ever hosted a Super Bowl.[72]

It was an incredible deal for Culverhouse, but the TSA didn't complain. The agency's other tenant, the Tampa Bay Rowdies, paid perhaps 12 percent and in 1976 averaged more than 16,000 fans per game. In June, the Rowdies drew 42,611 to a home matchup with the Cosmos, the New York team captained by the aging but still legendary star Pelé. Then, in August, on the same night the Bucs beat the Falcons, the Rowdies won the NASL's Eastern Division championship, setting up a Cosmos-Rowdies rematch in Tampa. The Rowdies played the Cosmos on Friday; the Bucs played the Dolphins on Saturday. "Pelé and Bob Griese back-to-back?" exclaimed one journalist. "Derek Smethurst and Steve Spurrier in the spotlight on consecutive days? Tampa Bay Rowdies–New York Cosmos and Tampa Bay Buccaneers–Miami Dolphins on the same weekend? Can you believe THAT?"[73]

For the weekend, stadium officials expected 100,000 people, and a sellout, perhaps, for the Bucs. Season ticket sales had peaked at 38,000, but for the Miami game fans gobbled up end zone seats and seats in the upper decks for eight dollars. The prices were high. In January 1976, for example, admission to nosebleed sections of the Super Bowl cost just twenty dollars, while Rowdies playoffs tickets were four. Even so, the Bucs sold sixty-five thousand tickets by Friday, and the rest the day of the game. Saturday, August 21, was "NFL Day" in Florida following an official proclamation by Florida governor Reubin Askew. There was also a stadium dedication ceremony featuring Senator Lawton Chiles of Lakeland, a guest appearance by former astronaut and Ohio senator John Glenn, and a "mini-Gasparilla" boat parade on the Hillsborough River, in which Joy Culverhouse and McKay's wife, Corky, served as judges.[74]

That night, the Bucs drew 71,718 fans, the largest preseason crowd at any NFL venue that year. (The Rowdies, by the way, drew 36,863.) Fans "arrived early and stayed late," wrote Tom McEwen, "and cheered their rookie Bucs as if they were defending Super Bowl champs."[75] However, the Dolphins were the champs, or at least the *former* champs. Winner of NFL titles in 1972 and 1973, and the only team to have ever had an undefeated season, the Dolphins were led by All-Pro quarterback Bob Griese. Griese was known for his accuracy. In three first-half drives, he was 8 for 11 for 100 yards and 3 touchdowns. Griese "cut through Tampa's defense Saturday night like a razor blade," wrote the *Miami News*. He was "so hot" he would "jerk the other team offside just by clearing his throat."[76]

Nevertheless, the Dolphins' defense versus Tampa Bay was uncharacteristically weak, the result of a linebacking corps that had already experienced two season-ending injuries, plus the temporary retirement of Nick Buoniconti, a perennial All-Pro. It held tough on the Bucs' first two drives, almost all running plays, but when Spurrier threw the ball the Bucs scored—again and again and again. The first was a nine-yard touchdown pass to Vince Kendrick following a 12-play, 60-yard drive. Spurrier then led a 10-play, 70-yard drive for a field goal, plus a short drive for a second field goal at the end of the half. The score at intermission was Dolphins 21, Bucs 12. "Spurrier was outstanding," said Miami coach Don Shula. Down 14–0, many teams "might have folded." But the Bucs didn't, he said. Spurrier "really kept 'em coming at us."[77]

In the second half, Shula replaced Griese with NFL journeyman Jim Del Gaizo, the Dolphins' fourth-string quarterback, who promptly led the offense to a touchdown. It was Miami's fourth touchdown in five drives. Spurrier responded with a twelve-play, 80-yard drive for a field goal and a 26-yard touchdown late in the fourth. The final score was Miami 28, Tampa Bay 21. "Give Tampa a moral victory," said Dolphins receiver Howard Twilley, the last player left from Miami's 1966 expansion team. "It's obvious they'll be competitive."[78]

Believe it or not, the preseason loss to Miami was the high point of Tampa Bay's season. On Monday, the team rose to nineteenth on the Dunkel Pro Index, while the 0-3 Seattle Seahawks remained last. In fact, Dunkel insisted that the fledgling Bucs were a three-point favorite the next week versus the Bears. (According to Jimmy "the Greek" Snyder, the Vegas prognosticator, the Bucs wouldn't be favored again until September 2, 1978—a period of two years.) Although just 4-10 in 1975, the Bears had a first-rate defense, led by All-Pro tackle Wally Chambers, which held Tampa Bay to 129 yards passing and 51 yards on the ground. In addition, the Bears had two interceptions, one for a touchdown, and sacked the frazzled Spurrier six times.

"We stunk," said McKay. "The offense couldn't have been worse. If we blocked anyone I didn't see it" and "if we would have played this way against Miami we would have been beaten 666–0. . . . It was our worst effort of the preseason."[79] Indeed, the Bucs were so bad they went three-and-out on nine of thirteen drives. They punted on ten drives, threw two interceptions, including one for a touchdown, and fumbled. It was a dismal performance. Nevertheless, the Bucs did score on a 92-yard kickoff return by Isaac Hagins, a Thursday waiver pickup from the Vikings who'd practiced with the team for one day. Known as "Tight Man" for his small yet muscular frame, Hagins returned a second kickoff a week later versus the Bengals.

On defense, Tampa Bay gave up 175 yards rushing, including 91 to Walter Payton, but limited Chicago to a single 44-yard field goal with 1:43 left in the fourth. The final score was Chicago 10, Tampa Bay 7. The fans blamed Spurrier. "Booooo!" they yelled. "Booooo!"—although on passing situations the quarterback didn't have time to throw. "Can't they see the guy is being knocked flat on his can by the defensive pass rush?" asked McKay. "Can't they see that when we've given Steve pass protection, he's usually hit his receiver?" The fans, he said, were "idiots."[80]

The next week versus the Bengals, in Tampa Bay's last preseason game, Spurrier opened with a 9-play, 93-yard drive for a touchdown but was otherwise ineffective. He was sacked twice and harried by a defense featuring four All-Pros, including two in the secondary, who held Spurrier and backups Larry Lawrence and Parnell Dickinson to just 8 of 23 passing for 89 yards. The lone bright spot again was Hagins, who had a 102-yard kickoff return for a touchdown, his second in two games. (Almost impossibly, the Bucs next kickoff return for a touchdown came 1,865 returns later—in 2007.)[81] Quarterback Parnell Dickinson ran the ball 6 times for 59 yards, but running backs Vince Kendrick, Essex Johnson, and Manfred Moore combined for just 89 yards on 27 carries, a 3.1-yard average. On defense, the Bucs gave up 279 yards passing and 3 touchdowns to John Reaves, a native Tampan and former University of Florida star who backed up Ken Anderson. In addition, Bengals running backs had 36 carries for 179 yards, rookie Chris Bahr kicked a field goal, and Cincinnati throttled the Bucs 24–13.

Still, the Bucs had had a decent preseason. At 1-5, they'd lost two games badly (versus the Bengals and Rams). They'd lost 10–6 and 10–7 to two NFC Central opponents (the Packers and the Bears), held their own in a shoot-out versus the Dolphins, and beaten Atlanta's first team. To some, including Cincinnati Bengals coach Bill Johnson, the Buccaneers were the best expansion team that they'd ever seen.[82] Odds were Tampa Bay would go 3-11. The last four expansion teams—Minnesota, Miami, Cincinnati, and New Orleans—had all gone 3-11, though in 1960, Dallas had gone 0-11-1. The Bucs would play their easiest games at home. They played Seattle at home, plus six teams whose record in 1975 was 31-53, including the 2-12 Chargers, the 3-11 Patriots, and the 3-11 Browns. (They also played the 3-11 Jets on the road.) No one, anywhere, predicted an 0-14 season, though editor Anson Mount II of *Playboy* called for 2-12. "Personally, I think we'll do better than that," said McKay. "Did he mention which two teams? I wish he would so I wouldn't have to worry about them."[83]

Chapter Four

The Aft Deck of the
Lusitania

I don't want to be no part of no Tampa Bay history mak-
ing. . . . No sir.

—O. J. Simpson, Bills running back

The futility of the Bucs' first season was epitomized on November 7, 1976. On a beautiful day at Denver's Mile High Stadium,
kicker Dave Green booted through a 35-yard field goal, giving
the Buccaneers a 13–10 lead. At 0-8, the Bucs were seventeen-
point underdogs, but surprisingly led the Broncos with 4:07
left in the third. This was a winnable game. Unfortunately, the
Broncos scored thirty-eight points in nine minutes. They managed two interception returns, a fumble return, a 71-yard pass,
a 9-yard run, and a field goal to suddenly crush the Bucs 48–13.
That's thirty-eight points in nine minutes. The NFL record, to
that point, was forty-one points in a quarter.

Denver had three defensive touchdowns, but John McKay
accused Broncos coach John Ralston of running up the score.
The two men had known each other in college. From 1963 to
1971, Ralston had coached at Stanford, where he was 2-7 versus McKay but had beaten the USC coach his last two years.

McKay hated him for it. "He's a prick," said the Buccaneer coach after the game. "He always was a prick. I hope he gets fired."[1] Standing on the sidelines, McKay pointed at Ralston and cursed. He then refused to shake hands. Back in the locker room, the seething coach was so mad that he gave players just fifteen minutes to shower, collect their things, and make it to the bus. They all made it, miraculously, but a person in the traveling party who didn't was owner Hugh Culverhouse, who ran through the parking lot throwing rocks at the bus and yelling "Stop! Stop! I own the team!"[2]

That was McKay: acerbic, imperious, "a cross," wrote one journalist, "between Richard Nixon and Captain Queeg."[3] On Mondays, McKay hosted the *McKay* television show, where he and Tampa's WTVT Channel 13 sports director Andy Hardy reviewed "highlights" from the previous day's game. Hardy wore an orange Buccaneers blazer. The carpet was orange. There was a desk and two chairs and on the wall above the set was "Bucco Bruce," the team's mascot. McKay did no preparation; each week he came to the studio in a gray Cadillac Seville driven by team assistant Dick Beam. When he walked in, the show began. Hardy: "So, Coach, there were bad snaps on both extra-point attempts against the Dolphins. I'm sure we don't want to throw blame on anybody, but . . ." McKay: "Yes, I do, Andy. One snap was high, the other was on the ground. We have a center who should be able to do better than that." Hardy: "Steve Spurrier showed he could run with the football on that play." McKay: "There's no law that says a quarterback can't run, Andy." Often, McKay answered questions with "Of course, Andy, you won't understand this, but . . ."[4] It went on all season long.

"That's just the way he was," says former WTVT sportscaster Pete Johnson, who worked with Hardy. "The station tried to improve the show by interviewing players or coaches, or introducing backstories, but McKay wouldn't let them. He also refused a hairstylist and a makeup artist, and wouldn't do a run-through." Worst of all, insists Johnson, McKay was "chippy with Andy," who feared that bored or annoyed viewers would switch to Channel 44, WTVT's rival station, instead of watching the show.[5]

McKay had, as one would imagine, a rocky relationship with the press. He was a phenomenal quote—I mean, who else called All-Pro tackle Dan Dierdorf "Dan Dusseldorf" or coach Bum Phillips "Bumblehead"—but he was volatile at times and mean. According to St. Petersburg *Independent* reporter Tim McDonald, McKay was "expansive, sullen, somber, friendly, intimidating, lucid, enlightening, abrupt, and just plain hilarious." The emotion he exhibited, wrote McDonald, "varied from week to week, from loss to win."[6] He couldn't stand to be second-guessed. "Why? Why? Why?" he once spat, in mock imitation of Hardy, who he claimed conducted the *McKay* show like "an inquisition."[7]

The question everyone asked, and not just Hardy, was why couldn't the Bucs score? That was a big one. In their first regular season game, at Houston, they had 108 yards of offense, total, and just 8 first downs. In fact, the team's first first down came in the second quarter, twenty-three and a half minutes into the game. Punter-kicker Dave Green, a preseason pickup from the Bengals who played in the Houston game, insists that in Cincinnati, the rule of thumb was that if he punted four or more times per outing, the Bengals were in trouble. But, in Green's first game with the Buccaneers, he punted *eleven* times. He was standing in the end zone, ready to kick, the ball at the Bucs' one-yard line, when the clock ran out.[8]

The problem was the offensive line. It had no cohesion. The Tuesday following the preseason game versus the Bengals, McKay cut Ira Gordon, the Bucs' starting guard and allocation pick from San Diego. (This was the same Gordon who'd promised to "whup" the Selmons.) Gordon was done, professionally, but in his place McKay started a rookie named Charlie Little, a fourth-round draft pick from the University of Houston. McKay believed that Little would struggle at first, but that in the coming years he would be one of the best linemen in the league. That was the plan, McKay's "five-year plan": lose now with inexperienced rookies and second- and third-year players to win later. As defensive coordinator Abe Gibron explained it, McKay was building from the ground up.[9] In all, the Bucs had fifteen rookies, seven of whom were opening-day starters—right guard Charlie Little, left tackle Steve Young, receivers Johnny McKay and Lee McGriff, fullback Jimmy DuBose, defensive tackle Lee Roy Selmon, and cornerback Mike Washington.

Former *St. Petersburg Times* sports editor Hubert Mizell insists that McKay's plan was a good one, but that on the field, versus NFL opponents, it was painful to watch.[10] Once, assistant public relations director Charlie Dayton was speaking to a senior citizens group when one person exclaimed, "What?! A five-year plan? Some of us don't have that long!"[11] The timeline wasn't ambiguous. McKay had a five-year contract and promised to quit, if he hadn't made the playoffs, when his tenure was over.[12] It helped, of course, that owner Hugh Culverhouse absolutely loved McKay. The men were friends; they often golfed together at Tampa's Palma Ceia Country Club, and McKay's wife, Corky, sat with Hugh and Joy Culverhouse in the owner's skybox. "As far as Hugh was concerned," said Joy, in a 1999 interview, "John walked on water. Hugh didn't know anything about football. That's why I think he had real hero worship for John."[13] Culverhouse's son, Hugh Jr., agrees. "Dad was starstruck." He sometimes accompanied McKay to watch McKay's other son, Richie, play in high school and later went with the coach to Princeton to watch Richie play there. Looking back, Hugh Jr. says, "Dad was closer to the McKays than he was to us."[14]

Still living in Jacksonville, Culverhouse came to Tampa several times a week. He and Joy had a suite at the Tampa Airport Resort near One Buc Place, but later moved to a luxury condominium complex on Bayshore Boulevard. Although not in the office every day, Culverhouse was an exceptionally "hands-on" owner; Bill Marcum recalls that the staff liked to joke that it couldn't purchase a paper clip without calling Jacksonville for permission. He was "a left-brained guy in a very right-brained business," he says. "He was always organized, and he always had a budget."[15] Although later known—and this is a typical post from JoeBucsFan.com—as the "cheapest, stingiest, stupidest, obnoxious, ugliest, incompetent and most selfish owner in the history of professional sports," Culverhouse wasn't stupid and wasn't, in his first few years, cheap.[16] According to *Sports Illustrated*, in the mid to late 1970s, the annual gross income of the average NFL team was $8.9 million.[17] Assuming the Bucs made $8.9 million and had expenditures of $7 million, which is what *Florida Trend* magazine estimated, Culverhouse had to squeeze the team to make money.[18] First, he owed $2 million a year for the next six years to the NFL, payments on loans to Citibank and the Exchange Bank of Tampa for his $4 million down payment, salaries for fifty or so players, including active players and those on injured reserve, plus salaries for ten coaches and a staff of thirty. He then had operating costs, including travel expenses for away games and a lease on One Buc Place.

The players were Culverhouse's single greatest expense. In 1977, the average NFL salary was $55,288, about $216,000 today, for an average outlay of approximately $2.75 million per year. The team with the highest payroll, reportedly, was Washington, at $3.6 million. The league's highest-paid player was O. J. Simpson at $733,358. Fran Tarkenton and Joe Namath each made $350,000, while veteran starters and most stars typically earned between $100,000 and $200,000 per year.[19] The Bucs had at least two players in the $100,000 range—Steve Spurrier and Lee Roy Selmon. The numbers were never published, but in 1977 Spurrier asked for a raise, reportedly, to $150,000, while Selmon made $182,000 as late as 1982. Veteran Pat Toomay was in the $75,000 range, while punter-kicker Dave Green, who had league experience, made $50,000. Low draft picks and free agents like Lee McGriff were in the $30,000 range, though the minimum league-wide was $20,000. (Vince Papale, the famed thirty-year-old Eagles rookie later portrayed in the 2006 Mark Wahlberg film *Invincible,* made just $21,000.)

Buccaneer fans may splutter a bit when they read this, but in 1976, Buc players were *not* underpaid, at least by league standards. "That was McKay's influence," says Culverhouse's son Hugh Jr. "Dad did what John said and that probably dictated a more generous salary structure. But later, after say '79, Dad's true character appeared."[20] While fair, at first, with salaries, the left-brained Bucs owner scrimped in a variety of ways. "This is a secondhand sofa," he once told journalists on a tour of One Buc Place. "I bought it out of the River Club in Jacksonville for four hundred dollars. It's not great looking, but it's comfortable and it'll do the job." Culverhouse also told journalists that the walls at the facility were painted white on purpose. That way, when players watched film, they didn't need a screen.[21]

Bill Marcum remembers a 1975 meeting with the manager of Tampa Airport, the team's early headquarters. Culverhouse had rented office space in the lobby and he and Marcum had asked the manager for tables and chairs, extra phone lines, that sort of thing. The manager agreed, but then Culverhouse made a final request. He said that since every piece of mail sent out by the Bucs would list the hotel in its return address, the hotel should pay for the letterhead. "My jaw hit the floor," says Marcum. "I mean, what did letterhead cost? And, no matter what it cost, that was your letterhead! That was a pro team's letterhead! But the manager, who needed the business I guess, said yes."[22]

On occasion, Culverhouse also used trainers and equipment managers to do non-team-related work. Trainers John Lopez and Tom Oxley were once told to move Culverhouse's bar from his condo near One Buc Place to his new apartment on Bayshore Boulevard. "There were all these bottles," remembers Lopez. "And Tom joked, 'Do you think he'd notice if we took a few?' And I said, 'Shoooot . . . He knows every bottle down to the ounce.'"[23] Once, Culverhouse called Oxley at home and told him to meet him at the airport. His back had gone out during a flight from New York, so he asked Oxley to treat him with warm gel packs heated up in the team's hydrocollator. As Culverhouse lay on the training table, awaiting treatment, he noticed that the hydrocollator was always in the on position. Ever the frugal owner, he told the trainer to go to the hardware store to buy a timer switch. When Oxley tried to tell Culverhouse that most likely they'd use more electricity turning it off and then on, Culverhouse replied: "Maybe so, but let me know what you find out."[24]

Oxley's most humorous story involves Joy Culverhouse, who in his words was a "very demanding woman." Joy liked to golf. She'd golfed on scholarship at Louisiana State and the University of Alabama, and had won the Florida amateur championship, at age forty, in 1961. According to Oxley, sometime in 1977, Joy was golfing at the Tampa Airport Resort when she teed off and struck a seagull, which she sent via greenskeeper to One Buc Place. The bird had a fractured wing, and she wanted the trainers to fix it. "What are we supposed to do with this?" asked Oxley. "I don't know," replied Lopez, "but I don't want to be let go for not taping a seagull's wing." In a pinch, the two men contacted a bird sanctuary, which didn't take seagulls, then found a South Tampa pet shop that took in the bird as a pet. Oxley heard later it had been run over by a Volkswagen bus.[25]

Tough, haughty, and headstrong, the fifty-five-year-old Joy bore a striking resemblance to famed Hollywood actress Katharine Hepburn. When, at a dinner with Hugh and Joy, Bill Marcum asked if anyone had ever told her that, she replied, tersely, "Of course."[26] As onetime Jacksonville resident and *St. Petersburg Times* editor Hubert Mizell insists, Joy had always been a more public figure than Hugh, who worked long hours and to some extent was a social recluse.[27] "Dad had never been a public person," says Hugh Jr. "But in Tampa, he'd walk into a pancake house and people would ask for his autograph. We're talking about a very insecure guy here whose wife had the notoriety. Now *he* was famous, and Mom, I think, was jealous. The funny thing is neither of them knew anything about football." One time, Hugh Jr. sat with his parents in the owner's box. The Bucs had the ball on a third-and-one, in what was an obvious running play, but Culverhouse yelled, "Watch this. . . . It's gonna be a pass!" "That's when it hit me," explains Hugh Jr. "He had no clue."[28]

Yet Culverhouse did know money. In September 1976, he petitioned the league to take Miami Dolphins games broadcasted in "his" viewing area off the air. As owner of the Bucs, Culverhouse could veto any game shown within a seventy-five-mile radius of Tampa whenever the Bucs played at home. "This is a business," he said. "Chicago does not allow Green Bay to be televised into their area" and "Miami does not allow our games to be televised down there."[29]

The Dolphins' blackout, which began in 1976, was in addition to a home blackout of any games that weren't sellouts, imposed by the league. Since 1973, the NFL had had a blackout policy in which home games could not be televised locally unless they were sold out seventy-two hours in advance. The policy seems strict, but it was Congress, and not the NFL owners, who passed it. Previously, the NFL had blacked out *all* home games, including playoff games, the Super Bowl, and even the Pro Bowl, regardless of attendance. The league was "protecting" the home team, said Rozelle, because "even the possibility that a game might be televised could hurt ticket sales."[30]

But with season ticket sales stuck at thirty-eight thousand—
or thirty-four thousand less than capacity—in 1976 the Buccaneers would black out all seven home games. They blacked out
seven more in 1977 and two more in 1978 before finally tele-
vising an October 1978 sellout versus the Vikings.[31] Thankfully,
Tampa Bay's away games were televised, but the lineup for
1976 was a murderers' row: at Houston, at Oakland, at Baltimore, plus a December matchup in Pittsburgh versus the Super
Bowl champion Steelers. Schedule-wise, the Bucs played once
against every team in the AFC as a member of the AFC West.
Then, in 1977, they switched leagues and played every team in
the NFC as members of the NFC Central. From 1978 onward,
when the league went to sixteen games, the Bucs played a "regular" schedule, with eight home-and-away games in division,
two interconference games, and six conference games, as members of the NFC. They were in the NFC Central until 2002.

———

The Buccaneers' first regular season opponent, the Houston
Oilers, had gone 10-4 in 1975 behind the third-best run defense and fifth-best overall defense in the league. Its star was
Curley Culp, an unbelievably stout 6'1", 265-pound nose tackle
and former NCAA wrestling champion whose aggressive play
helped popularize the "three-four" defense. In 1975, Culp had
eleven and a half sacks, a record for nose tackles, and was the
NFL's Defensive Player of the Year. Next to Culp was defensive
end Elvin Bethea, a six-time Pro Bowler who in 1975 had ten
sacks, including his fiftieth in five years, and backing them up,
at linebacker, was Robert Brazile, aka "Dr. Doom," a 6'4", 245-
pound hitter and the 1975 NFL Defensive Rookie of the Year.

Culp, Bethea, and Brazile, an elite threesome whose defense, in 1975, had held opponents to a league-best 3.4 yards per rush. (By contrast, the "Steel Curtain," the vaunted Steelers defense, had held its opponents to 4.2 yards per rush.)

Now they faced a bad Buccaneers team with a bad line and two rookie linemen whose quarterback gave the ball to the running back seven yards deep. "Sunday was ridiculous," wrote *Sarasota Journal* reporter Alan Lassila. "There were times when Curley Culp . . . and pals were streaking into the Bucs backfield faster than Spurrier could retreat."[32] As midseason pickup at quarterback Terry Hanratty explained it, "We just didn't have the manpower. McKay had a Southern Cal offense, but O.J. wasn't running and Ron Yary wasn't blocking."[33] For the game, the Bucs had 27 carries for 49 yards, an abysmally bad 1.8-yard average. Quarterback Steve Spurrier was chased, harried, harassed, slammed to the ground, knocked in the head, and sacked three times. His fourth-quarter replacement, Parnell Dickinson, was sacked two times.

Yet, almost unbelievably, Tampa Bay had missed at least four chances to score. Lee McGriff dropped a fingertip pass in the end zone. Mirro Roder bounced a field goal off the goalpost, while Spurrier threw two bad interceptions inside the Houston thirty. "When you get down there, you're supposed to get some points," said McKay. "Our defense played well enough. We had a chance to make it 7–7 and then 10–7, but we couldn't get anything."[34] On defense, however, the Bucs were impressive. Lee Roy Selmon had two first-half sacks. Pat Toomay nearly picked off a screen pass on Houston's first possession, and Ken Stone had an interception. The defense also forced three fumbles, which it recovered, and stopped Houston twice, on a third-and-one and a fourth-and-one, from the Tampa eight.

Although Houston had outgained Tampa Bay 188 to 62, and had 12 first downs to Tampa Bay's 5, the score at halftime was 7–0. It was 10–0 with eleven minutes left in the fourth. By that point, the Oilers had run sixty-three plays, nineteen more than the Bucs, who'd punted eight times. "It seems that after every game someone asks me how it would be if the offense was better," said Lee Roy Selmon. "Well, I'm not blaming anything on the offense. Sure, we had to play a long time on defense, but this isn't two teams, it's one. I'm as responsible for today as any offensive player."[35] Lee Roy was being nice. He was *always* nice. His brother Dewey, though, remembers how frustrating it was when the offense couldn't score.

"It wasn't a big deal at first," he says. "Those first few games we were learning. But you lose nine straight and people start pointing fingers. You know, saying, 'I'm doin' my job, what about you?' "[36] On more than one occasion, there were fistfights on the airplane. Dave Green remembers Mondays were film days. "You should have seen it," he said. "The defensive guys would have tons of film to watch, sometimes two or three reels, but the guys on offense. . . . They ran like thirty plays. They were in and out in no time."[37] Actually, at Houston, the Bucs ran fifty-eight plays, gaining 108 yards of offense, total, to the Oilers' 372. In addition, Spurrier and Dickinson were just 9 of 26 passing, for 59 yards. They were 1-for-16 on third down. "I'm worried about our lack of offense," said McKay after the game. "Our blocking was very, very poor. There was no consistency. As Alonzo Stagg probably said a long time ago, 'if you don't block, you lose.' "[38] At one point, a snide Houston reporter asked, "I thought you said you were going to win some games?" to which McKay replied, "Houston's been in the league six thousand years and still hasn't won a championship. The Bucs will be heard from."[39]

However, the next week, in Tampa, the Bucs lost 23–0 in sweltering heat to a bad Chargers team in front of 39,558 fans. During the game (and this has to be a record) *not one* wide receiver in a Buccaneer uniform caught a pass. In all, Bucs quarterbacks were 3 of 18 passing for negative 4 yards. "I wanted to put my best foot forward," said third-string quarterback Larry Lawrence, who went 0 for 4 with a sack and 2 interceptions in two disastrous series, "but I left a pile of dog manure and then stepped in it."[40] The defense again was spectacular. Bolstered in part by Richard "Batman" Wood, the former USC all-American at linebacker picked up in a trade with the Jets, it held San Diego to just three field goals with three minutes left in the fourth. The defense had three sacks, recovered two fumbles, and limited Chargers quarterback Dan Fouts to just 154 yards passing and no touchdowns.

The San Diego coaches and players praised the Buc defense for its hitting, but said the offense had no speed.[41] Unfortunately, the Bucs' fastest player was Isaac Hagins, its kick returner, but Hagins had been hurt at Houston and was out for the season. Receiver Barry Smith ran a 4.5 forty, but backed up J. K. McKay and Lee McGriff. The two "Macs" were possession receivers; they had, as one coach put it, "good, not great, speed" and excellent hands.[42] But neither player could go deep. "Sure," said McGriff, "we would have loved to have had someone who could have stretched the field, a Randy Moss type, but even if we had a Moss, Steve didn't have time to throw."[43] In one 1976 interview,

97

McGriff claimed that while other NFL receivers ran patterns seventeen to twenty yards down the field, the Bucs ran theirs in twelve. They had to. The blocking was *that* bad. It was so bad that *Orlando Sentinel Star* reporter Larry Guest quipped that the Bucs' offensive line was like the "South Vietnamese Army."[44]

Indeed, through two games, the Bucs had scored no points. They had 181 yards rushing, 54 yards passing, and were 3 for 30 on third down. They also missed three field goals and had punted twenty times. Announcer Jack Harris did a postgame radio show for the Bucs and recalls that the player of the game was usually the punter, Dave Green. "Now Dave was good," says Harris, "don't get me wrong, but when your punter's your MVP you've got a problem."[45] Ron Wolf attempted to help the offense by signing Morris Owens, a deep-ball threat at receiver waived in week three by the Dolphins. Owens ran a 4.5 forty and in 1974 at Arizona State had averaged an NCAA-best 21.5 yards per reception. But in Miami, he'd been beaten out by Nat Moore, Freddie Solomon, and Howard Twilley, the Dolphins' "Big Three." (To make room for Owens, who was a clear upgrade, the Bucs cut Mirro Roder, the kicker, and gave his job to Dave Green, who also continued to punt.) By season's end, Owens had 30 catches for 390 yards and 6 touchdowns, the best on the team.

Regrettably, Wolf did nothing for the line. He couldn't. There were no good players available. What was particularly tough was that starting tackle Dave Reavis, a third-year man from Pittsburgh who'd play in more than ninety games for the Bucs, reaggravated a knee injury and was out for the season. As a result, the Bucs had eight O-linemen, which for most teams was the minimum, while four—count 'em, four—were rookies. Blocking "continues to haunt us," said McKay, whose next opponent, ironically, was the Buffalo Bills, the absolute best blocking team in the league.[46] In 1975, the Bills led the NFL in total offense (and in rushing offense) behind superstar running back O. J. Simpson, who sat out the entire 1976 preseason demanding a trade. Simpson came back in September, practiced once, and signed a contract the weekend of opening day. Out of shape and, as he put it, "dead-legged," Simpson had had only sixty-six yards rushing in two games, and was wary of the Bucs. "Our coaches tell us that the way Tampa's defense has been playing, a break or two their way and we will become part of history. I mean, I don't want to be no part of no Tampa Bay history-making. . . . No sir."[47]

Hurting Simpson was the fact that Buffalo fullback Jim Braxton was out with a knee injury. A 6'1", 245-pound bruiser, Braxton had been a key member of Buffalo's "Electric Company" running game, the one that in 1973 had helped Simpson to a two-thousand-yard season, but Braxton's replacement had only been with the team a week. It was a disaster. Simpson was swarmed by the Bucs, who cornered, corralled, and ultimately held the running back to thirty-nine yards. The biggest story, however, was the Buccaneer offense—it scored, finally, on a first-quarter field goal by Dave Green. Apparently, McKay had told the team in the locker room that whenever they did score, he'd stop the game and give the player who did it the game ball. But when Green kicked his field goal, the mercurial Bucs coach failed to mention it. "So I said, 'Coach, hey . . . what about the game ball?'" recalls the kicker. "But then McKay says, 'Shit, Green. I didn't think it'd be you!'"[48]

In all, Green had three field goals and gave the Bucs a 9–7

lead with twelve minutes left in the fourth. But then Bills quarterback Joe Ferguson responded with a 5-play, 66-yard drive ending in a touchdown. The final score was Buffalo 14, Tampa Bay 9. "Our guys played their hearts out," said Steve Spurrier. But "a good offensive team would have had forty."[49] As it stood, the Bucs had 338 yards of offense to the Bills' 295. They'd run sixty-nine plays and faced first-and-ten, inside the Bills' thirty, seven times. Yet Bucs receivers dropped two passes in the end zone. Spurrier was intercepted at the goal line, and Dave Green was tackled, on a fake field goal, two feet from the first-down marker at the Bills' ten. "We ran better, we blocked better, and we played better as a team," said McKay. "We did what we said we were going to do defensively and we did it very well. We could've won and we should've won but we didn't. All I can say is we're trying."[50]

Without question, the Bucs had improved. The defense was phenomenal. The offense was moving the ball and the line was beginning to block. But Tampa Bay's next two games were at Baltimore and at Cincinnati, teams whose record in 1975 was a combined 21-7. Baltimore was the AFC Eastern Division champion. It had Pro Bowlers at the skill positions, and its quarterback was Bert Jones, a first-team All-Pro. Surprisingly, the upstart Bucs led 3–0 in the second, but the Colts scored on seven consecutive possessions, then added a safety. They also had thirty-one first downs to the Buccaneers' six, held Spurrier and Dickinson to 4 of 15 passing, and outgained the Buccaneers 458 to 89. The Bucs were so bad that receiver Lee McGriff had more passing yards on one play, thirty-nine, than either Spurrier or Dickinson had for the game. (Cut midseason, McGriff would finish his career 1 for 1 with 39 yards passing, but

no receptions.) The game ended 42–17. "Field position hurt us badly," said McKay, "dropped passes hurt us badly, no blocking hurt us badly, injuries hurt us badly, and penalties hurt us badly. But otherwise it was a perfect afternoon."[51]

The good news was that Tampa Bay scored two touchdowns late in the fourth. The first was a forty-four-yard fumble return by cornerback Danny Reece, while the second was a one-yard dive by running back Charlie Davis. The bad news was that two Buccaneer starters, defensive end Lee Roy Selmon and linebacker Cal Peterson, got hurt. Selmon, as usual, was the best Buc on the field. In less than two quarters, he had three tackles and a sack and forced Jones into several bad throws. Therefore, to protect Jones, the Colts attempted to stop Lee Roy by covering the gifted rookie with two blockers: a lineman who engaged the Buccaneer "up top" and a tight end who went for the knees. "It was a chop block," said Lee Roy. "I should have been watching for it," but "the guy just dove into my leg."[52] He sat out the following week at Cincinnati with strained knee ligaments, but reinjured the knee in November and was out for the year.

In all, eleven different Bucs were expected to miss the Cincinnati game due to injuries, in addition to nine Bucs out for the season on injured reserve.[53] "Our sidelines looked like a Civil War infirmary," jokes Pat Toomay, who claims that on good NFL teams, defenses typically played between thirty and fifty plays per game. Not so in Tampa, where the Bucs averaged an eye-popping sixty-eight. Toomay blamed ten weeks of two-a-days. The team had started the season "leg-dead and bone-tired," he insists, and so "down we went, suffering injury after injury."[54] As team trainer John Lopez remembers it, "We just kept running out of bodies," and it was Ron Wolf's job to bring players in. "He was like a ginseng hunter," says Lopez, "out there, in the forest, trying to find ginseng."[55]

The week of the Cincinnati game, for example, the Bucs signed free agent defensive tackle Larry Jameson, who had last played football in 1975 with the WFL's San Antonio Wings. Jameson signed on a Tuesday, played in the Bengals game on Sunday, then the following Tuesday was cut. One week, one game, his entire NFL career. Pat Toomay recalls standing in the huddle on week fourteen, in the Bucs' final game, and seeing a truck driver and a construction worker at the tackle positions, and a 180-pound linebacker plucked from the streets of Watts.[56] Bob Huckabee, the team ticket manager, remembers the Bucs being so desperate for players that they actually tried out a deliveryman. On the shelf above his desk, Huckabee kept the game ball from Tampa Bay's first-ever home game versus Miami. One day, McKay assistant Dick Beam asked Huckabee if he could use it, because the equipment room was locked. A short time later, he went outside and saw Beam and another guy practicing pass patterns. "When it was over, I asked 'Who was that?'" says Huckabee. And Beam said, "'He's our Coca-Cola guy.' I thought, 'No way,' but sure enough, a big Coke delivery truck was right outside."[57]

Needless to say, the game in Cincinnati was a catastrophe. With more than six thousand no-shows and a crowd far more interested in that evening's National League Championship game featuring Pete Rose and the Reds, the Bengals won 21–0. In first place and led by Pro Bowl quarterback Ken Anderson, they scored twice in the first, had a fumble return for a touchdown in the third, then coasted from there. They finished the game by running the ball eleven times in a row. "That's what teams did," explains Hubert Mizell. "They'd go up by two touchdowns, and rather than do anything crazy, they'd just sit on the ball. It was like 'why bother?' "[58]

The story in Cincinnati was an in-game argument between John McKay and offensive coordinator John Rauch. Apparently, McKay blamed Rauch for his team's offensive ineptitude, but insisted—absolutely insisted—that Rauch run the "I." According to Rauch's son, John A. Rauch, the Bucs' offensive coordinator sat in the coach's box and relayed plays to the field. But McKay grew so frustrated with Rauch's play-calling, he began ignoring the coordinator and wouldn't wear his headset. The coach sent plays to Spurrier, but wouldn't speak to Rauch.[59] Barry Smith, a receiver for the Bucs, insists "McKay was stubborn. It was his offense. So he did what he always did: pitch right, pitch left, run up the middle. But Rauch would say, 'It won't work! If your running backs can't get out of the backfield, your opponent's linebackers will cover your receivers. When that happens, it's really difficult to do anything out of the "I." ' "[60]

There were personal issues, too. Rauch wore hearing aids in both ears and was sensitive about it. Once, when McKay said something to him and Rauch didn't hear him, the head coach shouted, "You deaf son of a bitch!" and Rauch had to be restrained. Apparently, by the Cincinnati game, the belittled coordinator had had enough. Sometime, midway through the second quarter, with the Bucs down 14–0 and McKay calling run after run, Rauch quit. He simply exited the coach's box and flew home. On Monday, his replacement was pro personnel director Tom Bass, who says slyly, "Coach and I reached an understanding. He'd call the running plays, and if he wanted a pass play he'd call me in the booth. I mean, he was the head coach. He could do what he wanted to do."[61]

———

The next week, the Bucs played the Seahawks at home in what journalists called the "Expansion Bowl." Although 0-5, the Seattle franchise had outperformed Tampa Bay mightily both on and off the field. For one, it had averaged close to 60,000 fans per game through three home games, while Tampa Bay had averaged just 42,000 through two. (At Marcum's urging, Culverhouse had taken the unusual step of cutting ticket prices for students and senior citizens midseason. The new price, for nosebleed seats, was five dollars.) In addition, the Seahawks were led by rookie head coach Jack Patera, who started sixteen players from the veteran allocation draft, whereas McKay started nine. The result was a more experienced roster, better leadership, perhaps, and a marginally better team.[62]

It helped, too, that Seahawk scouts had found not one, but two diamonds in the rough: an undrafted rookie quarterback from Cal Poly Pomona named Jim Zorn and a rookie receiver and trade pickup from the Oilers named Steve Largent. A 6'2", 200-pound scrambler, Zorn had been cut by the Cowboys at the beginning of the 1975 season and spent the year living at home. As McKay described him, Zorn was a "a big kid with the ability to score. That's a plus not only with an expansion team, but anywhere—Dallas, Pittsburgh, what have you."[63] Through five games, he was 82 of 173 for 1,025 yards and 5 touchdowns, while Spurrier, by comparison, was just 38 of 89 for 431 yards and no touchdowns.

Zorn's favorite target was the sure-handed Largent, who entered the game with twenty-three receptions, the most in the league. Slow by NFL standards and just average in size, Largent had been a fourth-round draft pick out of Tulsa, but was traded to Seattle for an eighth-round pick late in the preseason. It was, quite possibly, the worst trade that any NFL franchise had ever made. Largent played fourteen seasons for the Seahawks, had 819 catches and 100 touchdowns, and has since been inducted into the Pro Football Hall of Fame. Although weak defensively—the Seahawks would finish the year twenty-eighth in the league, behind the Buccaneers, in team defense—they could clearly score. In game one versus the Cardinals, for example, Seattle had almost as many points (24) as the Bucs had had in their first five games of the year (26). The Seahawks had also scored eight offensive touchdowns to the Buccaneers' one.

Speaking at a "Meet the Bucs" luncheon at the Tampa Sports Club the Friday before the game, McKay claimed he wasn't interested in comparing the two teams. Instead, his focus was on collecting a core of talented players for the Bucs within three years, and being a playoff team within five. "Hey, a victory would give us all a boost," he admitted. But "our primary goal is not a win today. Our primary goal goes far beyond." As for the Bucs' scoring woes, McKay deflected criticism through jests. "You know all those people out at Tampa Stadium?" he quipped. "You know how they wonder what's going on out there on the field and why we're not scoring? Well, next time that happens, look down on the sidelines and see that gray-haired fellow. That's me. I'm wondering the same thing." He then paused for effect. "Like the fans, I figured at the start of the season we'd go 14-0. Then we had that first kickoff and didn't score and I said, 'Well, I'll be damned.' "[64]

Amazingly, tight end Bob Moore predicted an offensive explosion versus Seattle, but the next day, in a grueling 13–10 loss, the Bucs had more penalty calls than points. In fact, the team had twenty penalties, two short of the all-time NFL record set in 1944. Not to be outdone, the Seahawks had fifteen penalties. Altogether, the two teams had thirty-five total infractions for minus 310 yards. The game took three hours and twenty-two minutes. In all, there were two delay-of-game penalties, five offside penalties, sixteen holding penalties, two clipping penalties, three illegal procedures, five personal fouls, a noncontact foul (against McKay, for cursing), and a facemask. "It's not my bag to knock sports officials," wrote Tom McEwen in his column that week. But penalties "turned what may have been a 30–28 one way or another, into a clumsy, disappointing, three hours of anxiety and even anger that went into the book as a 13–10 decision."[65]

Statistically, the Bucs outgained the Seahawks 285 to 253 but made it inside the Seattle twenty only three times. Down 13–3 in the third, they drove from their own forty-six-yard line all the way down to the Seattle one, but were stopped on two consecutive runs up the middle. On third-and-one, running back Louis Carter attempted a third run, this one a dive, but was hit in midair short of the goal line. As he fell back, he looked to his right and saw Morris Owens, a receiver, standing alone on the goal line, so wisely enough he threw it. It was the first passing touchdown in Buccaneers history: a two-handed jump shot, from a stuffed running back, made on the fly. With the score 13–10, the teams traded punts through the fourth, and with less than a minute to play, kicker Dave Green attempted a 35-yard field goal to tie the game. But somehow, almost inexplicably, veteran Seattle linebacker Mike "Mad Dog" Curtis, an allocation pickup from Baltimore and a former All-Pro, ran through the line unblocked. He batted the ball down and the game was over.[66]

For their part, the Bucs were despondent, even glum. A lot of guys had hoped to "prove something," said Bob Moore. "I don't care what anyone says, there's a letdown after you've failed."[67] The fans blamed McKay for the loss, but it was Spurrier they booed. With each three-and-out, the stadium reverberated with boos. The fans threw trash at him: cups, napkins, programs, on one occasion a dead bird. The booing was so widespread that at one game, Spurrier's wife, Jeri, noticed their nine-year-old daughter, Lisa, was booing, too. "I said, 'Lisa, why are you booing?' And she said, 'I don't know, because everybody else is.' I said, 'Do you know who they are booing?' 'No.' 'They're booing your father!'"[68]

To back up and possibly replace Spurrier, who was day-to-day with a knee injury following the Seattle game, the Bucs waived third-string quarterback Larry Lawrence and brought in Terry "the Rat" Hanratty, a former Notre Dame star and career backup with the Steelers. Hanratty had been in the league seven years and played briefly in Pittsburgh's 1974 Super Bowl victory over Dallas. "I really came full circle," he laughs. "I started out on a 1-13 Pittsburgh team as a rookie, then finished my career with the Bucs. I tell you what, I always admired Chuck Noll, the Steelers coach, but I definitely gained a new appreciation for him when I got to Tampa." What perhaps surprised Hanratty the most was how incredibly simplistic McKay's offense was. He'd been with the team a week when McKay asked him to show the coaching staff what the Steelers were doing on offense. Eager to help, Hanratty began diagramming plays at the blackboard, but when he looked back, he says, everyone's mouth was open. "I mean wide open. They were like 'What?! They do what?!' And I said, 'Yeah. The Steelers have three hundred plays. They can audible to every one.' "[69]

Still living in Pittsburgh, Hanratty joined the Bucs as a free agent the week of the Seattle game, but McKay chose Parnell Dickinson as his starter. (Spurrier dressed but was not expected to play.) Like every other Buc, Dickinson had struggled mightily. In four appearances, the rookie quarterback had completed just 2 of 14 passes for 27 yards. He'd also thrown two interceptions and been sacked eleven times. But at home versus Miami, on the Bucs' opening possession, Dickinson, incredibly, went 3 for 3 with a touchdown on a nine-play, 74-yard drive. But, in the second quarter, with Miami leading 10–7, he suffered an ankle injury on a sprint-out to the sideline and was out for the game. His replacement was Terry Hanratty, but when Hanratty failed to move the team by halftime, he in turn was replaced by Spurrier. Hobbled by a chipped bone in his throwing hand, plus a sprained knee, Spurrier took the field down 17–7 in the third. (The crowd booed.) Yet with good blocking for once, and time to throw, Spurrier went 13 of 21 for 143 yards and 2 touchdowns to tie the game at 20. That's when Miami's Garo Yepremian, the goofy, Cypriot-born placekicker of "I keek a touchdown" fame, booted a 29-yard field goal for the win. The score was 23–20.

The Dolphins were a bad team. Just 2-4 on the season, they still had Bob Griese at quarterback, but the days of Larry Csonka and Jim Kiick, not to mention 17-0 seasons, were over.

Even so, veteran linebacker Nick Buoniconti, in his last year in a Dolphins uniform, said "I'm not taking anything away" from the Buccaneers, but this was "the low point in Miami Dolphins history."[70] The Bucs, despite the loss, were elated. They'd given up just one sack, and gained a season-best 334 yards. Plus the team had found a receiver, Morris Owens, who had 6 receptions for 88 yards and 3 touchdowns. Next up was Kansas City, at home, a 2-5 head case featuring the best offense and the worst defense in the AFC. The Bucs could hold the Chiefs, defensively, but the question remained: could they score? The answer was no, a resounding no. At halftime, the Chiefs led 6–0 on two Jan Stenerud field goals, but the Bucs' offense had ten total yards. And, with 12:18 left in the third, following a sack of Spurrier and two tackles for a loss, the Bucs had minus one yard—twenty-five plays, minus one yard.

"Hammering at the Chief defense with all the force of a wet noodle," wrote Lakeland *Ledger* reporter Patrick Zier, the Bucs "seemed bent on establishing themselves as the worst offensive team in pro football."[71] It was a horrible performance, which included, perhaps, the Bucs' worst play of the season: a sixty-five-yard kickoff by Stenerud that no receiver touched, and that the Chiefs recovered on the five. "I've never seen anything like that before," said an exasperated McKay. "I can't believe it. These guys are getting paid money. They should at least be able to fall on a football."[72] In the fourth quarter, the Bucs redeemed themselves by scoring three touchdowns, one an eight-yard reception by J. K. McKay, but the Chiefs won 26–19. Coach McKay was infuriated. The Bucs had been playing decent football, at least since the Miami game, but had taken what he called "forty-five steps backward" versus the Chiefs.[73]

Tired, angry, and frustrated, the caustic Buccaneer coach began to fray. He'd never lost before; losing wore on him. So he took it out on coaches, players, trainers, reporters, and even fans. He'd fired a ball boy, for example, twenty minutes into the first practice of the preseason.[74] But his behavior—volatile, mercurial, acidic—only escalated from there. The fans were "idiots." (He actually said that to the press.) The players were "chickenshits." (He said that to their faces.) One coach was so afraid of McKay, so stressed by working for him, he drank in his car. "Yeah, John McKay was a joy to be around," sniped offensive tackle Mike Current. "The diminutive one rode his ass into town, then acted as though he was one himself. . . . Did McKay bother us much at the time? You'd better believe he did!"[75]

Current wasn't alone. In February 1977, *Orlando Sentinel Star* reporter Larry Guest interviewed nine Buccaneer players, including seven starters, who "painted a consistent picture" of the coach. He was "foul-mouthed," "vainglorious," "arrogant," "tyrannical," "uncommunicative," "paranoid," "uncommonly demeaning," and "inconsistent." McKay was so bad, claimed Guest, that at one point a core of veteran players seriously considered a strike.[76] "In his brief trial with the Bucs," added St. Petersburg *Evening Independent* reporter Greg Hansen, "McKay has never been pleased with people—and opinions—that disagree with him." He "comes at you with teeth bared" and "exhibits all the politeness of a dog fight."[77]

He also drank—on the plane, in hotel bars with coaches and reporters at away games, at Malio's with *Tribune* editor Tom McEwen, and also at work. McKay "consumed alcohol like nobody's business," says Charley Hannah, a lineman who came to the Bucs in 1977. "He'd come out on the field with a cup with crushed ice and vodka and often go in and refill it during practice."[78] Once, on a return trip from an away game, McKay called equipment manager Pat Marcuccillo to the back of the plane. Marcuccillo assumed he was in trouble, so he raced down the aisle to see what the coach wanted. They'd run out of vodka, said McKay. There was no more vodka on the plane. When Marcuccillo asked what he could do about it, McKay told him that for future road trips, he was to carry a fifth of vodka with him at all times. "I'm looking at him and I'm starting to smile," recalls Marcuccillo, "but he says, 'Pat, I never want to run out of vodka again.' And that was it. I went back to my seat, and the next game Pat's got a fifth of vodka in his briefcase. We never ran out of vodka again."[79]

———

Still, McKay's meltdown following game nine, the team's 48–13 loss at Denver, was surprising even for him. In addition to calling Broncos coach John Ralston a "prick," the fifty-three-year-old McKay challenged Max Coley, the Broncos' offensive coordinator and former Oregon assistant, to a fight. "That's the first time I've ever seen a coach blame the other coaching staff for a loss," said Coley. "Evidently, he doesn't know the difference between offense and defense" because the defense "was doing the scoring."[80] McKay would apologize, but the blowup was national news. The Associated Press covered it, as did the *Los Angeles Times* and *Time* magazine, which described the Buccaneers as "urchins" and quoted Bob Moore as saying that playing for the Bucs was like being "on the aft deck of the *Lusitania*."[81] The one good thing was that Tampa Bay's 0-9 record, not to mention its loss to Seattle, virtually guaranteed the first pick in the 1977 draft. That was either Pitt running back Tony Dorsett or Southern Cal running back Ricky Bell.

A three-time all-American, as well as a first-team all-American as a freshman, by late 1976, Dorsett had gained more yards and scored more touchdowns than any other running back in Division I history. The better the opponent, the better Dorsett: in 1975, for example, in a surprising upset of number-nine Notre Dame, the Pitt running back had an astonishing 303 yards rushing, plus a 49-yard reception. He also had 224 yards versus Penn State at the end of the 1976 season and 202 yards versus Georgia in the national championship game. At 5'11", 190 pounds, Dorsett was one of the fastest players in football. He ran a blistering 4.38 forty and favored quick changes of direction over power. "He's a marvelous football player," said Army coach Homer Smith, who watched in amazement as Dorsett scored 4 touchdowns and put up 217 yards in a single half. "Maybe I've seen a performance like it on TV or in the pros, but I've never stood on the sidelines and watched anything like it."[82]

In contrast to Dorsett, an elusive, outside runner, the 6'2", 225-pound Bell was, as the Associated Press put it, an "out-of-control locomotive." "I consider myself rough and tough," he once said. Dorsett has "dazzling moves" and "super speed" but he's "more of a scatback." I'm a "power runner. I'll run over tackles if I can't get around them."[83] Indeed, Bell started his career as a linebacker, moved to fullback as a sophomore, then played running back his junior and senior years. His best year was 1975, when he came seemingly out of nowhere to rush for 1,957 yards and 13 touchdowns. His season total for yardage and his per-game total for yardage were the best in the country, and Bell outgained Archie Griffin, that year's Heisman winner, by more than five hundred yards. "As far as I'm concerned," said USC coach John Robinson, "he is the best football player of all time. He's so damn tough it's frightening." As proof, Robinson told the story of how he'd taken Bell out of a game once due to a dislocated shoulder. "He jammed it back in with the other hand," exclaimed Robinson, "and said, 'Why did you take me out?' "[84]

John McKay had recruited Bell out of high school. He was *his* guy, a USC guy, and Bell was bigger and stronger than Dorsett. He's "not what you'd call a pretty runner," explained McKay. "He's a pounder, a slasher," but in this league you need "a big back to build on. They don't come along every year. When you get a chance to take one, you better grab it."[85] The decision to draft Bell was made easier by Ron Wolf's November 1976 signing of former USC running back Anthony Davis, a speedy scatback like Dorsett who'd been playing in Canada. Bell had blocked for Davis as a sophomore when Davis, a senior, had been a huge star. Winner of two national championships in football and three in baseball, the flashy Davis had led the Trojans in rushing and scoring, as well as kick-return yardage, three straight years. However, at 5'9", 185, Davis was small. Scouts wondered if he could run the ball, regularly, or even if he could block. As a result, in 1975, behind two other backs, including Walter Payton, Davis went to the Jets in round two.

Davis demanded a three-year contract in the $1 million range, but the Jets offered a $60,000 signing bonus and just $30,000 a year. Therefore, Davis left the NFL to sign with the

Southern California Sun of the WFL, which offered a five-year, $1.7 million contract, including a $200,000 bonus and a Rolls-Royce. Although Davis played well, the team was short-lived, so in 1976 he moved again, this time signing a five-year, $1 million contract with the Toronto Argonauts of the CFL. (In the meantime, Davis's NFL rights went to the Bucs through the expansion draft.) Almost immediately, Davis clashed with coach Russ Jackson over playing time. Davis wanted twenty-five carries a game, but Jackson, who wanted to use Davis as a return man, gave him ten. What followed was a war of words in which Mike Trope, Davis's twenty-three-year-old agent, blasted Taylor for being incompetent, while Argos owner Bill Hodgson called Trope an immature boy.[86] Adding insult to injury, the fans saw Davis as a prima donna, so neither Jackson nor Hodgson complained when Davis asked for his release. He signed with the Bucs in November 1976, but because of league rules prohibiting players from playing in the NFL and the CFL in the same season, he wouldn't join the team until 1977.[87]

At the time of Davis's signing, the Bucs were 0-10 and had just played their worst game of the year, a 34–0 road loss to the woefully bad New York Jets. At 2-7 and in Joe Namath's last year at quarterback, the Jets were led by Lou Holtz, the future Notre Dame coach and ESPN commentator, who would resign at the end of the season. The game featured six Buccaneer turnovers—the score was 24–0 at half—including two turnovers inside the Buccaneer thirty. The Jets scored both times. "They just killed us," says tight end Bob Moore. "I couldn't tell you what the score was, but we couldn't do anything right." The worst play of the game, he insists, occurred in the third period. It was cold, Shea Stadium was empty, and he was running a

Between 1968 and 1974, promoter Bill Marcum brought no fewer than thirteen AFL and NFL exhibition games to Tampa. The games were incredibly well-attended and proved to NFL owners that Florida's Tampa Bay area could support pro football.

The original Tampa Bay owner was Hugh Culverhouse, a miserly Jacksonville tax attorney who paid just $16.2 million for the Bucs. The franchise was originally awarded to Philadelphia construction magnate Tom McCloskey, but when McCloskey backed out in 1974, the franchise went to Culverhouse.

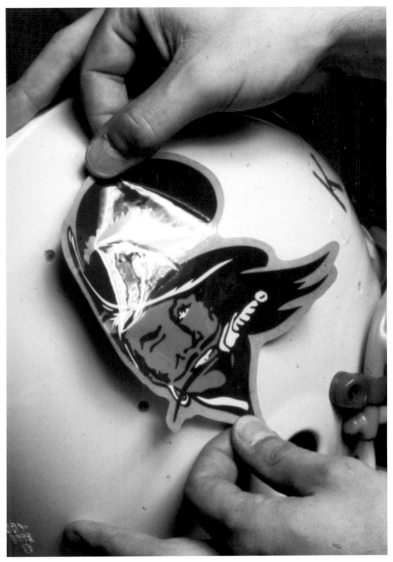

Designed by *Tampa Tribune* cartoonist Lamar Sparkman, the team's mascot "Bucco Bruce" was meant to resemble the swashbuckling D'Artagnan character from *The Three Musketeers*. One of Sparkman's original designs, bizarrely enough, was of a hangman's noose.

Bucs coach John McKay at an introductory press conference in Tampa in 1975. Known for his wry wit, McKay won four national championships at Southern Cal, but struggled mightily in his first two seasons with the Bucs.

Bucs coach John McKay (left) and Vice President for Operations Ron Wolf (right) greet the team's first-ever draft pick and 1976's overall number-one pick, Lee Roy Selmon. A star defensive end at the University of Oklahoma, Selmon suffered a knee injury in '76 and played just eight games for the year.

Team owner Hugh Culverhouse and Coach John McKay on a rainy day on the practice field at One Buc Place. The men were close friends, and despite the team's twenty-six-game losing streak, the owner supported the coach unconditionally.

The Bucs' defensive line coach was Abe Gibron, a rotund former Cleveland Browns star and Bears head coach who was a notorious eater. As one player put it: "He made me eat things that people in my part of the country are afraid to swim with."

The Bucs arrive in Los Angeles for their first preseason game versus the Rams. Looking to save money, Bucs owner Hugh Culverhouse leased the plane not from Eastern or United, but from McCulloch Corporation, the chain saw makers.

Veteran quarterback Steve Spurrier (#11), a trade pickup from the 49ers, spent most of the 1976 season on the ground. In the team's first regular-season game, a 20–0 loss at Houston, Spurrier was 8 for 21, passing for 90 yards and suffering 2 interceptions. He was sacked three times.

Due to poor line play, a nonexistent pass offense, and predictable play-calling, Buc running backs struggled to move the ball. The team's leading rusher for '76, Louis Carter (#32) had just 521 yards rushing and a single touchdown.

One of the few bright spots for the early Bucs was receiver Morris Owens (#85). The team claimed Owens off waivers early in the 1976 season. In 1977, when the terrible Buccaneer offense had just three receiving touchdowns, Owens had all of them.

One of the most popular early Bucs was nose tackle Dave Pear, an expansion pickup from Baltimore whose aggressive play and on-field antics excited fans. Pear—and not Lee Roy Selmon, believe it or not—was Tampa Bay's first-ever Pro Bowl selection in 1978.

Kicker Dave Green (#4) scores the Buccaneers' first regular-season points on a game-three field goal versus the Bills. Although McKay had promised to give the game ball to whichever Buccaneer scored first, he ignored the kicker, then said, "Shit, Green, I didn't think it'd be you!"

In October 1976, quarterback Steve Spurrier (#11) gets hit while throwing the ball in a 13–10 loss to Seattle. The Bucs' loss to the Seahawks, the league's other expansion franchise, virtually guaranteed the Bucs the number-one pick in the 1977 draft.

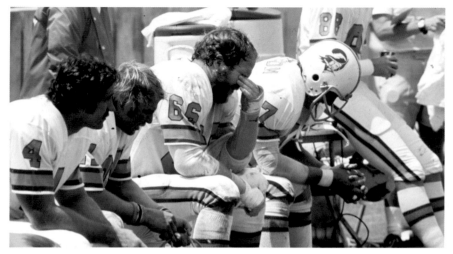

Another long day for Pat Toomay (#66), a veteran defensive end who started every game for the 1976 Bucs. Winner of Super Bowl VI with Dallas and an author to boot, Toomay described being sent to the Bucs as being "exiled to Siberia."

Offensive line coach Jerry Frei addresses what was by far and away the Bucs' worst unit. Beset by injuries and not very talented to begin with, the Bucs' O-line gave up fifty sacks in '76 while managing a not-very-good 3.5 yards per rush.

Angered by the team's losing streak and upset at McKay's supposed favoritism toward USC players, fans criticized the coach mercilessly. An ad in a local newspaper read "Wanted—Coach and Football Team—Personnel with California Experience Not Wanted, Apply No. 1 Buc Place."

Tampa television host Andy Hardy during a break of the *McKay* show. Bucs coach John McKay didn't like Andy and sometimes mocked the befuddled host on the air. McKay often began comments with: "Of course, Andy, you won't understand this, but . . ."

In 1977, a popular T-shirt in the Bay Area read "Go for O!" The shirt was designed by three friends in the marketing department at Tampa's Busch Gardens theme park, who, as a form of guerrilla advertising, flew "Go for O!" banners over home games.

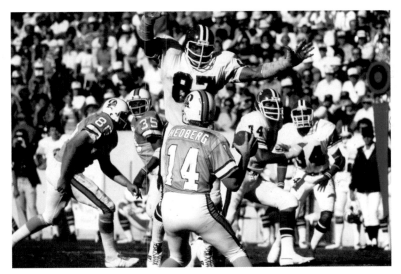

With two of its quarterbacks out due to injuries, the Bucs opened the 1977 season with rookie Randy Hedberg, an eighth-round draft pick from tiny Minot State in North Dakota. Hedberg went 0-4 as a starter with no touchdowns and ten interceptions. He never played in the NFL again.

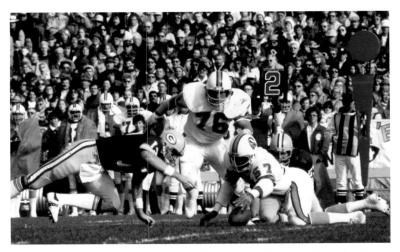

With stars such as Dave Pear (#76) and David Lewis (#57), by 1977 the lowly Bucs had the makings of an elite defense. But, as one player put it, "We'd make a stop, come off the field, and barely get our helmets off before someone yelled, 'PUNTING TEAM!' And we'd say, 'Ah shit!'"

Quarterback Gary Huff (#19), the Bucs' oft-injured starter during the 1977 season, leaves an October game versus the Packers with cracked ribs. A former Florida State star, Huff had a career 2-4 record with Tampa Bay, but led the team to its first two wins.

A workhorse back and one of the toughest players in football, Ricky Bell (#42) was the first overall pick in the 1977 draft. Chosen over Tony Dorsett, the future Dallas superstar, Bell was pilloried by fans through two mediocre seasons, but redeemed himself with a 1200-yard effort in 1979.

Joy Culverhouse (bottom left), Hugh Culverhouse, and John McKay celebrate with some eight thousand fans at an impromptu victory party at One Buc Place. The Bucs' win over the Saints in December 1977 ended the longest losing streak in the history of the NFL.

Following the Bucs' second-ever victory in their 1977 home finale versus the Cardinals, crazed Tampa Bay fans rushed the field and tore down the goalposts. Although just 2-26 overall, the hereto-fore woeful Bucs had energized the Bay Area.

hook pattern in the middle of the field. When he turned, however, a ball thrown by Terry Hanratty hit the ground in front of him and bounced straight up into his hands. Just as the whistle blew, two Jets linebackers who hadn't seen the pass made a beeline for Moore. "They turned and came after me like it was a live ball," he says with a laugh. "So I said, 'You're not gonna' hit me!' and I threw it straight up in the air. I just wung it. It was such a stupid play, such a ridiculous play . . . but it symbolized our season. For me, that was the lowest of the low."[88]

Indeed, in their last five quarters of football, the Bucs had given up seventy-two points but hadn't scored. Now they faced a playoff-caliber Browns team, plus the Raiders, the Steelers, and the Patriots, three clubs whose combined record was 27-8. "Look who we have to play," said tackle Mike Current, glumly. "If we don't get up for the next four games, we're going to get beaten a million to nothing."[89] In the end, the Bucs lost 24–7 to the Browns, 49–16 to the Raiders, 42–0 to the Steelers, and 31–14 to the Patriots. Apart from a Herculean effort versus New England, the games weren't close. *Sarasota Herald-Tribune* reporter Jack Gurney remembers following the team through loss after loss, and by season's end having nothing left to write. In fact, he and other reporters began writing leads *before* the games were played, including one, he laughs, about "the meek inheriting the earth." In 1976, Gurney nearly missed the Oakland game due to a traffic jam on the San Francisco–Oakland Bay Bridge. When finally he got to the press box he saw maybe eight plays, but still wrote a complete article on the contest. "In my defense," he says, "there wasn't anything to write. They had like three first downs for the game!"[90]

The highlight of the Raiders game was, well . . . there were no highlights. Buccaneer tight end and former Raider Bob Moore, a fan favorite in Oakland, was met at the airport, on the tarmac, by Raider linebacker Phil Villapiano in a black limousine hearse. Raider players had bought the hearse in the early 1970s for use as a party barge, and for the rest of the evening, the two men partied with other Oakland players. But as they rushed out to make Moore's curfew, they found that a TV news crew had assembled outside. "They thought it was a funny story," said Moore. "You know: 'Former Raider Returns.' But McKay saw it and was pissed. I think he'd been mad at me since the Denver game, when I gave the *'Lusitania'* quote to *Time* magazine. He didn't care that I had said it. He was mad that he hadn't said it. He was the one with the quotes."[91]

The big story the following week in Pittsburgh was the triumphant return of Terry Hanratty, the Steeler-turned-Buc and Pittsburgh bar owner, who faced "Miracle on Ice" odds. Actually, it was worse than that. The Steelers were the defending Super Bowl champions, twice over. After a slow start and several close losses, plus an injury to quarterback Terry Bradshaw, Pittsburgh had won seven games in a row. It had eleven Pro Bowlers, including eight on defense—a defense ESPN.com has described as the best defense ever.[92] December 5, 1976. Three Rivers Stadium. Arguably the best defense ever, versus perhaps the worst offense ever. Jack Lambert, Mel Blount, L. C. Greenwood, "Mean" Joe Greene—the "Steel Curtain" versus the "Yucks."

McKay had told Hanratty that his first start would be against the Jets. Instead, Hanratty, who went 1 for 4 for minus-one yard in two quarters of play, got Pittsburgh. The Steelers' team prankster, Hanratty had spent the week on Pittsburgh radio jawing facetiously with Lambert, the Steelers' barbarian-like linebacker who was, without a doubt, the scariest player in the league. "I feel real good," said Hanratty. "I don't know how I'll feel Sunday night, but tell Lambert I'll be looking for him—off the field."[93] Other Steelers, including the oft-injured Bradshaw, weren't nearly so sanguine. "No one in their right mind would want to play against this defense," said Bradshaw. "I don't think it's a safe thing." In fact, "I've entered Terry into my prayer life."[94] Hanratty's wife, Rosemary, lamented, in mock seriousness, "Have you *seen* Tampa play? Oh, it's just so tragic to watch them. It strikes terror in my heart. Terry behind that offensive line and Jack Lambert standing there grinning . . . The last time I saw them the receivers were so slow they couldn't complete their routes."[95]

Luckily for Hanratty, the Bucs ran the ball on almost every play. At halftime, they had one first down. The Steelers led 28–0 and had downed the ball, on purpose, in field goal range, to end the first half. The final score was 42–0. "There is only one difference between what happened to Custer and his men at Little Big Horn and what happened to McKay and his men at Three Rivers," quipped one journalist. "Custer had better weather."[96] For the Bucs, nothing good had happened in Pittsburgh. Nothing. Not one play. In fact, the team's best play was a pass interception by Steelers cornerback Mel Blount. Blount fumbled at the nine, but rather than pick the ball up, Hanratty kicked it out of the Pittsburgh end zone for a touchback. It was, as one reporter put it, the "play of the game."[97] Dave Pear got hurt. Louis Carter got hurt. Jimmy DuBose got hurt. And Jimmy "Psycho" Sims, a recent pickup at linebacker who hadn't learned the defense, blitzed on every down. (To his credit, Sims had five tackles and three assists and started the next week versus New England. He never played in the NFL again.) When asked after the game if he was embarrassed, McKay replied "Embarrassed? I was embarrassed before I got here."[98] He just wanted to go home.

Incidentally, at home, in the season finale versus New England, the Bucs faced a 10-3 Patriots team that had already made the playoffs. The Patriots knew they would win—they were eighteen-point favorites—so rather than prepare for the Bucs, they arrived in Tampa two days earlier than scheduled so players could go to the beach. Pat Toomay remembers that Bucs players just didn't want to be there. In fact, they were ready to leave. The team parking lot, he insists, "looked like the staging area for a bunch of Okies fleeing the Dust Bowl." Toomay had his own car packed and planned to be out of Florida, on his way home to Texas, by midnight. He wasn't the only one. "The lot was full of loaded U-Hauls, station wagons with bulging luggage racks, pickups hauling flatbed trailers heaped with furniture and other household stuff," he explains. "The diaspora couldn't be accomplished quickly enough."[99]

Nevertheless, the game was a close one. The Bucs led 14–7 in the third and were tied 14–14 midway through the fourth. But at the 6:15 mark, Steve Spurrier threw an interception to Patriots corner Sam Hunt, which Hunt returned for a touchdown. New England added a field goal, and though they led 24–14 with four seconds left in the fourth, quarterback Steve Grogan called a time-out. Grogan was one touchdown short of the all-time NFL record for rushing touchdowns by a quarterback and stopped the game to run the ball in from the one. Adding insult to injury, Patriots linebacker Steve Zabel, in a classless move worse even than Grogan's, kicked the extra point. It was a bad end to a bad season.

"McKay wasn't really that mad," remembers Dave Green, the Buccaneers' kicker. Rather than give a speech, the coach merely asked the team which players were planning to stay in Tampa during the off-season. They expected that McKay would tell them to stay in shape, or work out, or eat right, but when a handful of players raised their hands, the coach said, "Good. Come by the office in the morning for some fake noses and sunglasses so nobody'll recognize your sorry asses." Green laughs. "That's exactly what he said!"[100]

Chapter Five

Go for 0!

The on-looker can't help but wonder whether consecutive losing will have permanent results. Will marriages break up? Will off-season jobs become a shambles? . . . And what about the city of Tampa? Will the name enter the lexicon as a swear word, as in "Go Tampa yourself!" . . . Only time will tell.

—John Clancy, *Oui* magazine

In September 1977, at the beginning of Tampa Bay's second season, three friends in the marketing department at Tampa's Busch Gardens theme park had an idea. They'd been drinking, remembers Thom Stork, a member of the group, when one of them said, "Hey, what if we lost every game again this year? What if we broke the record? Maybe we should somehow encourage this . . . you know, as a community!" Stork was a Bucs fan to the core. His ex-wife had sold preseason exhibition tickets for Bill Marcum, the promoter, and Stork had seats on the fifty-yard line. (Forty years later, in today's Raymond James Stadium, he sits in almost the same seats.) "I can't recall which one of us it was," he insists, "but someone said, 'Why don't we sell T-shirts? Why don't we sell T-shirts that say, 'Go for 0!'"

The Yucks!

It was a joke at first, but when the Bucs opened 1977 with their fifteenth loss in a row, the men decided to act. With an opening investment of $450, they hired an artist, checked with the U.S. Copyright Office to see if anyone had used the slogan, and printed a hundred shirts. Because "Bucco Bruce" was copyright protected, the design they used was a seventeenth-century galleon, a pirate ship presumably, sinking bow-first. In orange letters, the words read: "Tampa Bay 1977. Go for O!" The shirts were a huge hit. At the team's first home game, the men sold every one. They pulled wagons through the parking lot, selling T-shirts to tailgaters, and took out ads in the sports section of the *Tampa Tribune*. They even had a plane pulling a "Go for O!" banner fly over Tampa Stadium.

On a whim, the men sent shirts to Hugh Culverhouse and John McKay. (McKay threw his in the garbage.) They also sent shirts to NBC's *The Tonight Show* and *Today* show, and both programs used them on air. "*The Tonight Show* was a big one," says Stork. "That was great press, because Johnny Carson was always ripping on the Bucs. But my favorite was the Pro Football Hall of Fame. We sent a T-shirt to the museum there, so when you walked in, right there in the Tampa Bay exhibit, there was a T-shirt that read 'Go for O!' "[1]

Go for O! Losing. Losers. That's what America thought of the Bucs. "Tampa Bay was the worst franchise in the history of the world," wrote future Buccaneer and Hall of Fame nose tackle Warren Sapp. "Growing up, I was a huge Dallas Cowboys fan, but on Sundays we got Bucs games on TV. . . . Oh, I used to pray that lightning would come down and strike the tower so I could see the Cowboys. But it never did, so I had to watch the Bucs, the *Yucks* we called them, losing week after week. The only member of my family who wanted me to be drafted by that sorry-ass franchise was my brother, Hershel. Hershel was a huge Bucs fan," but "I just looked at him like, the Yucks? You are out of your mind."[2]

Although Johnny Carson had been spoofing the Bucs since the end of the 1976 season, it was in 1977 that America's Bucs fetish finally picked up steam. Comedians Red Foxx, Bill Cosby, David Brenner, Don Rickles, and Charles Nelson Reilly all lampooned the team, as did the absurdist host Chuck Barris of *The Gong Show*. The Bucs were a plot device in the sitcom *What's Happening!!* and were a punch line in the Hollywood film *Semi-Tough*. At one point, the Bucs even appeared in Congress, when Wisconsin senator William Proxmire compared the performance of the Bucs to the performance of the Federal Reserve. The Fed, said Proxmire, was the "Tampa Bay of the Federal Government."[3]

In December 1977, journalist Jack Gurney observed that the "Go for O!" phenomenon was reminiscent of the furor surrounding the 1962 Mets, the bumbling-yet-beloved Major League Baseball team that finished sixty and one-half games out of first place. "It's been fifteen years since New York City was swept by Mets-mania," he wrote, "a peculiar phenomenon" in which fans rooted for a team "that couldn't hit, field, run the bases, or win very often." Now, like the Mets, the Bucs "are in that twilight zone of sports" in which people see them as the "defeated darlings of football."[4]

Nevertheless, while the name "Tampa Bay" was synonymous with losing, relatively few Americans knew where the region was. In the early 1970s, for example, a group of Tampa officials visited Manhattan to pitch municipal bonds to a Wall

The Yucks!

Street bond trader. Before listening to the pitch, the trader asked, Tampa, that's "somewhere near Fort Lauderdale above Miami, right?" "No sir," replied one of the visitors, "it's on the west coast." Hmm, he said, so it's "near San Diego, is it?"[5]

The reason for this was that even though people had moved to the Bay Area in record numbers, the region's national identity was weak. Near the tip of Florida, on the east coast, was Miami, famed for its "Calle Ocho" Cuban district, its nightclubs and cruise ships, and of course Miami Beach. North and east of Tampa, in central Florida, was Orlando, a somewhat nondescript city with one notable exception, Walt Disney World, the most popular amusement park in the United States. But Tampa–St. Petersburg–Clearwater? What was its identity? What did people outside of Florida think about when they heard "Tampa Bay"?

The answer was, not much. The answer is still not much, for as late as 2013, the Stanford Research Institute, the same institute that studied the Bay Area in 1973 as to its suitability as a future NFL site, reported that Tampa–St. Petersburg–Clearwater lacked "a cohesive . . . regional identity."[6] Tampa Bay is a "mish-mash," wrote *Tampa Tribune* business reporter Michael Sasso in 2012, "a couple big cities, laid-back beach towns, some cigar history, lots of hospitals, a military base, and a ton of back-office jobs for banks and corporations." As a result, branding the area has been "a surprisingly difficult task."[7]

The main fear in 1977, among some residents, was not a lack of identity, but that Tampa Bay's ungodly losing streak would somehow brand Tampa the "City of Losers," as if losing was what it did. Pittsburgh, for example, was the "City of Champions," having won two Super Bowl championships, a

World Series championship, and an NCAA football championship in six years. Repeated thousands of times in print, on
news programs, in the sports media, and especially by *Monday
Night Football* host Howard Cosell, Pittsburgh was "Title-town
USA," the "City of Champions." So then, what was Tampa?
Loserville? In a letter to the *Tampa Tribune* in December 1977,
a reader from Lakeland complained that by losing, the Bucs
had made Tampa "the laughingstock of the nation." And it
was because of the Bucs, this person wrote, that "most intelligent people" had realized Tampa wasn't "city enough" to support a team.[8]

John Clancy, a writer for the adult magazine *Oui,* put it
best: "The on-looker can't help but wonder whether consecutive losing will have permanent results," he wrote. "Will marriages break up? Will off-season jobs become a shambles? Will
players be able to recover, even in the off-season, or will they
start punching people in restaurants for imagined slights? You
have to wonder if these players will ever shake off the feeling of
total worthlessness, this mustard-gas attack to the psyche that
comes from losing week after week. And what about the city of
Tampa? Will the name enter the lexicon as a swear word, as in
'Go Tampa yourself!' or as a synonym for disaster, as in 'That
was a real Tampa!'? When traveling, will citizens of Tampa say
they are from someplace else, like Miami? Only time will tell."[9]

Bucs locker room announcer Jack Harris, who in 1977 replaced Andy Hardy as host of the *McKay* show, insists losing
was always a concern, but that win or lose, "we were just happy
to be there. You know the saying 'any press is good press'?
Well, when it's twenty degrees in Chicago, we could at least
say, 'Ah man, we lost, but it's eighty in Tampa. We're going to

the beach.'" That's why, he insists, whenever NFC Central opponents would play in Tampa, their fans came to the region in droves. (This was especially true of Packers fans. In 1997, for example, an estimated twenty thousand Green Bay supporters flew from Wisconsin to Florida for a December matchup with the Bucs.) "So, even though we lost a lot," says Harris, "the Bucs were a huge advertisement for the region."[10]

Former Tampa city councilperson and mayor Sandra Freedman agrees. "What did the Bucs mean to me?" she asks. "Well, for once, whenever I was outside of Florida, I didn't have to explain where Tampa was anymore. People just knew."[11] Indeed, in 1973, the *New York Times* used the term "Tampa Bay" in its articles forty-five times. In 1977, due in part to the Rowdies, who played the New York Cosmos in the NASL playoffs that year, but mostly to the Bucs, it would use the term 297 times, an increase of 560 percent. With similar increases in papers throughout the country and references during NFL games, comedy shows, and news programs, the woefully bad Bucs had put the Bay Area on the map.

"I can't tell you what the coming of the Bucs has meant for us," says former Tampa mayor Dick Greco, who served from 1967 to 1974 and again beginning in 1995. "And not just for Tampa, but for the Bay Area as a whole. It's incalculable. Do you think that if we hadn't gotten the Bucs back in '74 that we would have had the Republican National Convention here in 2012? I don't. Would we have gotten the Tampa Bay Devil Rays in St. Petersburg or the Tampa Bay Lightning here in Tampa? There's no way." Forty years ago, says Greco, people didn't know where Tampa was. But the Bucs changed that. Not by winning, he admits, but by simply being in the league. "Sure, all that Johnny Carson stuff was bad, but we were joked about and joked about until people knew where we were."[12]

———

Tampa Bay's second training camp opened in late July 1977, roughly two weeks later than the Bucs' infamous "Junction Boys" camp of 1976. The shortened training session—this one eight weeks instead of ten—had nothing to do with McKay. In 1977, a new collective bargaining agreement between the NFL and the NFL Players Association mandated that veteran players were not required to report to camp until July 22, two weeks before the first preseason game. "It was sometime before that," remembers Pat Toomay, "maybe a day or two. I was driving in from my home in Texas, but the closer I got to Tampa, the slower I drove. Mentally, I just didn't want to be there."[13]

Ten minutes north of the city, he pulled over. The realities of a second camp in Tampa raced through his mind. "The oppressive heat. McKay's caustic sneer. I couldn't face any of it."[14] So Toomay called his wife. "That was it," he says. "I was done. I was throwing in the towel. My wife listened to me and started laughing. So I said, 'What's so funny?' And she said, 'Ron Wolf just called and you've been traded to the Raiders!' I said, 'The Raiders? The *Oakland* Raiders!?' I almost cried. It was like I'd died and gone to football heaven."[15]

Although Toomay was one of only five players to have started all fourteen games for the Bucs, in the off-season he'd lost his job to Lee Roy Selmon after McKay had switched from a "four-three" defense to a "three-four" defense, and moved Lee Roy to right defensive end, where Toomay played. Wolf had also drafted Alabama defensive end Charley Hannah with the team's third pick, and since Hannah could play both end positions, Toomay was out. Yet, as Hubert Mizell explains, "There was more to it than that. McKay just didn't like veterans, especially outspoken veterans. He called them 'Old Pros.'"[16]

"Seventy-six was a weird year," explains Dana Nafziger, a free agent tight end who came to the Bucs in 1977. "The team had all these expansion guys, these older guys coming in and out, because of injuries. But, by the time I got there, most of those guys were gone." In fact, Nafziger remembers McKay cutting Cal Peterson, Jim Peterson, and Jimmy Gunn, three starting linebackers, on the same day. "I thought, *If these guys are getting cut, what the heck am I doing here?* But McKay wanted youth. He wanted his own players there. Not guys who'd come to Tampa out of necessity, or guys someone else had given him. McKay wanted youth."[17] Indeed, by the beginning of season two, he had cut or traded numerous key veterans, including Pat Toomay, Steve Spurrier, and Mike Current, and had kept just twenty-seven original players, including ten from the 1976 expansion draft, on his forty-five-man squad.

In August 1977, he traded Current for a troubled twenty-four-year-old tackle named Darryl Carlton, a former University of Tampa star and number-one pick of the Dolphins. At 6'6", 270 pounds, Carlton had recently recovered from second-degree burns over 20 percent of his body, the result of a January 1977 automobile accident following a high-speed chase with police. Talent-wise, Current and Carlton were a wash, but since Carlton was eight years younger than Current, Current had to go. "He's a great player and a fine man," said a Bucs administrator. "But he's almost thirty-two years old. That's a long way in this business from twenty-four."[18]

The same could be said for Steve Spurrier. In April, the Bucs waived the thirty-one-year-old quarterback in favor of former Florida State star and twenty-five-year-old Bears backup Gary Huff. Spurrier played briefly for Denver and Miami during the 1977 preseason, but by early September his playing career was through. He started coaching as a University of Florida assistant in 1978. "At first I was anxious to grow with the team," said Spurrier. "I knew about the Dolphins, about how they built from expansion, and I thought there was no reason we couldn't do that at Tampa. But then I found out they wanted to go with youth. I found out I was out of the place."[19]

The son of an air force recruiter, Huff had been a three-sport star at Tampa's Leto High School before attending Florida State. There, he played sparingly on FSU's freshman squad but wowed observers as a sophomore when, in a game versus Florida, he threw three touchdown passes in seven minutes. Over the next two years, he set FSU marks for passing attempts, completions, passing yards, passing touchdowns, and total offense, and was the second quarterback chosen, with the thirty-third pick, in the 1973 draft.[20] Alternating between starter and backup for a bad Bears team, the strong-armed Huff had twelve touchdowns and thirty-four interceptions in twenty-two career starts. When, in 1976, Chicago coach Jack Pardee named Bob Avellini the starter, Huff didn't throw a pass all year. In Tampa, he started as the preseason number one, but in July, the team also signed Mike Boryla, a former Stanford star and Eagles backup, whom Philadelphia had let go.

A onetime basketball player and son of former New York Knicks coach and NBA player Vince Boryla, in 1975 the twenty-four-year-old Eagles quarterback had been 2-3 as a starter, but somehow made the Pro Bowl. That year, so many quarterbacks had been hurt, NFL officials had trouble finding people who could play. The league asked Roman Gabriel, James Harris, Steve Bartkowski, Archie Manning, Roger Staubach, and Fran Tarkenton to play, before naming Boryla, an almost completely unknown backup, as a reserve. According to Ernie Accorsi, the future Giants GM and league official who named Boryla to the team, NFC coach Chuck Knox was incensed. He said, "Ernie, this guy can't play. I'm not playing him. So don't expect to see him. How did you come up with him?" Accorsi replied, "Coach, there was no one else."[21] Nevertheless, with 5:39 in the fourth, down 20–9, Knox put Boryla in the game. In two quick drives, he threw touchdown passes to Terry Metcalf and Mel Gray, and handed the AFC a surprising 23–20 defeat.[22]

"For two years, we've had the top NFL draft choice with no quality quarterbacks available," said Ron Wolf. "That made the Boryla deal too good to pass up."[23] Indeed, Tampa Bay had entered the 1977 draft needing, among other things, a quarterback, but after picking USC running back Ricky Bell first overall, the two supposedly elite passers available (Tommy Kramer of Rice and Steve Pisarkiewicz of Missouri) were gone by the second round. So the Bucs selected USC linebacker David Lewis with the team's second pick and Alabama defensive end Charley Hannah third. With no picks in rounds four through seven due to trades, the Bucs selected Minot State quarterback Randy Hedberg in round eight and Arizona State receiver Larry Mucker in round nine. (No other pick made the team.) "We got what we wanted," Wolf said. Bell and Lewis are "instant starters," and Hannah "is right up there" with them. He'll "play a lot of football for us this year."[24]

Nevertheless, the Bell pick was controversial. In spring 1977, respondents to a *St. Petersburg Times* poll favored Pitt running back Tony Dorsett over Bell by a margin of two-to-one.[25] And since Seattle, choosing second, had traded its pick to Dallas for a first-round number-fourteen pick and three second-round picks, critics asked why the Bucs hadn't done the same. The team had so many holes—and not just at running back—it was easy to wonder whether four good players, instead of one great player, would have been better for the team. The Dallas deal, hypothetically, could have netted the Bucs a good young quarterback with the first pick (Kramer), a star defensive back such as Nolan Cromwell with the second pick, as well as two potential starters with picks three and four. But Bell was *the* pick. This was never a doubt. "For the Tampa Bay Bucs, Ricky Bell is their Man for All Seasons," joked one reporter. "A Cure for All Ills . . . It makes no difference that what the Bucs need is a defensive secondary, a quarterback, and a reliable place-kicker." Therefore, "prescribing Ricky Bell for what's wrong with the Bucs is like getting a plumber for a heart attack. The team needs an iron lung, not an iron horse."[26]

Obviously, Tampa Bay's biggest needs were on offense. In 1976, it had the twenty-eighth-ranked running game and the twenty-eighth-ranked passing game in the league. It'd been last—dead last—in points, yards, plays, number of yards per play, yards rushing, rushing touchdowns, and yards per rush. While Bell was a huge help, the Bucs were opening the season with a new quarterback, tough under any circumstances, and a new offensive line. In fact, Dan Ryczek, the center, was the only starting lineman in 1977 to have played for the Bucs in 1976. (Dave Reavis, the team's left tackle, had spent the pre-

vious year on injured reserve.) "It was a new line," says Ryczek, "a completely new line. There were some talented guys
there, like Reavis. But the same lack of consistency we had in
'76, we had again in '77. You can move guys, you can bring
in guys, but no matter how talented they are, building a line
takes time. It just does."[27] As September pickup and starting
guard Jeff Winans put it: "One-on-one, I'm not afraid to match
us with anybody in the league physically. But this isn't a one-
on-one game. It's eleven-on-eleven, and if one guy messes up,
you blow it."[28]

However, on defense, the second-year Bucs were astound-
ingly good. They'd been good since 1976—holding O.J. to just
thirty-nine yards, for example, or being in games, into the
fourth, on six different occasions. But with such a bad offense,
one that punted, fumbled, missed field goals, or threw interceptions 138 times, it was impossible to see it. Not so in 1977,
when the Bucs quickly emerged as one of the best young defenses in the league. The architect was Tom Bass, who moved
that year from offensive coordinator to linebackers coach, and
oversaw the defense. A big man with a bald head, thick beard,
and somewhat menacing visage, Bass was an artist at heart. He
served on the board of the Florida Gulf Coast Symphony, and
for years was a contributing editor of the league's Super Bowl
program.[29]

Originally from Los Angeles, in the mid-1950s Bass played
guard at San Jose State but contracted polio and quit his junior
year. Doctors told him he wouldn't walk again, but after intense pool exercises and time in the weight room, he emerged
with a limp. In the early 1960s, he was a graduate assistant
at San Diego State University under innovative coach Don

Go for O!

Coryell, and from there jumped to the pro ranks with the Chargers. In 1968 he joined the Bengals as defensive coordinator under owner and coach Paul Brown. Bass's philosophy, in terms of defense, was "bend but not break." It worked well with the Bengals, an expansion team, and beginning in 1977, it worked perfectly for the Bucs. "Yards don't bother me," he once said. "The main thing I preach to our people is 'touchdowns allowed.' If we can hold people to field goals, we can win games."[30]

Fortunately for Bass, the Bucs had Lee Roy Selmon, a once-in-a-generation foundational player who anchored the defensive line. During the off-season, the talented Lee Roy had returned to Oklahoma to finish his degree requirements and rehabilitate his knee. He came back stronger than ever, and in 1977 had his first great year. Defensive linemen Dave Pear and Council Rudolph were back, but at linebacker, the Bucs had added three new starters: Dewey Selmon, David Lewis, and Cecil Johnson. In the spring of 1977, Dewey had returned to Oklahoma with Lee Roy, where he entered an MA program in philosophy, did linebacking drills with his brother Lucious, and worked with the track team. He came back to Tampa a svelte 240, quicker in pass coverage, and the hardest-hitting linebacker on the team.

"Dewey's extremely strong and a punishing tackler," said McKay. "How many teams have a fast, 240-pound linebacker?"[31] Bass explained that Dewey's switch from nose tackle to linebacker was "kind of unusual," but that Dewey was "smart enough and mean enough" to make the change. "I used to tell people what the difference was between Lee Roy and Dewey," says Bass. "The difference was when Lee Roy knocked

133

you down, he helped you up. But Dewey . . . Dewey would step on you."[32]

The Buccaneers' other new linebackers were David Lewis, the team's second-round USC pick, and Cecil Johnson, a rookie free agent out of Pittsburgh. At 6'4", 235 pounds, the effervescent Lewis ran a 4.6 forty and was as good with reporters off the field as he was hitting running backs on it. According to Ron Wolf, Lewis was the best linebacker in the draft, but a player who'd fallen unexpectedly to the second round. "I'm not going to beat around the bush," said Wolf. "The rest of the NFL blew it."[33] More traditionally sized at 6'2", 220 pounds, Johnson had played at Pittsburgh, where, as a freshman, he'd once knocked Tony Dorsett out cold. But time at too many positions, including a senior campaign as an undersized defensive end, had left Johnson out of the draft.[34]

The last and only returning starter at linebacker from 1976 was Richard "Batman" Wood, who came to the Bucs in a week-three trade with the Jets. At 6'2", 230 pounds, the metro New York native had been a three-time all-American at USC, where he once told teammates, "I'm Batman. I'm from Gotham City." The nickname stuck, and for years Wood drew bat emblems on his socks and wristbands, and even his face. "Our linebackers were really good," says Bass. "But it wasn't something we saw coming . . . at least, not at first."[35] In fact, the Bucs would evaluate ten different linebackers during the preseason, and tried, unsuccessfully, to acquire the Rams' Jack "Hacksaw" Reynolds through a trade.

Reynolds was a talented yet disgruntled Pro Bowler who, in August 1977, was in a contract dispute with owner Carroll Rosenbloom. In July, Reynolds had testified with other players against Rosenbloom in federal court, seeking to nullify the league's new collective bargaining agreement, which limited free agency. In response, Rosenbloom traded Reynolds to the Bucs, but the seven-year veteran, unwilling to play in Tampa, refused. "Reynolds Traded to Mongolia," read one headline, which Reynolds's attorney insisted was incorrect. Tampa, he said, was actually *Outer* Mongolia. "Money is an issue," explained Ron Wolf, playfully, but the "biggest issue" was Reynolds's wife. "She hyperventilates—a traumatic stage they tell me. They maintain that the trade scared her."[36]

Although Wolf tried for a time to trade Reynolds to the Colts, Hacksaw's failure to report to the Bucs meant that any deal, with any team, was through. Reynolds returned to the Rams in November 1977. But, for as good as Reynolds was, the Bucs didn't need him. By midseason, the team's linebacking corps had gelled, and its defensive backs, Jeris White, Mike Washington, Cedric Brown, and Mark Cotney, were playing their best games of the year. Overall, the second-year Bucs had the youngest defense in the league. The average starter was twenty-four, with 1.6 years of experience, while Cecil Johnson had just turned twenty-two. "I accept the fact that we're young and understand why we're losing," said David Lewis. But "what I'm happy about is that even though we haven't won a game . . . no team has been more physical than us. For us, it's not a matter of defeats; it's a matter of mistakes. We're making mistakes, but we won't be doing that next year. . . . Next year, we're going to lower the boom."[37]

———

September 1977. Tampa Stadium, the Bucs' last preseason game. Quarterback Mike Boryla was hurt and out for the season. Likewise, quarterback Gary Huff had a sprained knee, so McKay named Randy Hedberg, the Bucs' eighth-round draft pick out of tiny Minot State, the starter. Minot (pronounced "my not") was one hour south of Saskatchewan in the distant Drift Prairie region of North Dakota. In 1977, it had just nineteen hundred students and played football in the NAIA North Dakota Athletic Conference against Mayville State Teachers College and the Wahpeton School of Science. At 6'3", 200 pounds, Hedberg had grown up in nearby Parshall, North Dakota, where his German and Scandinavian grandparents had homesteaded. Known for its "world-famous" rock sculpture museum, Parshall had twelve hundred residents, mostly farmers, who lived within the boundaries of the Fort Berthold Indian Reservation. It had a car dealership, a couple of grocery stores, some hardware stores, and "a whole bunch of bars," said Hedberg, "three, I think."[38]

Although admittedly a long shot, scouts compared Hedberg to Bengals quarterback Ken Anderson, a two-time Pro Bowler from diminutive Augustana College in Illinois. Hedberg had been a four-year letterman at Minot and an NAIA all-American, but Tampa was a big step up. Still, the fair-haired Dakotan made the most of it. First, he beat out two Division I quarterbacks, free agents Scott Gardner of Virginia and David Jaynes of Kansas, then unseated Parnell Dickinson to make the team. Thus, with neither Huff nor Boryla available, McKay named Hedberg the starter.

He began slowly, handing off to Bell and completing three passes for twelve yards. But late in the second, Hedberg went 4-for-4 with a touchdown on a 7-play, 50-yard drive. The score was 7–0. Then Bell scored in the third, the defense battered

Bert Jones, and the Bucs held the Colts to just five first downs. They won 14–0. Hedberg "did a marvelous job," said McKay. "Our line protected him well, but he still had to scramble, and he did. He didn't seem nervous. He'd come over to the sidelines and we'd tell him to do something, and he said, 'okay.' "[39] Hedberg's final stats were pedestrian: 10 of 25 for 148 yards with 1 touchdown and 1 interception. But he'd managed the game with poise, throwing balls away when he had to, scrambling when his receivers were covered, or simply eating sacks.

In fact, Hedberg had been so cool, teammates called him the "Iceberg," though running back Anthony Davis preferred, for some reason, the "Lonesome Polecat." The fans ate it up. Within a week there was a Randy Hedberg fan club, and supporters wore buttons that read, "Why Not Minot?" In North Dakota, the Minot radio station KCJB joined the Buccaneers' radio network, and Hedberg did so many interviews, he developed what he called "telephone ear."[40] The high point, perhaps, was a grandiose September 1977 newspaper article in which the *St. Petersburg Times* asked, "Is a clean-cut, 6-foot-3 farm boy from the wheatlands of North Dakota the pied piper who will lead the Tampa Bay Bucs out of the NFL badlands?" In the background was a cartoon drawing of Mount Rushmore, with a worker holding a picture of Hedberg, and wondering "Maybe Too Soon?"[41]

It was. The next week, in the Bucs' season opener at Philadelphia, the shell-shocked Hedberg ran for his life. He was "sacked four times," observed one reporter, "decked a half dozen other times," and twice "lay on the hard artificial carpeting, unable to move. . . . Welcome to the NFL, kid."[42] Although 10 of 25 passing for just 66 yards, the beleaguered

Hedberg received no help—literally, no help. The blocking was "horse manure," said McKay, with receivers dropping balls and drawing penalties, Dave Green missing a field goal, and Ricky Bell fumbling at the Eagles' ten. The score was Philadelphia 13, Tampa Bay 3. The Bucs' lone bright spot, as usual, was the defense. Lee Roy Selmon had two sacks and Dave Pear had one. Cedric Brown and Cecil Johnson each had interceptions, while the Bucs forced fumbles, including two in Eagles' territory, three times.

"We had an aggressive defense," remembers Mark Cotney, a safety. "We were hard hitters and good tacklers, but didn't press a lot. We just didn't have the depth, and we didn't have any Darrelle Revis types who could play man-to-man." While Cotney is quick to insist the defense wasn't perfect, it was the offense, he says, that struggled. "Those first few years were a doozy," he explains. "We'd make a stop, come off the field, and barely get our helmets off before someone yelled, 'PUNTING TEAM!' And we'd say, 'Ah shit!' "[43]

The next game, at home versus Minnesota, was the 1977 season in a nutshell. On a soggy field in front of 66,272 fans, the Bucs forced six punts, had two sacks, two interceptions, and a fumble recovery, but lost 9–3. Likewise, they lost 10–0 to Washington, 13–0 to Green Bay, 10–0 to the New York Giants, 16–7 to Detroit, and 10–0 to Chicago. The highlights? Tough defense, but a painfully inept offense that was, without a doubt, the worst in the history of the league.

"Sack. Sack. Sack. Sack. Sack," wrote Hubert Mizell. "Sack. Sack. Sack. Sack. Sack. Slip. Interception. Penalty. Slip. Interception. Penalty. Penalty. Slip. You've just scanned a major portion of the Tampa Bay Buccaneers' offensive script."[44] It seems

Go for O!

impossible, because the 1976 Bucs had scored just 125 points, the second-lowest point total since World War II, but in 1977, the new and improved Bucs managed just 103 points, or 7.4 points per game—the poorest-producing offense since 1944, when the Brooklyn Tigers averaged under 7. But Brooklyn had an excuse. Its coach, its quarterback, and most of its key players had been in uniform, in the military, while the Bucs . . . the Bucs were just bad.

With McKay calling the plays, in 1977 the Tampa Bay offense scored just seven touchdowns—seven—while the defense scored four. To put that into perspective, four different NFL running backs and five different receivers that year had more touchdowns than the Bucs. The Bears' Walter Payton had more yards rushing than the Bucs. And Richard Wood, a Buccaneer linebacker, had as many touchdowns in 1977 as the team's star running back, Ricky Bell. Although injuries at quarterback had devastated the team offensively, the Bucs' most glaring problem was the "I." It was too predictable. "I'll tell you," said Jeff Winans, a tackle, "it gets pretty discouraging when you line up and the defense knows exactly what play you're going to run. That happened a couple of times Sunday. We had this one play, 29-pitch we call it, and we were gonna run it. Soon as we get down, I hear their defense yellin' 'Goin' left!' They knew exactly what we were going to do."[45]

Following a 10–0 loss to the Redskins in which the Tampa Bay offense gave up ten sacks and generated just 138 yards, opposing lineman Bill Brundige said, "I leave Tampa admiring the defense. It's a winner. But the offense? Coach McKay is going to learn that the I-formation isn't going to work. He isn't at Southern Cal anymore playing Stanford."[46] Reporters quipped that "Student Body Right" was actually "Minus-Two Right" and printed letters from fans that were, in a word, brutal.[47] "I would like to remind John McKay that he is in the big time," insisted one Largo resident, "not at USC. Everyone in the stadium knows his plays—run through the middle, run outside, pass, Green kicks."[48] A fan in Lakeland called it the "run two, pass one" offense and blasted McKay for being unimaginative.[49] "Why doesn't John McKay open up the Tampa Bay offense?" asked a St. Petersburg resident. "The Bucs are 0-22 and McKay is strictly a ground-game man. Why doesn't he go for the bomb once in a while?"[50]

Others wanted short, quick passes or screens—something, anything, besides the run. But Hedberg had been woefully ineffective at quarterback; so had his backup Jeb Blount. In eight combined starts the two quarterbacks had zero touchdowns and seventeen interceptions, and were sacked thirty-two times. That left Ricky Bell. The talented running back had started the season slowly. He had 15 carries for 53 yards at Philadelphia, but due to a chipped bone in his ankle and a shoulder injury, finished the year with 436 yards rushing and a less-than-impressive 2.95 yards per rush. He had two touchdowns.

Bell's running mate, Anthony Davis, averaged a slightly better three yards per rush, but was moody, truculent, and one of the least popular players on the team. Although fans disliked Davis—he was, as one journalist put it, a "better press agent (for himself) than a football player"—they were downright angry at Bell.[51] After all, *he* was the first pick. And while Bell had trouble running the ball, Tony Dorsett had more than a thousand yards rushing and was the NFL's Offensive Rookie of the Year. Thus, rather than cheer for Bell, fans in Tampa Stadium booed.

Lakeland *Ledger* reporter Patrick Zier called it an "orchestrated crescendo" of boos, which drove the rookie nuts.[52] "Coming to an expansion team," he said, "and being hurt and having the fear of not living up to my own expectations was more than I could handle. I never went out or tried to get involved with people here. I dwelled on feeling sorry for myself."[53]

No one felt sorry for McKay. He'd chosen Bell, and Bell was the seventh former USC player on the team. In fact, five of his coaches were Trojans, including first-year quarterbacks coach Bill Nelson and co–offensive line coach Skip Husbands, as well as administrative assistant Dick Beam. "Certainly, there was an arrogance there," claims Glenna Hancock, who worked in public relations for the Bucs. "McKay was from *the* Southern California. So naturally, players he recruited were the best. His coaches were the best. But if you keep saying: 'This is how we did it at USC,' 'this is how we did it at USC,' but you don't win, people are going to grumble."[54] In his 2000 memoir, tackle Mike Current agreed. McKay "continually told us how badly his past USC teams would have beaten us," he wrote, "and the only players he treated with any civility were USC graduates. After all, how bad could they be if he had coached them?"[55] Once, after a close loss to Buffalo, he stormed into the locker room and screamed, "I won four fucking national championships at Southern Cal!" His face was red and his hands were shaking. "He just looked at us," said receiver Lee McGriff, "then walked out of the room. That's when a player next to me said, 'OK then, let's win one for the coach!' "[56]

The press called Tampa Bay "USC East," and once, after a game versus the Dolphins, Don Shula quipped: "Getting ready to play the Bucs is like getting ready to play Southern Cal."[57]

"The whole USC thing was a drag," says Ron Martz, a reporter with the *St. Petersburg Times*. "I think it brought the team down. Fans felt McKay was showing favoritism to USC guys who didn't deserve it. They disliked J. K. McKay for being the coach's son, and felt, rightly or wrongly, that there were better receivers available. I actually felt sorry for J.K. Then they sign Bell, who struggled, so I'd say the atmosphere, at times, was sort of poisoned."[58]

Safety Mark Cotney explains: "Sure there was talk. But I didn't pay any attention to that. I couldn't. I was interested in how Mark Cotney played safety. Because, when your boss is John McKay, you never feel safe. He would cut you. He would cut you at the drop of a hat for anything." As Cotney recalls, the team was in practice once, during the preseason, when a tight end standing next to McKay said jokingly, "Boy, that cigar stinks!" In a rage, McKay turned to the player and said, "What did you say? Get your ass off the field now! Take off your pads and go home!"[59]

The one player who could have criticized McKay—both for his offense on the field and for his caustic demeanor off it— was Lee Roy Selmon, but Selmon was too mild, too respectful, and maybe even too afraid. As defensive end Charley Hannah recalls, the Bucs had a team meeting once in which McKay, in a frenzy, threatened to cut anyone who hadn't learned their playbook. "We're all going back to our rooms," explains Hannah, "and someone says, 'Hey, let's go get something to eat.' But Lee Roy says, 'No, no . . . I can't go. I'm going to study. I don't want to get cut.' I thought, 'What! Cut Lee Roy? There wasn't a team in the league who'd cut Lee Roy!' But Lee Roy seriously believed McKay would cut him."[60]

Go for O!

As for Hugh Culverhouse, the Bucs' owner supported McKay unconditionally. And why not? Even with a twenty-six-game losing streak, average attendance at home games had increased in 1977 from 44,169 to 52,637, and midway through the 1977 season, the Bucs had the third-highest attendance figure in the league. What's more, in October 1977, the NFL signed a four-year, $576 million broadcast deal with NBC, ABC, and CBS, and voted to expand the season to sixteen games. Suddenly the franchise Hugh Culverhouse had paid $16 million for was worth at least $25 million, perhaps even more.[61] By late 1978, the Bucs were bringing in so much money that Culverhouse was able to buy out Marvin Warner, the team's 48 percent co-owner.[62] "I must say, the first two years we didn't anticipate, nor could we, the extent of the disappointments," explained Culverhouse in a 1981 interview. "I guess my job was to counsel and comfort John." Often, after a loss, "we'd be here until two, three, four in the morning," and "I'd remind him of our plan to go with youth. We knew it would take time and yes we made mistakes. But overall, we were making improvement, and by Tuesday we'd be on top again."[63]

Support for McKay, however, was one thing; support for Ron Wolf and other front office types was another. In early 1977, Culverhouse fired marketing director Bill Marcum, the person who in many respects had landed the franchise, and decided that winter that he was going to fire Wolf as well. Only really wanting Marcum for his ticket list, Culverhouse had clashed with the marketing director over pricing, and the two men disliked each other. But Wolf's firing was a McKay decision. Although mum on the subject publicly, the imperious Bucs coach was not secretive about the fact that he wanted complete control, not only over coaching decisions, but also over personnel. "John McKay and Hugh Culverhouse were contemporaries," wrote Wolf in his 1999 memoir. "They socialized together" and "as the months went by, John McKay's authority within the organization grew and my authority diminished. He had Hugh Culverhouse's ear, and I didn't."[64] According to Wolf, McKay took control of the team gradually, though Glenna Hancock, the team's public relations assistant, insists that was the coach's plan all along. In late 1975, she and McKay assistant Dick Beam were driving around Tampa buying groceries and other supplies to ready the McKay home prior to the coach's arrival. "I'm taking him here and there," she recalls, "when out of the blue Beam says, 'You know what, Glenna? Within a year, no one'll be left who was original to this team. Coach McKay is going to come in and put his own people in place.' And I remember saying, 'What? You're talking about my job!' And he said, 'I doubt it'll go that deep. But Coach McKay will be head coach and general manager in a year.'"[65]

Although Wolf had drafted well (bringing in Lee Roy Selmon and David Lewis), had made some good trades (for Richard Wood and Mike Washington), and had done well in the expansion draft (with Dave Pear, Mark Cotney, and Dave Reavis), McKay criticized the exec for signing Steve Spurrier.[66] While McKay never said so publicly, he also blamed Wolf for signing Gary Huff. Huff, the former Bears quarterback and Bucs preseason number one, had come into camp with tendonitis in his throwing arm, though neither Bears general manager Jim Finks nor Huff had said anything prior to the trade.[67]

Nevertheless, Huff played well in the preseason, but tore knee ligaments in an exhibition loss to Atlanta, then suffered torn rib cartilage and cracked ribs in a game-six loss to the Packers. When he came back in November, again versus Atlanta, he had trouble throwing the ball. On a sunny 68-degree day, at home, in front of 44,000 fans, Huff "led" the 0-24 Bucs to their worst offensive performance in two years, worse even than the infamous Colts and Steelers games of '76, and worse than the Randy Hedberg opener of 1977. In four quarters of play, through 47 plays, the Tampa Bay offense managed just 78 yards—47 plays, 78 yards—a 1.65-yard average. "If the Bucs had been allowed seven downs instead of the customary four," wrote one journalist ruefully, "they still would have faced seventh-and-a-foot on their average series."[68] Sacked 3 times, Huff went 4 for 11 for 38 yards, with no touchdowns and 3 interceptions. Hedberg went 1 for 12 with no touchdowns and 1 interception, and Bell had 11 yards. The final score was Atlanta 17, Tampa Bay 0.

"This was our worst effort in two years," said McKay. "Our offense left me talking to myself."[69] Naturally, the fans booed, hurling insults at the team from behind the bench, where season ticket holders sat, and from the corner passage into the team's tunnel. A vocal minority threw trash and loose change; one fan yelled racial epithets at Bell, prompting teammates to restrain the running back from climbing into the stands. McKay had a soda dumped on his head, and standing in the tunnel he challenged the person who threw it to a fight. "We've brought the abuse on ourselves by not winning," explained McKay after the game. "People wouldn't be reacting if they didn't care," he said, adding that "the racial slurs and hate are coming from teenagers, something ninety-nine percent of fans wouldn't even think of doing."[70] That was probably true. But after twenty-five straight losses, the atmosphere at home games had grown ugly.

"I used to position myself in Tampa Stadium to get a good view of McKay walking off the field," wrote reporter Tim Mc-Donald. "The verbal garbage that was heaped on him from the southeast corner of the end zone, the entrance to the team's dressing room, was unbelievable. There was actually violence in the air. It scared me. I'm sure it scared him."[71] Signs that had previously read "Throw McKay in the Bay" now read "Slay McKay," and once, when Gary Huff lay writhing on the ground with a rib injury, fans cheered. "I moved here from Wisconsin and was a Green Bay fan," wrote one person to the *Tampa Tribune*. "Now I am a Bucs fan. But I will never live down what we, the fans, did to our players and coaches on Sunday. . . . [We] cheered when Huff got hurt. That's like cheering a traffic accident."[72] Defensive end Charley Hannah remembers packages mailed to One Buc Place containing dead animals and fecal matter and wondering if some crazed fan would send something "more assertive," such as a mail bomb. Ron Wolf even joked about it. "Certainly, those comments" made by Johnny Carson and other critics "don't sit well with us," he said in a 1977 interview. "But when you can no longer laugh at them, you're in trouble. Of course, I have a good secretary who starts my car."[73]

In November 1977, comedian George Carlin appeared at the St. Petersburg Bayfront Auditorium. In front of a packed crowd, Carlin recited a series of fake headlines, including one that read "Football Team Dies in Sudden Death Overtime." The crowd laughed politely, but when a man in the back yelled the "Tampa Bay Bucs!" the audience burst into applause. "Okay, so this is your Tampa Bay team," wrote *St. Petersburg Times* reporter Rick Abrams, "and you're angry. Angry to the point of absurdity. Good. Because the only way to sensibly analyze the Buccaneers is with an eye of absurdity. New York had the Mets, we have the Bucs—the team that turned Tampa Stadium into the Gilligan's Island of football."[74] Locker room announcer Jack Harris agrees that "it *was* absurd," and tells the story of Bucs' first play-by-play announcer, Ray Scott. Scott had been Green Bay's announcer during the Vince Lombardi years, but somehow landed in Tampa covering the Bucs. "It'd be like third-and-forty," recalls Harris, "and the quarterback would drop back and get sacked for a thirty-yard loss, and Scott would moan, 'HOW MUCH ADVERSITY CAN ONE . . . TEAM . . . TAKE?!?' You just had to shake your head and laugh."[75]

Reporter Jack Gurney insists that the funniest player on the Bucs was punter Dave Green, who, like Scott, had a penchant for the absurd. Green's cheering section was in the end zone, and most of his fans were in wheelchairs because that's where the wheelchair section was. "So one time, I was back there behind the goalposts. The line's set, the center's hiking the ball, and Dave is right on the white line. Most guys would have been terrified, but he just looks at me and says, 'Pssst! Hey! You wanna change places?' I almost died."[76]

Green remembers the wackiest play of his career, a play that for decades was synonymous with the Yucks. It occurred in 1978—and not in 1977, oddly enough—during the fourth quarter in a close game at Minnesota, the Bucs leading 16–7, when Tampa Bay kicker Neil O'Donoghue lined up for a field goal. Kneeling at the seventeen-yard line, Green was the holder. As he called for the snap, however, the ball sailed up and over his head, past O'Donoghue, and out to the middle of the field. The players gave chase, in a mad scrum, when the lanky, 6'6" O'Donoghue tried to kick the ball out of bounds. Instead, he whiffed and fell, while Viking linebacker Fred Mc-Neill picked the ball up and returned it to the Tampa Bay ten.

"Now, Metropolitan Stadium was huge," explains Green, "but everyone in it was laughing. You could hear it. But because I'd been spun around and blocked, I didn't even see the play. I just saw snippets. So as I came off the field, I asked Lee Roy, 'What the hell happened?' And I could see his shoulder pads bobbing up and down. He was also laughing. And he says, 'That was the funniest damn thing I've ever seen!' " Although Green didn't know it at the time, that was *the* biggest blooper in the forty-year history of the Bucs. That evening, the clip appeared on nightly news programs nationwide. But since the team was en route from Minneapolis, Green didn't see it. "I get home and it's late and my wife's lying in bed. Now she's seen the clip, and she's kind of mad about it. I mean, I'm the one who played, right? But she turns to me and hisses, 'Aren't you embarrassed?' "[77] Well, yes, said Green, he was—and so, in 1977, were the Bucs.

The week after the Atlanta game, the team lost 10–0 to the Bears, at home, for its twenty-sixth straight defeat and its twelfth loss of the 1977 season. In six home games, the bumbling Buccaneer offense had scored three points. In fact, it'd gone scoreless for twenty-two straight quarters. It was O-for-October and O-for-November, and had scored fewer points per game, at home games, than the Tampa Bay Rowdies, the NASL soccer team. The worst thing was that the defense had played spectacularly, holding Bears great Walter Payton to 101 yards on 33 carries, and taking a 0–0 tie four minutes into the fourth. But Randy Hedberg threw an interception, setting up a field goal, the Bucs went three and out, then the Bears managed a fake punt for their one good drive of the game. The final score was Chicago 10, Tampa Bay 0. "We were determined not to give up the ball in our end of the field," said McKay, "and we were determined not to let them pass from punt formation. So what do we do? We give up the ball in our end of the field and we let them pass from punt formation. Other than that, we could have played for a month and a half and they couldn't score a touchdown on us."[78]

Lee Roy Selmon insisted that all the Bucs needed was a point—a single, solitary point. "I felt we handled them quite easily," he said. "All we needed was one point and we wouldn't have had to pass in the fourth quarter. They wouldn't have been able to intercept. But we couldn't get a point."[79] Yet again, like a broken record playing the same song for the umpteenth, nausea-inducing time, the Buccaneer offense was atrocious. It had just 135 yards total. Randy Hedberg was 4 of 15 passing for 36 yards and 2 interceptions, and its deepest drive was to the Bears' twenty-eight. (The team threatened to score only once.) "I think those last few home games were a turning point," says Dewey Selmon, "all those 10–0 and 14–0 defeats. That's when the guys on defense realized that if we wanted to win, we had to carry the ball into the end zone ourselves. Now, I'm not blaming the offense. They tried hard and we were teammates, but that's just how it was."[80]

———

The Yucks!

In 1977, the New Orleans Saints were one of the worst-performing franchises in the league. Founded ten years earlier, the Saints had won a record three games their expansion year, but had followed that up with nine losing seasons in a row. In ten years, they had had five coaches and four GMs, one a retired NASA astronaut named Richard Gordon, who'd never run a team. The Saints' owner, John Mecom Jr., was the thirtysomething son of a Texas oil magnate, who made (or who let his general managers make) one bad decision after another. For example, in 1967 the team traded its first pick, ever, for a backup Colts quarterback named Gary Cuozzo. Cuozzo was beaten out in the preseason by an expansion draft quarterback, while the Colts chose future All-Pro defensive end Bubba Smith. In 1968 and 1969, the Saints lost their two first-round picks as compensation, under the Rozelle Rule, for signing free agent receiver Dave Parks, and in 1971 they traded the previous year's pick, receiver Ken Burrough, for Oilers running back Hoyle Granger. Burrough would play eleven seasons for Houston and make two Pro Bowls, while Granger played one forgettable year for the Saints and was cut.

However, Mecom lucked out in 1971 by selecting the talented Ole Miss quarterback Archie Manning, the father of future stars Eli and Peyton Manning, with a first-round number-two pick, but after six arduous seasons all Manning had done was suffer. Through November 1977, his record as a quarterback was 16-49-3. He'd had numerous surgeries, including two in 1976 that left him out for the season, and he'd been sacked at least two hundred times. In fact, Manning led the league in sacks in 1971, 1972, and 1975. Although roughed up physically, he maintained an impressive workout regimen and was widely regarded as one of the best quarterbacks in the league. Everyone wanted him, and Mecom, in a rare moment of clarity, signed the quarterback to a million-dollar contract extension in the summer of 1975.

In early 1976, following a dismal 2-12 season and the firing of coach John North, Mecom hired the accomplished former Chiefs coach Hank Stram. Stram was a noted disciplinarian and a sharp dresser who wore suits on the sidelines. In the 1960s, he'd won three AFL championships and a Super Bowl championship, but he struggled through the 1976 season in New Orleans and again in 1977. That year, the Saints were 3-9, in last place in the NFC West division, when the 0-26 Buccaneers came to town. The spread was eleven, and though Tampa Bay had been shut out four of its last five games and had scored just fifty-three points, Stram was nervous. A loss to the Bucs would undoubtedly end his Saints career.[81] Adding insult to injury, a week earlier, Archie Manning had supposedly said that losing to the Bucs would be a "disgrace." "I don't want to be the laughingstock of the league," he explained, "and that's just what we'll be if we're the first team to lose to Tampa Bay."[82]

Although Manning would later insist he'd never said the word *disgrace,* McKay used the slight, real or imagined, to motivate his team. "When Coach McKay told us what he had said," claimed Lee Roy Selmon, "a powerful look came over our dressing room. Everybody seemed to burn inside, saying to themselves that it's time to end all this losing."[83] According to offensive coordinator Tom Bass, even the coaches were angry. Just prior to the game, during warm-ups, he and McKay chatted with Stram and Mecom at midfield. At one point, Stram showed Mecom his sport coat, and started teasing the Saints' owner, jokingly, that he had the better tailor. "They're going on and on about leather patches," says Bass, "and McKay's standing there with this ugly orange windbreaker on. Now that really pissed me off. So as we walked away, I turned to McKay and said, 'Coach, we're gonna' kick their ass.' I could feel it."[84]

Played on Sunday, December 11, 1977, in the half-empty Louisiana Superdome, the game began as all Bucs games began, with punishing plays on defense followed by no offense whatsoever. On Manning's first drive, for example, David Lewis and Dewey Selmon stuffed talented Saints running back Chuck Muncie on two consecutive plays; then Lee Roy Selmon recovered a Manning fumble on third-and-six. But, starting in New Orleans territory, the anemic Bucs managed just one first down and missed a 33-yard field goal from the Saints' sixteen. On the next New Orleans drive, Dewey stopped Muncie again, Cedric Brown tackled running back Tony Galbreath on a draw, and Council Rudolph sacked Manning at the New Orleans ten. Two Saints drives, four total yards. It was at that point, starting at the Saints' twenty-six, that Tampa Bay ran the ball on six consecutive plays, five for Ricky Bell and one for Louis Carter. The two running backs gained just twelve yards, but Tampa Bay finished the drive with a field goal. The score was 3–0.

On New Orleans' third drive, the Buccaneer defense stopped the Saints again, for their third three-and-out, but in spite of good field position at the New Orleans' forty-three-yard line, the Bucs were forced to punt. That's when corner Mike Washington intercepted Manning on a first-down pass, a bomb that went in and out of the receiver's hands at the Buccaneer forty. Washington snagged the ball, then lateraled it to safety Cedric Brown, who returned it twenty-seven yards to the New Orleans thirty-three. With that, the quarter ended. In four drives, the Buccaneer defense had obliterated the Saints, who'd had three three-and-outs, a fumble and an interception, and gained just eleven yards. Even more impressive, not one Saints play had occurred in Tampa Bay territory during the first quarter. As for the offense, it ran nine consecutive times on the following drive, and made it to the Saints' eight before kicking a field goal. Gaining in confidence and momentum, the upstart Bucs led 6–0.

From that point, the teams traded punts, the Saints went three-and-out, then late in the second, the Bucs had their one good drive of the game—their best, in fact, of the season. Seemingly out of nowhere, Gary Huff hit Morris Owens for a thirty-nine-yard completion, then passed to Jimmy Dubose for eight and Louis Carter for five, before again hitting Owens in the end zone. The Bucs' 13–0 lead, amazingly enough, was the largest lead in the history of the franchise. The Tampa Bay fans in the crowd, all two hundred of them, including a sixty-person contingent from the Sarasota "Block and Tackle Club," erupted. "From across the huge indoor stadium they looked like an orange postage stamp," wrote one reporter, "but on the sideline their message came across loud and clear."[85] Laughing and hugging, the players cheered, too, but the game wasn't over yet. With a grim determination, the defense returned to the field. "We knew that if the offense got us thirteen points," said Dewey Selmon, "there was no way anybody was going to beat us. We would have had to beat ourselves at that point and we weren't about to let that happen."[86]

At halftime, the Saints replaced Manning with backup quarterback Bobby Scott, but Scott's first attempt was a swing pass for minus four, and his second attempt was intercepted.

Throwing from the Saints' forty-two, Scott threw the ball down the left sideline to speedy receiver John Gilliam, but cornerback Mike Washington stepped in front of Gilliam and returned the ball for a touchdown. It was Washington's second interception of the game, and the first "pick-six" of his career. The score was 20–0. "We knew that when Gilliam came into the game," explained Washington, "they would try to go short to him. So when they threw to him we were in a type of defense where I was in a good position to intercept. I just stepped in front of him, and was gone."[87] For Tampa Bay, the second Washington pick was the play of the game, arguably the most important play in the two-year history of the franchise. For all intents and purposes, the twenty-six-game losing streak was over.

Tom Bass exhorted the defense from the sidelines. So did Wayne Fontes, the defensive backs coach, and burly Abe Gibron, who coached the line. "Get after them now!" screamed Bass. "Get after them now, don't let up."[88] They didn't. On the next series, David Lewis hit Scott on a blitz, the ball popped up, and Richard Wood intercepted. The teams traded punts through the third, but early in the fourth, with the Saints backed up at the four, Wood made another interception, then fought his way like a fullback into the end zone. He spiked the ball over the crossbar. Green missed the extra point, but the score, with fourteen minutes left in the fourth, was 26–0. "We've got a blankety-blank, bleepedy-bleep defense," exclaimed David Lewis after the game. "No, seriously, the offense played well," too.[89] Actually, it hadn't. The offense had scored just thirteen points on six trips inside the New Orleans thirty, but by this point it didn't matter. Manning scored two touchdowns in the fourth, but gave up the Saints' third pick-six to lineman Greg Johnson with two minutes left to go. The Bucs ground out the clock and won by a final score of 33–14.

The response on the sidelines, in the stands, and throughout the Bay Area was pure, unadulterated joy. Players hugged and laughed, and several lay on the field, rolling about in ecstasy like children, while Hugh Culverhouse and Abe Gibron cried. Sitting in the locker room, McKay lit a cigar. "This is an emotional moment," he said, his voice quivering. "I'm glad we won for the fans and the players and the coaches because they all waited so long for this." And "whatever Archie Manning said, I agree with him. He said it would be a disgrace to lose, and it is. If only we can get some more guys to make statements like that . . ."[90]

The thing that every Buc remembers, to a man, was the plane ride home. A boom box blasted disco music, players danced in the aisles, and Culverhouse, in a rare show of generosity, bought steak and champagne. Nobody ate. "It was just raucous," says Jack Harris. "Of course, we always had booze on planes, but this time everybody just got rip-roarin' drunk. I was sitting on the top of the back of the seat and Abe Gibron was dancing in the aisle when the pilot said 'Okay, we're about to land, so you're going to have to sit down.' But nobody did. Nobody listened to him. It was the only time I've ever seen a plane land with people standing up."[91]

What the Bucs didn't know at the time was that an estimated eight thousand fans, from all over the region, had come to Tampa to greet them. And this was at nine at night on a Sunday. To fans such as Ray Brooker of Sebring, a city one hundred miles east of Tampa, it didn't matter. "As soon as the game was over me and my wife, Denise, got in the car and shot right over here," he said. "This is history and we definitely wanted to be part of it." Fans went to the airport, but as word spread that players were exiting the facility by bus from the tarmac, they reassembled en masse at One Buc Place. There were traffic jams in the parking garages and bumper-to-bumper traffic up and down Westshore Boulevard, the route from the airport. It was a scene the *Tampa Tribune* described as "fandemonium."[92]

Equipment manager Pat Marcuccillo was the first employee to make it to the building. Driving ahead of the team in his own car, it was his job to open One Buc Place before the players got there. But, as he neared the headquarters, his assistant yelled, "There's somebody on the roof!" And "wouldn't you know it," he says, "the goddamn Buccaneer cheerleaders were on the roof! [They were actually next door, on the roof of a different building.] They were up there dancing. And there were people everywhere. There were so many people, the cops had to block off the street." When he finally got through, he says, his car was a wreck. The antenna was gone, there was a headlight broken, and the side mirrors were gone. According to Marcuccillo, the building fared even worse. "It looked like it'd been mortared," he insists. "There were no flowers left. There was no grass left, no bushes. People kept coming in and I'd say, 'I don't know who you are! You gotta leave!' But they wanted anything they could get their hands on, just so they could say they were there. It was incredible."[93]

As the team arrived in three different buses, under escort, the crowd went nuts. "Let's go Bucs! Let's go Bucs!" they chanted, aided by one fan who'd hooked a CB loudspeaker to his car. In the background, the Buccaneer marching band played "When the Saints Go Marching In." One by one, players exited, signing autographs, shaking hands, and getting patted on the back. Then McKay, wearing a houndstooth hat given to him by Alabama coach Bear Bryant, addressed the crowd from the roof of a car. However, amid a new round of cheering, including a raucous chant of "Hooray for McKay," no one heard him. "I couldn't have anticipated this reception," said Culverhouse, who also spoke. "Not in my wildest dreams. When Coach McKay got in the car with me, his first words were 'Mr. C., I've never seen fans like this. I can't believe what I am seeing.'"[94] Despite their excitement, the crowd, shockingly enough, was orderly. Hundreds lined up at 10 p.m. to buy tickets at the hastily opened ticket office, but one idiot fan stole McKay's hat from his head. It was never recovered.

The next week, the scene at One Buc Place and in the locker room was euphoria. Crews from all three networks were in Tampa to film the Bucs, and Howard Cosell conducted an interview with McKay during the halftime show of *Monday Night Football*. Johnny Carson was on vacation, but Bill Cosby, his fill-in, did a five-minute monologue specifically on the Bucs. "Put it on the blimp!" he crowed. "Get horsemen going through the town. Let little children run through the neighborhoods sitting on cans and pots announcing Tampa Bay won the game. . . . Let's all hear it for Tampa Bay!"[95]

Op-eds in local newspapers praised the fans, and noted what a unifying effect the victory had had. "The Bucs won!" exclaimed the *St. Petersburg Times*. "Everyone knew it already but the word nonetheless was passed from neighbor to neighbor, stranger to stranger, on a late Sunday afternoon in the happy neighborhood of Tampa Bay. In Tampa, St. Petersburg, Clearwater, and Tarpon Springs, in Pasco and Manatee Counties and in other points around," residents "shouted to people they hadn't spoken to in months: 'the Bucs won!' "[96]

The *Times'* sister paper, the St. Petersburg *Evening Independent*, had this to say: "After two seasons of professional football," the Buccaneers "have proven to critics that: 1) they can compete and win, 2) the five-year plan of Coach John McKay and owner Hugh Culverhouse is reasonable, and 3) the Bay Area is far better with the Bucs than without them. . . . Growing with a newborn pro football franchise isn't easy," but "the Bucs are entitled to some credit: No other enterprise has done as much to unify the Bay Area."[97]

The icing on the cake? The next week, at home at Tampa Stadium, the surging Bucs trounced the St. Louis Cardinals, a 7-6 NFC East team that had almost made the playoffs. For once—in a 17–7 victory in which Gary Huff threw a sixty-one-yard touchdown pass to receiver Morris Owens—the Buccaneer line did not give up a sack. Indeed, after ninety-eight sacks over two years, its performance was, at least for the Bucs, unprecedented. However, the biggest spectacle wasn't the team's performance; it was the fans. High on triumph, but drunk most certainly on beer, they stormed the field as the game ended and tore down the goalposts. (That's right. Fans of a 1-12 team that had just beaten a 7-6 team tore down the goalposts.) Some took sod, actual pieces of sod, as souvenirs. "It was sort of a Hollywood script," said McKay after the game. "We win the final two games of the season and still get the number one pick." But "we're most appreciative of the fact that we could win at home for the fans. They never got to see us win before. But I guess a lot of people can say that."[98]

Chapter Six

We Is the Champions!

Two times the Buccaneers had 80-yard touchdown drives.
E-i-g-h-t-y yards, two times. That's even hard for me to
type. Did the Bucs drive 80 yards twice in their first two
years? I can't remember. Eighty. Eight-oh.

—Hubert Mizell, *St. Petersburg Times*

Quarterback Doug Williams was Tampa Bay's first pick and the overall seventeenth pick in the 1978 NFL Draft. Tall, smart, and athletic, the rawboned Louisiana native was a first-team all-American at Grambling who starred in both the East-West Shrine Bowl and the Senior Bowl before coming to the Bucs. The problem was that Williams was black. As of 1978, no African-American quarterback had ever been taken in the first round. In fact, the highest any black quarterback had been taken, purely as a quarterback, was Karl Douglas, a former Texas A&I (now Texas A&M–Kingsville) star selected by the Colts in the third round.[1] What's more, only nine black players, including Parnell Dickinson, the former Buccaneers backup, had actually started a game at quarterback in the fifty-eight-year history of the NFL.[2] Nine. The explanations, such as they were, were racist. Blacks weren't smart enough, they were

159

lazy; while black quarterbacks were exceptional athletes and runners, they just couldn't lead a team.

But Williams was intelligent. He'd made the dean's list in college and had been scouted closely by Ken Herock and Joe Gibbs, the future Redskins coach and the Bucs' recently hired offensive coordinator, who had also observed Williams at work as a student teacher. And the 6'4", 215-pound quarterback was anything but lazy. Grambling coach Eddie Robinson said that Williams was the first person to arrive at practice and the last person to leave. He went to class and to church without prompting and his priorities were in order.[3] But more than anything else, the twenty-two-year-old Grambling star was a leader, and his effect on the 2-26 Bucs was profound. His very first pass, in preseason game two versus the Colts, was a touchdown. His second pass was a seventy-yard incompletion, a towering bomb that sailed over the receiver's head, but which earned the quarterback a standing ovation.

Confident and poised, the typically reserved Williams had what players described as "a presence." If the Bucs had a captain, a commander, Williams was it. Doug "takes charge," said center Steve Wilson in a September 1978 interview. "He's a presence in the huddle and on the field," and "we sense his leadership in every respect."[4] (And this, remember, was a *rookie* he was talking about.) Within a year, the Bucs were "Doug's team." It was "Doug's locker room," and where Williams went, the coaches, the players, the fans, indeed the entire Bay Area followed. "Doug Williams was my idol," said future Buccaneers coach Jon Gruden, whose father was a running backs coach for the team and later director of player personnel. "The way he conducted himself, the charisma with which he played quarterback, his toughness, the way he stood in there and absorbed hits and led his team in tough situations . . . that was something I always admired."[5] Tackle Darryl Carlton called Williams "a morale booster," and claimed just six weeks into the season that sick or not, injured or not, "we just gotta protect a man like that."[6]

The Williams pick was controversial for two reasons. The first was that the Tampa–St. Petersburg region, though bursting with transplants and home to tract communities that were, in some instances, no older than the Bucs, was still firmly rooted in the South, specifically the Deep South. Despite the 1954 *Brown v. Board of Education* decision banning segregation in public schools, it wasn't until 1971 that schools in Hillsborough and Pinellas were fully integrated. In June 1967, just five months before Tampa Stadium opened, Tampa police shot Martin Chambers, an unarmed nineteen-year-old African-American youth, in the back. The Chambers shooting touched off three days of riots in Tampa's Central Avenue business district, in which residents battled police and state troopers, as well as a five-hundred-man National Guard contingent sent to the city by Florida governor Claude Kirk.[7]

In 1968, a report issued by the National Advisory Commission on Civil Disorders, also known as the Kerner Commission, stated that though African-Americans made up 20 percent of Tampa's population, "there was no Negro on the city council; none on the school board; none on the fire department" and "none of high rank on the police force." It also found that six of every ten houses in Tampa inhabited by African-Americans were "unsound" and that "a majority of Negro children" attending schools in Tampa "never reached the eighth grade." The situation had improved somewhat by the time Williams arrived in 1978, but racial tensions in schools and neighbor-hoods and discrimination in job and housing markets contin-ued to be the norm.[8] In 1976, for example, Dixie M. Hollins High School in St. Petersburg closed temporarily due to per-sistent fighting between black and white students, something that had gone on at Hollins in one form or another since 1971, and in 1977, the white power terrorist organization the Ku Klux Klan burned crosses in five mid-Florida counties, includ-ing thirteen crosses in Hillsborough County alone.[9]

"It's evident that Florida is one of the most racist states in the country," wrote Williams in his 1990 autobiography, *Quarterblack: Shattering the NFL Myth.* "I would make the statement to my teammates, 'You can't go no farther south than Flor-ida.'" As Williams explained it, many Bay Area residents sim-ply couldn't imagine an African-American quarterback being in charge of the Bucs. "There hadn't been any black presi-dents," he wrote. "No governors were black. There weren't many black Congressmen. So here was a black guy who was in complete control of the Tampa Bay Bucs. That just didn't sit right with a lot of folks."[10]

On occasion, Williams received what he called "nigger let-ters," in other words, racist hate mail, and once even received a rotten watermelon in a box. The note read: "Try throwing this to your niggers. Maybe they can catch this."[11] To his credit, McKay defended his quarterback vociferously, criticizing jour-nalists for asking what he felt were racist questions and for describing Williams not as a quarterback, but as a *black* quar-terback. When a fan yelled "Hey, McKay, why don't you go back to Southern Cal and take your niggers with you!" the fiery coach attempted to fight the fan in the stands.[12]

Yet the issue didn't stop at race. Many debated whether the Bucs should have chosen a quarterback—black or white—at all. At 2-12, the 1977 Bucs had "earned" the number-one pick in the 1978 draft, which, presumably, was all-American Texas running back Earl Campbell. But the Bucs didn't need Campbell. For better or worse, they already had a back in Ricky Bell. What they needed was a quarterback, and Doug Williams was the best player, at that position, in the draft. "One look at Doug and it didn't take an expert to see he was the best quarterback to come along in several years," said McKay. "I'd have picked Doug if he was Chinese. Correction. Make that tall and Chinese."[13] Knowing teams would pass on Williams due to race, and that most likely the gifted Grambling quarterback would still be available in the mid-first round, McKay traded the Bucs' number-one pick to Houston for its first-round number seventeen pick, its second-round number forty-four pick, third- and fifth-round picks in 1979, and a second-year tight end named Jimmie Giles.

A twenty-three-year-old graduate of Alcorn State, Giles was a superathletic, three-sport star who, at 6'3", 240 pounds, had played just two years of football in college. He had "rough edges," admitted McKay, but had good hands, ran a 4.6 forty, and could block. "If I were to put him at fullback," he explained, "it would shatter you. He would be an excellent fullback. But he will be an excellent tight end. . . . Eventually, he will be one of the very best, if he doesn't get in the old bugaboo of 'I'm a receiver.' Tight ends must block."[14] Indeed, a key aspect of McKay's run-first I-formation was the availability of big tight ends who could block. At USC, each of his four national championship squads had featured NFL-caliber tight ends, including the future All-Pro and Eagles star Charles Young, who in 1973 was the sixth pick in the draft. In 1977, the Bucs were last in the NFL in rushing, the result, mainly, of injured and inept quarterbacks and a bad offensive line. However, that year, tight end Bob Moore had gotten hurt. Then backup Jack Novak had gotten hurt, which left undrafted rookie Dana Nafziger, a Cal Poly–San Luis Obispo grad, the starter. Nafziger would play five years for the Bucs, mostly as a tough second-teamer, but his emergency stint at tight end meant that the running game had suffered. "This isn't a knock against Nafziger," explained McKay, but as a tight end he "wouldn't have started for most of my teams at Southern Cal."[15]

But Giles was a different story. So was Williams, for after a slow start to 1978, the 0-2 Bucs upset the Vikings on the road, in Dave Green's infamous botched field goal game. By midseason their record was 4-4, and in second place in the NFC Central, they were no longer the Yucks. Their best game, perhaps, was a 30–13 road win versus the Chiefs in which Williams completed 14 of 23 passes for 223 yards and a touchdown. Leading drives of 80, 80, 23, and 47 yards, Williams ran the McKay offense to a "T," going 7 of 13 on third-down conversions and gaining a team-record 21 first downs. "Why are the Bucs getting better?" asked Lakeland *Ledger* reporter Patrick Zier. "Because their offense is getting better. And why is their offense getting better? Ask Coach John McKay and he will tell you: 'Doug Williams.' Ask Richard Wood of the long-suffering Buc defense and he will tell you: 'Doug Williams.' Ask Morris Owens, who has seen every quarterback Tampa has ever had and he will tell you: 'Doug Williams.'"[16] With good quarterbacking, better line play, and improved blocking at tight end, not to mention fullback, the Bucs' running game improved, from 28th in the league in 1977 to a relatively respectable 19th.

In a 33–19 home win versus Chicago in week eight, for example, Ricky Bell had 97 yards on 27 carries, a Buc record. He also caught 3 passes for 45 yards and scored a touchdown, and was given the game ball. Overall, the 4-4 Tampa Bay offense had scored seventeen touchdowns in eight weeks. This was so-so for an NFL team but a marked improvement over the previous year, when the team had managed only three. Meanwhile, the Buc defense was, well, the Buc defense. Tough, smart, and aggressive, through week eight it was the number-two-ranked defense in the league, holding Walter Payton to 34 yards on 15 carries, and sacking opposing quarterbacks 16 times. And, compared to week eight of the 1977 season, it had given up nearly five hundred fewer yards, the result, mainly, of more offensive possessions and Pro Bowl–level seasons by Lee Roy Selmon and Dave Pear. "People have been saying for a long time what a good defense the Buccaneers have," said Doug Williams, after an 11-for-19, 2-touchdown effort versus the Bears. "Now, maybe they'll begin to realize we have a football team," too.[17]

Unfortunately, two weeks later at Los Angeles, Williams suffered a broken jaw on a nasty hit by Rams defensive end Fred Dryer and was sidelined, his mouth wired shut, until the last game of the season. With no offense and injuries to Lee Roy Selmon, backup quarterback Mike Rae, and Ricky Bell, among others, the Bucs went 5-11. Progress, yes, but not what the 4-4 McKay team had expected. "I'll give it to you in one word," said McKay in a December 1978 interview. "Frustrating."[18] In fact, at the beginning of the season, McKay had written in a notepad that a 9-7 record would win the NFC Central, but now, every time he opened the notepad, he cried. McKay, of course, was joking. For one, he had Williams coming back, as well as fifteen different starters, including nine on defense. The defense was so good, and so deep, that in April 1979 McKay traded nose guard Dave Pear, who'd just been to the Pro Bowl, to the Raiders. He then moved Charley Hannah, the team's starting defensive end, to offensive line.

By this point, the 1979 Bucs had just ten of the team's original players, including two 1976 expansion picks (Dave Reavis and Mark Cotney), left on the squad. Although primed for what *Sports Illustrated* believed was a 6-10 season, the Bucs shocked observers by rattling off five straight wins, their biggest being a 21–6 home whupping of the Rams. "Unbeaten, Untied, and Unbelievable" exclaimed *SI* on its October 1, 1979, cover. The picture, fittingly enough, was of Dewey Selmon laying a vicious hit on Rams running back Lawrence McCutcheon, the same Lawrence McCutcheon who'd torched the Bucs in the franchise's first-ever game in 1976. "Anybody who takes them lightly is a fool," said Rams defensive end Jack Youngblood, a University of Florida grad from Jacksonville. "The Bucs are legitimate. Doug Williams is a good quarterback, very good. They have good running now and effective passing. And when you make mistakes they sure as hell capitalize."[19] Quarterback Pat Haden predicted a Rams-Bucs rematch in the playoffs and said, magnanimously, the Bucs "have been down so long, they've endured so many hard times, I know they're enjoying this."[20]

By week thirteen the Bucs were 9-3, in first place in the NFC Central Division by two games. With four games left, including three at home, they needed just a single win to clinch it. But in a home game versus the Vikings, trailing 23–22 with only nineteen seconds left in the fourth, Minnesota defender Wally Hilgenberg blocked a point-after attempt by kicker Neil O'Donoghue. The crowd, which only seconds earlier had witnessed a gutsy Williams score and which was preparing itself for overtime, turned apoplectic. Boos rained from the crowd. "You suck, McKay! You suuuccccck!" fans yelled, and as he walked to the locker room, he heard the now-infamous line: "Hey, McKay, why don't you go back to Southern Cal and take your niggers with you!" Buc players herded the coach into the locker room while he barked, madly, "Go fuck yourself! You go fuck yourself!"[21] He was insane with anger, the pressure of coaching the Bucs, of building a winning team so quickly, then losing a game and being booed for it, having finally got to him. It was unfair. "I'm sick and tired of people booing me," he said. "I'm not the one playing. I wish they would boo the people who can't block."[22]

Over the next two weeks, the Bucs lost 14–0 to the Bears at home, then 23–7 to an incredibly bad, 1-13 San Francisco team (which, incidentally, was Coach Bill Walsh's first San Francisco team) on the road. Although Ricky Bell passed the thousand-yard mark, Doug Williams went 15 for 43 for the stretch with 1 touchdown and 9 interceptions, the absolute worst performance of his career. "I think I've been trying too hard," explained Williams. "I have to just relax and do what I was doing before. I realize it. The people realize it. I got a letter in the mail with 'Relax' written all over it."[23] However, Williams couldn't relax. On the contrary, he and his teammates were afraid of becoming what *Tampa Tribune* editor Tom McEwen called the

"Chokeneers." With three straight losses, wrote McEwen, the Bucs were "on the verge of choking themselves out of the play-offs." He continued: "There was a time when plenty would have bet" the Bucs would "have won all of the last four and marched into the playoffs the Cinderella team of the NFL." But now, "call them the Tampa Bay Chokeneers. . . . That is precisely what they have become."[24]

Sensitive to being a loser, or, once again, a laughingstock like the 0-26 Yucks, McKay bristled. "I think it's a bunch of bullshit," he said, in an expletive-filled rant. And "I don't know anybody laughing at us. We lost three football games. . . . We're 9-6 and if you look at the standings there are a lot of teams with records not nearly as good."[25] However, the pressure, he admitted, was intense. The team was down mentally, and Williams, its leader, was in a slump, while only five Buc starters had ever been to the playoffs. No one knew what to do. "I don't know what's happened," moaned offensive tackle Darryl Carlton. "Our players seem passive, not nearly as aggressive as they should be. In the locker room they holler and scream and say 'Go out there and take no enemies,' but when we go out on the field it turns right around. We got to regroup. I mean really regroup."[26]

Luckily, on December 16, 1979, the Bucs played a 7-8 Chiefs team with a rookie quarterback and the worst passing offense in the league. If anything, the Bucs could play man coverage on the corners and limit the Chiefs' running game by putting eight or even nine men in the box. The problem was that Kansas City's defense was a good one, giving up just 108 yards of rushing per game, and the fewest rushing touchdowns (8) in the NFL. With no Buc offense to speak of, the teams' final contest in Tampa was going be a war. And then, it rained, two inches of rain in less than three quarters of football. The field was drenched, the players were drenched, and 63,000 fans, many in shorts and T-shirts, stood shivering. What they saw was one of the lowest-scoring games in the history of the NFL, a 3–0 slugfest decided by a late Buccaneer field goal with seven minutes left in the fourth. True to form, the Tampa Bay defense was spectacular, holding the Chiefs to just eighty yards of offense and four first downs, a franchise low.

While a shaky Doug Williams was 5 of 13 passing with 2 interceptions, the star of the game was Ricky Bell. Shaking off a bad performance at San Francisco, the workhorse back had 137 yards on 39 carries, a then NFC record, and ran almost every play, 9 of 11, on the team's winning drive. "We is the champs!" yelled McKay, his fist in the air, his pants covered in mud. "It was a beautiful, blazing, sun-shining day, and I'm proud of all my players. Now somebody lead me to a hot shower before I get pneumonia."[27] The scene on the field, in the stands, and in the locker room was pandemonium. Players hugged and wept, while Jimmie Giles and David Lewis, two of the Bucs' more exuberant personalities, rolled in the mud. They were delirious with joy. "There is no way to describe my feeling," exclaimed Giles. "This is the finest game the Tampa Bay Bucs have ever played. And it might be the finest game the team ever plays. Even if we go on and win in the future, there will never be anything to match this time and this moment. The first time is just fantastic."[28]

In the locker room, a grinning Hugh Culverhouse gushed, "This is glorious. This is just glorious!" over and over again. "I didn't think we could do it in just four years," he explained.

"My hope has always been to be competitive after five. But I've always been an incorrigible optimist, and now I believe anything is possible."[29] And anything *was* possible, at least for the Bucs. The team that had won seven games in three years was now 10-6, in first place in the NFC Central Division, and a playoff contender in year four, one year ahead of schedule. It had the league's number-one defense, which gave up fewer yards (246.8) and fewer points (14.8) per game, and fewer yards per play (3.9), than any other team in the league. Bell had 1,263 yards on 283 carries, a workmanlike 4.5-yard average, while Lee Roy Selmon was the AP, UPI, and Pro Football Writers "NFL Defensive Player of the Year." (He was also, of course, a Pro Bowler and a First-Team All-Pro.) John McKay was named the *Football News* "Coach of the Year," while the UPI voted David Lewis and the AP voted Dewey Selmon "Second-Team All-Pros." And finally, in April 1980, the NFL Players Association gave its "Strength in Unity Award" to the Bucs' offensive line for giving up the fewest sacks in the league.[30] It gave up twelve, after a three-year average of *fifty*.

This was a good team, a McKay team, a team that ran the ball (and ran the ball) and played good defense, then once in a while threw the deep pass over the top. Offensively, the 1979 Bucs were no different than McKay's USC teams, or his infamous 1976 or 1977 teams, but now he had the right personnel. "You know, it's a fine line," explains former receiver Lee McGriff, "between having strong convictions and a belief in what you are doing, and saying, Okay, this isn't working." Most coaches would have changed course after an 0-14 season, says McGriff, but not McKay. "The way he saw it was that the system worked. It'd always worked. It'd won four national

championships and damn it, it was going to work here! And
I can tell you from experience, he had no problem cutting a
hundred guys a year. He'd cut two hundred if he had to. And
when the offense didn't work, it wasn't his fault. It was the
players' fault. And that had a lot to do with his impatience, I
think, with his anger and embarrassment. When he said 'I won
four fucking national championships,' what he was really saying was 'you guys are messing me up!' "[31]

The question, then, was: could a McKay offense win a Super
Bowl? Critics said no, but on December 29, 1979, in front of a
sellout crowd at Tampa Stadium, in their first—I repeat first—
nationally televised game, the Bucs upset the Eagles in the NFC
divisional round 24–17. And, as if on cue, the Bucs' offense
began the game with an 18-play, 80-yard drive, scoring on a
Ricky Bell touchdown and eating up nine and a half minutes
of clock. In one drive, Tampa Bay ran the ball sixteen times,
Bell ten of them, using what *Sports Illustrated* called "that old
USC Student Body Right."[32] As usual, the defense was superb,
holding the Eagles to just forty-eight yards rushing and gang
tackling so ferociously that after a first-quarter hit of Leroy
Harris, an Eagles running back, officials called an unnecessary-
roughness penalty on the entire defensive squad. "The helmet
is a weapon," explained linebacker Richard Wood after the
game. "The shoulder pad is a weapon. You come out to catch a
pass, you have to pay the price."[33] In all, the harried Eagles receiving corps dropped ten balls for the game. (By contrast, the
2014 Super Bowl champion Seattle Seahawks dropped twelve
balls for the *season*.) The most amazing stat, perhaps, was that
Tampa Bay's "no-name" secondary held 6'8" receiver Harold
Carmichael, a four-time Pro Bowler and member of the NFL's

All-Decade Team, to just three catches, none in the first half. "We tried to keep him from getting off the line quickly," said safety Cedric Brown, "and when he did catch a pass we made sure to give him a good lick."[34]

Forcing five punts, three three-and-outs, and a fumble, the hard-hitting Bucs defense frequently gave the offense the ball. It responded with 55 rushes, the most in a playoff game since 1949, and ate up more than thirty-six minutes of clock. Ricky Bell had 2 touchdowns and 142 yards on 38 carries, a playoff record, while a nifty nine-yard touchdown from Williams to Giles iced the game in the fourth. It was an impressive victory, all according to plan. "I knew that sooner or later" McKay "was going to win in this league," said linebacker David Lewis. "McKay told the team, 'Sure we're going to take some lumps.' That's what's made us. You can't go through the horrors that we've been through and not get strong. We've been to the pit. We've been embarrassed to go home." Even so, the press called Tampa Bay's victory "shocking," "astonishing," "stunning," "amazing," or, as the *New York Times* put it, a "wonderment."[35] "Don't laugh," it wrote, "but the Tampa Bay Buccaneers are one win away from the Super Bowl. . . . The National Football League's greatest contribution to national humor, a team that lost its first twenty-six games and gained more punch lines than yards, qualified for the National Football Conference championship game."[36] The shock soon went global. In Tehran, Iran, American hostages entering their second month of captivity were visited and given news updates by Rev. William Howard, the leader of an ecumenical delegation, who said many of them "were surprised to learn that Tampa Bay was in the running."[37]

One team that wasn't in the running was the Dallas Cowboys, the preseason NFC favorite upset 21–19 by the Rams. Since Tampa Bay had beaten the Rams and had a better record (10-6 versus 9-7), it would now host the NFC Championship Game at home. "Don't pinch yourself," wrote journalist Jack Gurney, "and don't blink. This might not be happening." In fact, "there are no adjectives left to describe the meteoric rise in the fortunes of this young Buccaneer franchise. . . . It has happened so fast, heads in the Tampa Bay area are spinning."[38]

In fact, they were spinning, in one instance due to carbon monoxide poisoning. In January 1980, as five thousand people braved 30-degree temperatures while waiting forty-eight hours in a ticket line, a group of four Buc fans nearly died after falling asleep in a car with the engine running. When paramedics revived the fans, they refused a trip to the hospital, to keep their spots in line. Police in dozens of communities reported hectic but still orderly scenes at Bay Area ticket outlets, but, as a precaution, escorted Tampa Stadium ticket vendors away from the facility once tickets ran out.[39] In all, the Bucs sold 28,000 tickets—the rest going to 44,000 season-ticket holders—in four and a half hours. At Tampa Stadium, at department stores in St. Petersburg, Bradenton, Sarasota, and Lakeland, at banks in Venice, at nonprofits in Clearwater and Spring Hill, and at sporting goods stores in Ocala, among others, the scene was essentially the same: Bucs fans spending the night, with blankets and bonfires and space heaters, waiting for tickets. Russell Rine, who'd driven fifty miles into Tampa to sit for two days, told the *Tampa Tribune*, "I vowed that if the Bucs made the playoffs they deserved my support. So here I am. . . . I haven't been bored a bit. I'm just enjoying these people and making friends. Besides, I've got this bottle of Jack Daniel's. . . . This is going to be the baddest party in the state of Florida tonight."[40]

Without a doubt, the once-woeful Bucs, now heroes in 1979, had brought the Bay Area together. People spoke of "Bucs Fever" and "Bucs Mania" and everyone, everywhere, wore orange. Through Christmas and New Year's, the most-requested song on Tampa-area radio stations was the team's unofficial fight song, "Hey Hey, Tampa Bay!" which got more requests than Bing Crosby's "White Christmas" or the Rupert Holmes hit "Escape (The Piña Colada Song.)"[41] In Sarasota, a city sixty miles to the south of Tampa, Mayor Fred Soto declared December 31, 1979, to January 6, 1980, "Tampa Bay Buccaneer Week." The team held a pep rally, complete with an autograph session and a cheerleading performance by the Swashbucklers, at a mall in St. Petersburg.

"Never has Tampa been so united," declared an article in the *Tampa Tribune* titled "Buccaneer Fever Sweeps Tampa Bay." "Ask a cab driver, a doctor, a postman, a garbage collector, a lawyer, a child, a clerk, a retired person from Michigan. They're all talking Buccaneers."[42] A week earlier, at the start of the Eagles game, CBS announcer Jack Whitaker put it best: "John McKay is the only professional coach ever to survive a twenty-six-game losing streak, the only coach to go from nothing in four years to a playoff. And in the process, the Tampa Bay Bucs have solidified the towns that fringe on the edge of Tampa Bay" and "these communities now share something else than just a drive to the airport."[43]

As the Bucs took the field against the Rams, fans on one side of Tampa Stadium yelled "TAMPAAAA!!!" while fans on the other side yelled "BAAAYYYY!!!" "TAMPAAAA!!!"

We Is the Champions!

"BAAAYYYY!!!" "TAMPAAAA!!!" "BAAAYYYY!!!" It was mesmerizing. And though the upstart Bucs lost 9–0, and were outrun, out-hit, and out-possessioned by a better football team, the fans gave the Buccaneers a last-minute standing ovation. They even yelled "TAMPAAAA!!!" "BAAAYYYY!!!" as Rams quarterback Vince Ferragamo downed the ball and the Rams ran out the clock.[44] "Did you hear Tampa Bay's fans cheering for them at the end?" exclaimed Rams tackle Dennis Harrah. "That cheering made me feel good for the Tampa Bay players. Because we never know what our fans are going to do. They might boo us in the Super Bowl."[45] Critics called the game boring, noting that no conference championship had ever been won without at least one team scoring a touchdown, but admitted, grudgingly, that in spite of an 0-26 start and a four-year record of 18-44, the Bucs had arrived. "We shouldn't be able to sneak up on anybody anymore," said McKay in a 1980 interview. "And I think anyone who still feels that the Bucs are a one-year fluke is sadly mistaken."[46]

———

Over the next three years, the Bucs made the playoffs two times, winning the NFC Central in 1981 and qualifying with a 5-4 record, in a strike-shortened year, in 1982. In both instances, they lost to the Dallas Cowboys (38–0 and 30–17) on the road. However, by 1983, the key defensive players who had taken the Bucs to the 1979 NFC Championship Game had either aged or retired, and Doug Williams had left the Buccaneers for the United States Football League (USFL). Still, there were eight original Yucks from the 1976 or 1977 teams left on the squad. They included offensive linemen Dave Reavis and Steve

Wilson, defensive end Lee Roy Selmon, safety Mark Cotney, cornerbacks Mike Washington and Cedric Brown, and linebackers Cecil Johnson and Richard Wood, who all had been signed, drafted, and/or traded for by former Bucs vice president Ron Wolf. In 1978, Wolf returned to his position as player personnel director of the Oakland Raiders. In the coming years, Wolf would help Oakland win two Super Bowls, in 1981 and 1984, and select, among others, Matt Millen, Howie Long, Marcus Allen, and Greg Townsend—four All-Pros and two Hall of Famers—in consecutive drafts. In 1982, Bucs defensive coordinator Tom Bass went to the Chargers, as did linebackers David Lewis and Dewey Selmon, and running back Ricky Bell.

Bell, who had a breakout year in 1979, played sluggishly in 1980 and was outperformed by talented rookie James Wilder in 1981. He played sparingly in his final season with the Bucs and in early 1982 was traded. However, unbeknownst to everyone, including Bell, the MVP of the Bucs' 1979 team was sick; he had been, presumably, when he came to the Bucs as the number-one pick, and might even have been sick at USC. For up to ten years, doctors surmised, Bell had been suffering from a rare disease known as dermatomyositis, an inflammation of the muscles and skin, which in turn had led to poor blood flow and an even rarer disease known as cardiomyopathy, a weakening of the pumping mechanism in the heart.[47] It explained his listlessness and fatigue, and why he would come home from practice, fall on the couch, and go to sleep. "Me and Ricky lived in the same apartment complex," said teammate David Lewis. "That last year in Tampa, I spent a lot of time helping him into his apartment. I didn't think anything of it. I just thought it was soreness and wear and tear. He played a tough position, and got hit a lot. It never occurred to me that something might be wrong with him."[48] Things came to a head in 1982, in San Diego, when a poorly performing Bell went on the injured reserve list with swelling in his extremities, and lesions on his fingers and toes. Bell was diagnosed with dermatomyositis in 1983, and died, a shell of his former self, in 1984. He was twenty-nine years old.

Naturally, the Bucs who knew Bell were shaken, even distraught. "One of the trainers came and told me," said Richard Wood. "I didn't know what to do so I got down on my knees on the field and said a little prayer."[49] John McKay described Bell's death as "a great tragedy," and said that while Bell "was one of the finest football players" he'd ever coached, he was "an even finer man."[50] "I think about Ricky quite a bit," explained running back Anthony Davis in a 2004 retrospective. "He was a great player. But as a person, Ricky was a diamond. The question always bugs you. Out of all of us, why did it have to be Ricky? He was the good one, the jewel. Why him?"[51] Quarterback Doug Williams insisted that Bell was the one Buccaneer most responsible for the team's remarkable turnaround in 1979. "Ricky Bell was a physical terror," insisted Williams, and "whatever Tampa Bay did in 1979, the bulk of it should go to Ricky Bell. He was a horse, and we rode him. The thing people never saw was his leadership. There were times for me, when I got booed, when I was disgusted, but Ricky was there for me. He said, 'Keep your head up. It'll get better.' He pulled me through some things mentally. That was Ricky. Quiet, but effective."[52]

Although the loss of Ricky Bell was a blow for the Bucs spiritually, the loss of Doug Williams was an even bigger blow on the field. As of 1983, Williams had been the starting quar-

terback in thirty-three of Tampa Bay's thirty-six regular season wins. Tough as nails, he had overcome a broken jaw as
a rookie, plus a torn bicep in the NFC Championship Game,
and had managed to start fifty-seven games in a row. He'd also
improved as a passer, immensely, been the team's MVP twice,
and had a career record of 33-33-1. Although not an elite quarterback by any stretch, Doug Williams was, quite simply, the
Johnny Unitas of the Bucs, the most important player the franchise had ever had—and that included Lee Roy Selmon. As the
St. Petersburg *Evening Independent* put it: "If there is one name
that is synonymous with the Tampa Bay Buccaneers—besides
John McKay—it is Doug Williams. If there is one man who
has meant more to the Tampa Bay Buccaneers in the past four
years than John McKay, it is Doug Williams. . . . The word *franchise* comes to mind."[53] Yet for some reason—a stingy owner
perhaps?—in 1982, Williams was the forty-second-highest-
paid quarterback in the league, at $120,000 per year, which
meant that if each team had a starter, there were fourteen
backup quarterbacks who made more money than him.

It was inexcusable, which is why, in May 1983, Williams demanded a five-year contract at $600,000 per year. Owner Hugh
Culverhouse countered with $400,000 per year, plus "a piece
of a real estate deal," then pressured Williams by trading a first-
round pick to the Bengals for seldom-used backup quarterback
Jack Thompson, the "Throwin' Samoan."[54] The tactic would
have worked, but in March 1983, with former ESPN president
Chet Simmons as its commissioner, the USFL began its inaugural year. With twelve teams, including one in Tampa called the
Bandits, whose coach, incidentally, was Steve Spurrier, veteran
NFL players who once had no leverage now had somewhere

to go. The league's biggest signees were college superstars such as Herschel Walker and Doug Flutie, but through the course of 1983 it landed perhaps two hundred "Old Pros," including former Browns quarterback Brian Sipe, Colts quarterback Greg Landry, and Chiefs free safety Gary Barbaro. In all, the USFL featured at least two dozen former Bucs, including Richard Wood, Anthony Davis, Gary Huff, and Lee McGriff. Doug Williams signed on with the league's Oklahoma Outlaws in August 1983. He received a five-year contract, in the $600,000 range annually, with the first three years guaranteed.[55]

Although nowhere in the league of say, Boston's infamous Babe Ruth trade, the failure to sign Doug Williams was, for the Bucs, a catastrophic mistake, a *Hindenburg*-level mistake, the football equivalent of the Yugo—bad, bad, bad, bad, bad. In 1983, the Bucs went 2-14, then followed that up with thirteen losing seasons in a row, an NFL record. From 1983 to 1996, they were by far the worst franchise in the league, going 64-159, a .287 win percentage, and finishing in last place in the NFC Central Division eight times. In addition, they had the league's worst record three times and lost ten games in a season twelve years in a row. "In this ever-shifting world," joked *Orlando Sentinel* columnist Mike Thomas in 1995, "the Bucs are my anchor. The Reagan Revolution revamps America. The Bucs lose. The Communist Empire crumbles. The Bucs lose. We go to war in the Persian Gulf. The Bucs lose." So, whenever the Bucs do lose, wrote Thomas, "I set my beer down, get out of my recliner and give the Bucs a standing ovation." They are "the worst team in the history of professional sports."[56]

Fans called it the "Curse of Doug Williams," blaming Culverhouse and vacating the stadium in droves. After selling out twenty-eight of twenty-nine home games between 1979 and 1982, the Bucs wouldn't sell out again until November 1986, when the Super Bowl champion Chicago Bears, a team with a Beatles-like following in those days, came to town.[57] (Author's note: I was at this game, a fourteen-year-old orange-clad reject, and sat so high up in Tampa Stadium I could touch the skybox. I remember it was stiflingly hot, and that a Bears fan in our section was wearing a Doug Flutie jersey over a gorilla suit.) The low point came in 1985, when the Bucs drew fewer fans for the year than the Tampa Bay Bandits and had a lower per-game attendance average (37,457 versus 42,283) than the 1976, 0-14 Yucks.[58]

The culprit, of course, was Hugh Culverhouse, who, beginning in 1982, received some $14 million annually as his cut of the NFL's new five-year, $2.1 billion television contract.[59] He presumably made hundreds of thousands off NFL Properties—though incomes from T-shirt sales and other forms of licensing were rarely made public—and perhaps $4 million more from concessions, parking, skybox rentals, in-stadium advertising, and tickets. In 1986, however, Culverhouse's player payroll was just $9 million.[60] If you included coaches' salaries, salaries for staff and administrators, equipment costs, travel costs, facilities upkeep (which did not include the stadium), and advertising, through the mid-1980s, Culverhouse made—and this is a low estimate—approximately $4–5 million a year. In fact, in 1992, a series of NFL financial documents released as part of lawsuit revealed that in 1989, when the Bucs went 5-11, the team's seventh losing season in a row, Culverhouse made a $6.3 million profit, second only to the Bears, while his payroll was the twenty-seventh lowest in the league.[61]

Although there were exceptions—in 1987, for example, Culverhouse gave number-one pick Vinny Testaverde the richest rookie contract in history—his modus operandi was to keep salaries low, which is why Doug Williams went to Oklahoma and why his replacement, Jack Thompson, made just $210,000 a year. But, as offensive lineman Charley Hannah insists, there was more to it than that, because not only had Culverhouse replaced Williams with a lower-earning quarterback but, by trading for Thompson, he'd also avoided taking a first-round pick, a salary for whom in 1984 was on average $431,665.[62] "Now McKay made some mistakes," says Hannah, "and I'm not saying he didn't. But clearly, Culverhouse's definition of winning was waaayyy different than McKay's was, because no matter what the team did, Culverhouse had a winning year. And I think that was hard on McKay. It was certainly demoralizing, because I don't believe McKay thought when he took the job that there was anyone in America who wouldn't at least try to win games. But, that was Culverhouse."[63]

Left without a quarterback, his defense aging and his talent pool drying up, McKay announced his retirement in November 1984. At 44-88-1, his was the worst record out of the thirty-seven coaches, all-time, who'd coached one hundred or more games in the league. But, in his defense, the irascible, headstrong, querulous, and demanding coach did what he said he would do: build a playoff-caliber team in five years—though he actually did it in four. "His way of building the Bucs," wrote journalist Patrick Zier, was "as ruthless as a Russian five-year plan." McKay made "supreme sacrifices now in favor of a big payoff later."[64] However, either due to impatience or arrogance, McKay didn't stick to the plan. In 1978, he traded a first-round pick to the Bears for defensive end Wally Chambers, though Chambers had a bad knee and was at the end of his career. Chambers would play two years for the Bucs, while Dan Hampton, the player the Bears took with the Bucs' number-four pick, was a six-time All-Pro. Perhaps even more galling, in 1983, during the Doug Williams negotiations, McKay traded a first-round 1984 pick (which turned out to be the number-one *overall* pick) for Jack Thompson. Thompson would start sixteen games for the Bucs, winning three, while the number-one pick, sent from the Bengals to the Patriots, was the five-time Pro Bowl receiver Irving Fryar.

These were mistakes, but Tampa Bay's biggest mistake, apart from Doug Williams, was Booker Reese. In 1982, in what was the zaniest draft screwup in history, the Bucs selected Sean Farrell, a talented O-lineman from Penn State, with the overall seventeenth pick in the draft. However, the Bucs had meant to select defensive end Booker Reese, a freakishly athletic, but still raw talent from tiny Bethune-Cookman College in Florida. According to Don Banks, author of the *Sports Illustrated* article "The Most Botched NFL Draft Pick Ever," the mix-up occurred when Pat Marcuccillo, the team's longtime equipment manager and draft representative, picked Farrell by mistake. It seems Marcuccillo was given a card with the names Booker Reese and Sean Farrell written on it, but didn't hear the exact pick over the telephone due to background noise at the New York Sheraton hotel. Instead of "we're not going with Farrell," Marcuccillo only heard "Farrell," so that's the player he chose.[65]

Although the Penn State lineman wasn't the team's first choice, he should have sufficed, but Herock, McKay, and defensive coaches Abe Gibron and Wayne Fontes compounded matters by trading their first-round 1983 pick to the Bears for a second-round 1982 pick in order to get Booker Reese. The Bucs got Reese, who underperformed terrifically in two forgettable years, while the Bears chose a ten-year starting receiver in Willie Gault. Other disastrous picks followed. In 1985, the Bucs chose defensive end Ron Holmes with a first-round number-eight pick, while Pro Bowlers Al Toon (#10), Jim Lachey (#12), Eddie Brown (#13), Ethan Horton (#15), and Jerry Rice (#16)—yes, the Hall of Famer Jerry Rice—went to other teams. In 1986, the Bucs chose Bo Jackson with a first-round, number-one pick, but due to what Jackson considered underhanded negotiating tactics on the part of Culverhouse, the Auburn great refused to sign with the team, playing pro baseball instead. Other busts included Vinny Testaverde (1987, #1), Broderick Thomas (1989, #6), Keith McCants (1990, #4), Charles McRae (1991, #7), Chris Chandler (whom the Bucs traded a 1992 #2 pick for), and Eric Curry (1993, #6.)

But was it the player or the team? Because, as more than one journalist noted, the Bucs for years had no general manager, no one with football expertise who had veto power over player personnel decisions and who had "answer-only-to-the-owner" oversight for who coached and who played. In 1976–77, Ron Wolf had been "Vice President of Operations," but in addition to personnel, his bailiwick, his duties had also included public relations and day-to-day front office administration.[66] When he left, forced out by McKay in a power struggle, five consecutive coaches—John McKay, Leeman Bennett, Ray Perkins, Richard Williamson, and Sam Wyche—had complete operational control, not just over X's and O's, but over draft picks, free agent signings, and trades. Culverhouse held the purse strings, but it was the coaches who ran the team. "A major part of the Bucs' problem," wrote one observer in 1992, "has been that the team has never had a pure personnel guy, a thinker with a long-range plan making the franchise's key decisions. Instead, that authority has always . . . rested in the hands of a coach, and always the coach has blown it."[67]

Under McKay, the system worked, but from the beginning of 1985 through the end of 1992, the Bucs had four head coaches. (That's *four* head coaches in *eight* years.) Over that same period, they had three player personnel directors, five defensive coordinators, four offensive coordinators, and seven quarterback coaches. The team was a mess. Under Coach Leeman Bennett, for example, the suddenly woeful Bucs had back-to-back 2-14 years in 1985 and 1986. In fact, through Bennett's first thirty-two games in Tampa (which turned out to be all of them), he had the same coaching record, 4-28, that McKay had in his first thirty-two games with the Yucks. And, in a shout-out to the 1976 team, the Buccaneer's tenth-anniversary team was 27th in offense, 28th in defense, and scored the third-fewest points of any offense in the league. Tampa Bay is "the blue-light special" of the National Football League, wrote journalist Mike Bianchi. "They are like the kid in school who used to wear his shirts inside-out because he didn't know any better. They are the fat refrigerator repairman who shows off half his rear end when he leans over to see what you have in the crisper. They are the old lady in the Plymouth Valiant in front of you. She is oblivious to her coat sash, which is slammed in the car door and has been flapping in the wind for the last eight miles. They are a joke."[68]

The Bucs were such a joke that talented players just didn't want to play there. There was Bo Jackson, of course, and gifted tackle Paul Gruber, a two-time Associated Press All-Pro, who, during a contract dispute in 1993, sold his house. "I want to go somewhere where there's a chance to win," he said.[69] And Gruber was being civil. In 1986, guard Sean Farrell, in what became the greatest "get-me-outta-here" moment in Buccaneer history, told an astonished booster club at Disney World, "I know what I want this Christmas. I want to get the hell out of Tampa Bay."[70] Farrell was lucky—in 1987, the Bucs traded him to the Patriots—but players who stayed faced instability in coaching and rarely developed into first-rate, NFL-level pros. An example of this was Vinny Testaverde, a Heisman-winning quarterback from Miami taken first by the Bucs in the 1987 draft. In five seasons as a starter, Testaverde failed miserably in Tampa, winning just twenty-four of sixty-eight games, while throwing 72 touchdowns and 106 interceptions. Fans mocked Testaverde for being stupid, and screamed "a-ha!" in 1988 when the team revealed that the interception-prone quarterback was color-blind. Adding insult to injury, WFLA, a Tampa radio station, put up blue billboards throughout the Bay Area that read: "Vinny thinks this is orange!" (An equal-opportunity critic, the station also ran a sign featuring a picture of a screw with the words "Hugh Culverhouse" next to it.)[71]

Ironically, as soon as Testaverde left Tampa Bay, he improved. In 1994, the former Buc went 9-4 for the Browns and in 1995 trounced his former team with a 256-yard, 2-touchdown performance with no interceptions. Overall, the once-maligned quarterback would play in two Pro Bowls and a conference championship game, throwing for more than 30,000 yards and 198 touchdowns in a fifteen-year post-Buccaneer career. Likewise, the 0-6 quarterback Chris Chandler went to two Pro Bowls and a Super Bowl after being waived by the Bucs, while quarterback Steve Young, Tampa Bay's first selection in the 1984 Supplemental Draft, was 3-16 in Tampa but 91-49 in San Francisco. He also went to seven Pro Bowls and a Super Bowl (which he won), and was a two-time NFL MVP. The coup de grâce, however, and the ultimate sign that the Bucs were indeed cursed, was Doug Williams's truly masterful performance for Washington in Super Bowl XXII. In 1986, following the end of the USFL and the Oklahoma Outlaws, Williams returned to the NFL as a backup quarterback under former Tampa Bay offensive coordinator turned Washington coach Joe Gibbs. At first Williams played sparingly, but in 1987, with three wins in relief, including a 27–24 come-from-behind victory in the last game of the year, Williams won the starting job for the play-offs. He responded with two close wins, then in the Super Bowl completed 18 of 29 passes for 340 yards and 4 touchdowns. Washington won the game in a blowout, while Williams, the quarterback Culverhouse had jettisoned for the paltry sum of $200,000, was the game's MVP.

In 1989 Doug Williams retired from football. He returned to Tampa in 1992 for his official induction into the team's "Krewe of Honor," a hall of fame whose three members were Lee Roy Selmon, John McKay, and Ricky Bell. Grateful and magnanimous, Williams thanked the long-suffering fans, who had watched the Bucs go 36-108 without him. Although Williams joked he wasn't "into voodoo," in the stands there was a banner that read: "Hey Doug! Thanks, but how about removing that curse?"[72] Yet, curse or no curse, nothing changed for the Bucs until 1994, when owner Hugh Culverhouse died of cancer, and the team was purchased in early 1995 by financier Malcolm Glazer. What had cost Culverhouse $16 million to start now sold for a then-record $192 million.[73] If you adjusted for inflation—$16 million in 1974 was worth $49 million in 1995—Culverhouse still made a profit of 291 percent. Not bad for the Yucks. With John McKay's younger son, Rich McKay as general manager, the Bucs had a once-in-a-lifetime draft in 1995, selecting Hall of Fame linebacker Derrick Brooks and Hall of Fame nose guard Warren Sapp. A series of picks between 1993 and 1997 produced Pro Bowl players John Lynch, Trent Dilfer, Mike Alstott, Donnie Abraham, Warrick Dunn, and Ronde Barber, and in 1996 McKay hired Vikings assistant Tony Dungy as coach. That year the team went 6-10 but in 1997, with a 10-6 record, the once-pitiful Bucs had their first winning season in fourteen years. "People have asked me if I'm following in my father's blueprint," explained McKay in 2001. "I don't know, but that is how we have gone about it, going after defensive players first and a defensive-minded coach. And on offense, we believe in establishing the run first and then pass. That was my father's formula."[74]

Interestingly enough, Rich McKay built the Bucs just as two new expansion teams, the Jacksonville Jaguars and the Carolina Panthers, came on board. The two new franchises, which had been chosen over Memphis, St. Louis, and Baltimore, cost $140 million each, plus a 50 percent cut in the teams' share of TV revenues for three years, which was $50 million.[75] But, because the franchises had cost so much, then-commissioner Paul Tagliabue argued that owners should give the teams the most generous expansion plan possible, that the Panthers and Jaguars should each receive twenty-eight extra picks in the 1995 and 1996 drafts, including two extra picks in rounds one and two and an additional pick in rounds three through seven in 1995, plus extra picks in rounds three through seven in 1996.[76] By contrast, the Bucs and Seahawks had extra picks only in rounds two through five in 1976 and no additional picks in 1977. The clincher, however, was that by 1995, the NFL Players Association, through lawsuits and negotiations, had forced NFL owners into accepting unrestricted free agency. In return, the players agreed to a salary cap, which in 1995 was $37.1 million per team.[77]

Although Jacksonville and Carolina would build their rosters with players taken in the expansion and college drafts, they would sign, collectively, *twenty* free agent starters. (Carolina signed nine and Jacksonville signed eleven. They included top-shelf NFL veterans Sam Mills, Mark Carrier, and Jeff Lageman, among others, as well as Bryan Barker, who in 1994 was the best punter in the NFC.) "They certainly had a lot more salary-cap room than I did when I came here," said Bill Tobin, a vice president with the Indianapolis Colts, in July 1995. "They'll get better quicker than any expansion teams in history. Established teams have lost some of their stars to them, so it's a two-edged sword. Not only has that made the expansion teams better, but it's weakened the teams they're competing with."[78] The grumbling was league-wide—though the NFL's Management Council had created the plan and the owners had ratified it—but no one grumbled more than Ron Wolf, now the Packers' general manager, who had lived through two long years with the Yucks. "It's the most liberal stocking procedure ever granted," he exclaimed. "They got a fifty-two-card deck" while other teams "are playing with forty-card decks. It's not supposed to be that way. . . . A person should crawl before they walk. They didn't even have to walk. They are strutting."[79]

In year one, for example, both Carolina and Jacksonville beat the 'all-time NFL record for expansion-team victories in a season. Jacksonville was 4-11, while Carolina was an incredible 7-9. In 1996, year two, aided by good draft picks and even better free agents, including Wesley Walls and Kevin Greene of the Panthers and Leon Searcy and Keenan McCardell of the Jaguars, the two teams not only made the playoffs, but made it all the way to their conference championship games, à la the 1979 Bucs.

Still, Tampa Bay general manager Rich McKay, whose own team had finished 6-10, for its fourteenth losing season in a row, wasn't impressed. "When the Bucs began, it was impossible under the old rules to obtain a veteran starter," he explained. "Jacksonville has fifteen, and Carolina has fourteen. Tampa Bay had zero."[80] He continued: In 1976, the Bucs "were given enough ammunition to fire a popgun." But now, under the new rules, the Panthers and Jaguars could "set off a neutron bomb."[81] Nevertheless, McKay insisted that the owners' plan to help the two franchises was the correct one. He knew because he'd lived through it. He'd seen the 0-26 alternative. "I would much favor these results than the way it was in '76," he said. Because "one of the NFL's greatest failures, if there are any, was the way they treated expansion teams in those days. You can't give a new city a new franchise that they paid all this money for, invested all this emotion to get the franchise, and then nothing. It just wasn't right."[82]

What was right, however, was the improved state of the

Buccaneers. A new coach, new players, new management, new stadium . . . heck, even the uniforms were new; beginning in 1997, orange was out, Bucco Bruce was out, and skulls, cross swords, and pewter pants and helmets were in. Bruce "was wimpy," said one former player. "Guy like that comes ashore, and he isn't going to do anything. You could beat him up and steal his boat."[83] In 1999, the Bucs went 11-5, won the NFC Central, and lost 11–6 to the Rams in the NFC Championship Game. They followed that up with 10-6 and 9-7 seasons, but in early 2002 fired Tony Dungy, who at 54-42 was the team's all-time winningest coach, in favor of Jon Gruden, a talented, thirty-eight-year-old Raider coach. Seeking a Super Bowl, the Glazer family, said the always measured Dungy, "thought it was time for a change."[84]

To that end, the Glazers spent big, sending $8 million in cash plus two first- and two second-round picks to the Raiders for the right to sign Gruden, who was at that point under contract. They also added veteran free agents Keenan McCardell and Joe Jurevicius at wide receiver, Michael Pittman at running back, and Ken Dilger at tight end. The new players complemented the Bucs' already-elite defensive corps, which as of 2001 featured four All-Pros: Warren Sapp, Derrick Brooks, Ronde Barber, and John Lynch. It was a huge gamble—the Bucs, after all, were sacrificing the future for the present—but in 2002 the team went 12-4, winning the NFC South and the NFC Championship and beating the Raiders 48–21 in the 2003 Super Bowl. It was unbelievable. Literally. "Sunday's news ranks somewhere between man biting dog and Iraq freezing over," wrote *Orlando Sentinel* reporter David Whitley. "Or imagine the ugliest kid in high school showing up at the twenty-year class reunion with Catherine Zeta-Jones on his arm. Could these Bucs be the descendants of 0-26, Hugh Culverhouse and Bucco Bruce?" So go ahead and "pinch yourself, get out the scissors, snip out these paragraphs. You might want to show them one day to your great-grandkids. The Tampa Bay Buccaneers are world champions."[85]

In honor of the Bucs—and in search of what one reporter called "absolution"—in 2002 Hugh Culverhouse Jr., the fifty-one-year-old son of former Bucs owner Hugh Culverhouse Sr., donated a whopping $1 million to the Grambling State University football program, where former Buccaneer Doug Williams was coach. "Let's say it like it is," admitted Culverhouse, a partner in a law firm in Miami. "Doug deserved better treatment. That goes without saying. Doug should've been with the Bucs."[86] Insisting that when Tampa Bay made the Super Bowl, he "was screaming and yelling and crying all at the same time," Culverhouse explained, "the Bucs gave me what I wanted: vindication. This gets rid of years of shame."[87]

Epilogue

From the Yucks to the Bucs and Back Again . . .

Well, the only way to handle this season and still remain a
Bucs fan is to embrace the suck. Just like every other season.

—Buc1987, respondent, JoeBucsFan.com

History hasn't been kind to the Bucs. Apart from a Super Bowl title in 2003, and runs to the NFC Championship Game following the 1979 and 1999 seasons, Tampa Bay victory celebrations have been few and far between. In fact, of thirty-two current NFL teams, the Bucs have the lowest all-time regular season win percentage (.385) and hold modern NFL records for the league's longest losing streak (26 games), most consecutive ten-loss seasons (12), and most losing seasons in a row (14). They also hold records for most points allowed in a game (62), most points allowed in a half (49), and most points allowed in the first quarter (28)—and these were from three different games, two in the 1980s and one in 2014. They've had the fewest passing touchdowns in both a fourteen-game (3) and a sixteen-game (5) season; gone the most consecutive games without scoring a safety (191) or a kickoff return (498); and were victims of the greatest halftime comeback and greatest third-quarter comeback in league history. And finally, as of 2015, Tampa Bay has won seventy-four fewer regular season games all-time than its sister franchise the Seattle Seahawks. (Although, to be fair, the teams' Super Bowl tally is 1-1).

Even by Buc standards, the thirteen seasons since the 2003 Super Bowl win can only be described as bad. Five head coaches, six offensive coordinators, six defensive coordinators, nine starting quarterbacks, and last-place NFC South finishes eight times. With a dismal 2-14 record in 2014, the franchise's fifth two-win record in forty years, the Bucs were once again the worst team in the league. But that's not all. As more than one observer has noted, the heirs of Malcolm Glazer, who own not only the Bucs, but also the English Premier League team Manchester United, have seemingly turned into Hugh Culverhouse, pocketing money from ticket and merchandise sales and TV contracts but refusing to invest in the team. In the five-year period from 2004 to 2008, the Glazers spent $449 million in player salaries, the absolute lowest figure of any team in the league.[1] And, in 2010, when the league's collective bargaining agreement temporarily expired, the Glazers used the opportunity to ignore what had been the payroll minimum, $112.1 million, to spend just $80.8 million.[2] For the year, the team spent $54.5 million less than the Super Bowl champion Packers.

Off the field, the news from Tampa Bay has been no less perverse: in 2013, the Bucs had a MRSA outbreak in the locker room, which, it is alleged, ended two players' careers, while a *Tampa Bay Times* investigation found that Aramark, the team's concessions vendor, paid a homeless shelter for laborers, but the laborers were never paid. (As one headline put it: "Buccaneers Employ Indentured Servants as Concessions Workers.")[3] In 2014, after a 20–3 home loss to Green Bay, seven fans were hospitalized following a lightning strike, and in 2015, cornerback C. J. Wilson was placed on the "reserved/retired" list after losing his index, middle, and ring fingers in a fireworks accident.[4]

With nineteen wins in the past four years—just two more wins than the team had in its first four years—the Bucs have come full circle. As Kenny Stein, a correspondent for *Bleacher Report*, put it, they've gone "from the Yucks to the Bucs and back again," with "back" being the operative word.[5] But here's the catch. Will there ever be another Yucks? Not just a bad Buccaneers team, but a team everyone, everywhere, even people outside of sports, just knows is bad? Probably not. Today, writers are quick to claim that this club or that club is a "national laughingstock," but who actually noticed in 2003, apart from baseball fans, when a brain-dead Detroit Tigers team went 43-119 to finish forty-nine games out of first place?

The fact is, few, if any, teams today are transcendently terrible; few capture the national consciousness or tickle the funny bone quite like the original Yucks. The only parallel, perhaps, is the 1962 New York Mets, the ill-fated National League expansion team that lost an astonishing 120 games, the most in pro baseball since 1899. Composed of castoff veterans and a gaggle of talentless rookies, the Mets were coached by Casey Stengel, a seven-time World Series winner with the Yankees, who had a McKay-like comicalness of his own. He even sounded like McKay. "The only thing worse than a Mets game," he once said, "is a Mets double-header." Or, my personal favorite, "Nobody knows this, but one of us has just been traded to Kansas City."[6] It seems apocryphal, but McKay *and* Stengel both supposedly uttered the funniest line in sports history, though there is no direct record of them saying it and no one knows if they did. It is as follows: "What did you think of your team's execution, Coach?" The answer: "I'm in favor of it."

In what was a career of quotes, McKay's execution quote was by far and away his most famous. He *may* have said it—it was first referenced in a November 1979 Cleveland *Plain Dealer* article in which Browns coach Sam Rutigliano "shared a story from the coaches' fraternity relating to John McKay, after his Tampa Bay Bucs lost a game recently"—but the details are vague.[7] Rutigliano didn't say which game (and it wasn't versus the Browns, who hadn't played the Bucs since 1976, when Rutigliano was a Saints coach), or when McKay had said it. The quote appeared again in October 1980 as a humorous snippet in the "Scorecard" section of *Sports Illustrated*, whose editor, Jerry Kirshenbaum, attributed it to a September 1980 home loss to Cleveland.[8] (A connection to the Rutigliano quote, maybe?) Yet no other journalist, not a Browns writer, nor a single one of the dozen or so Bay Area beat reporters who covered the Bucs at the time, ever mentioned it.

It showed up again in November 1980 in a John Clayton article in the *Pittsburgh Press*, and in November 1981 in a *San Diego Union* article by Barry Lorge, but both writers used "once, after a bad loss" phraseology and neither cited a date.[9] It didn't matter; by this point, McKay's execution quote was firmly ensconced in Buccaneers lore. For nearly four decades, it's been a regular feature in team retrospectives, where it's linked mostly to the 1976–77 Yucks. The funny thing is, the quip didn't originate with McKay, even if he had said it. It dates from an 1894 newspaper story in The Dalles, Oregon, referring to a young girl learning the piano, and once was a punch line in a 1936 stage performance by the Marx Brothers. In fact, the joke was so popular, and apparently so widespread, that when Groucho Marx asked the audience what it thought of his execution, a dozen people yelled: "We're in favor of it!"[10]

Quote or no quote, what is clear is that the 1976–77 Bucs, like the 1962 Mets, were the sports equivalent of Neville Longbottom, the sad sack character from the Harry Potter series, or, for older generations, Charlie Brown. Lovable losers. One would think that Americans despise losers. That's what General George S. Patton believed. But research suggests that for all other teams apart from the home team, Americans prefer losers; "not because we like backing losers," as one scholar put it, "but because we love to see losers beat the odds. It all has to do with an evolved trait: our sense of fairness."[11] So, if this is true, why then were the Yucks so lovable, while, say, the 2003 Detroit Tigers were not? Or, to put it another way, when the terribly inept Tigers lost, why didn't America care?

The answer, I believe, is twofold. First, in this day and age, due to free agency in all four major sports, not to mention longevity issues in football, teams can go from worst to first, or from worst to the playoffs, in a single year. From 2003 to 2014, for example, at least one NFL team finished last in its division, only to win that division the following season.[12] In fact, the 2006–07 Miami Dolphins lost seventeen straight, finishing 6-10 in 2006 and 1-15 in 2007, but added stars Chad Pennington at quarterback and Joey Porter at linebacker, among others, to finish the 2008 season at 11-5.

Second, and perhaps most important, in 1976 the average American household received, let's say, a dozen channels. Today that number is 189.[13] With Netflix, Amazon, and Hulu, plus movies and clips and shows direct from the Internet, there's simply too much to watch. Therefore, no single show, no program or entertainer can direct our attention to a bad sports team like Johnny Carson could with the Yucks. With more than five and a half million viewers a night, more than eight times the viewership, in recent years, of a 6 p.m. *SportsCenter*, Carson was the most popular man in television, bar none.[14] What he said at night was watercooler talk in the morning; when he laughed at something, America laughed, too. "Johnny's monologues were part of the *Zeitgeist*," wrote Carson biographer Laurence Leamer. "One day, social historians will turn to his quips and commentaries in trying to understand popular culture in the last third of the twentieth century."[15] So thanks, Johnny, wherever you are. Because of you, the Yucks weren't just bad, they were famously bad, the absolute worst team, ever, in America's most popular sport.

But—and this is a very big but—for current Buc fans, there's hope. In 2015, the team chose controversial Florida State quarterback Jameis Winston with the overall number-one pick in the draft. A 6'4", 227-pound behemoth with a rocket for an arm, Winston opened the season with a 42–14 home loss to the Tennessee Titans, whose own rookie quarterback, Marcus Mariota, had been passed over by the Bucs and drafted second. For a team that had lost all eight home games the previous year, it was a miserable performance, the franchise's worst opening-day outcome since 1996. "Part of you simply wants to throw up your hands and say, well, what else is new?" wrote

Tampa Bay Times columnist Tom Jones. "But another part of you demands answers. How can this happen? How can the Bucs be this bad?"[16]

But during week two in New Orleans, the team rebounded. In a surprising 26–19 upset of the Saints, Winston went 14 of 21 for 207 yards and a touchdown, while the Tampa Bay defense throttled Saints quarterback Drew Brees. With three victories in November, including an impressive 45–17 road victory over the Eagles, the heretofore atrocious Bucs were a respectable 6-6, Winston a surprise candidate for NFL Rookie of the Year. (Unfortunately, this was the high point of the Bucs season. The team would finish 6-10.) Although it's way too early to tell, for many Bucs fans, including team great Jimmie Giles, Winston is "Doug Williams reincarnated," that once-in-a-generation player who maybe, just maybe, will turn these current Yucks back into the Bucs.[17] We'll have to see.

Acknowledgments

As my first acknowledgment, I wish to clearly state that in spite of the book's title, I *love* the Bucs. In fact, I've loved the Bucs since 1982, when, as a nine-year-old resident of Punta Gorda, a town one hundred miles south of Tampa, I met Doug Williams, when he and several other Bucs came to our local high school to play a charity basketball game. I don't remember the contest, not even a second of it, but I vividly recall standing in front of Williams at a post-game autograph session. I walked up, handed him a 3" x 5" index card, and froze.

Sitting in front of me, on a folding chair, was (to my nine-year-old sensibilities) the "baddest" dude I had ever seen. He was like Superman, but cool. I was smitten. For the next year, I hoarded his football cards, and begged my mom for his poster, his collector's cup, and, of course, his jersey. I then began watching the Bucs religiously. By the time Williams, my hero, left Tampa Bay for the USFL, it was too late. I bled orange, several shades of an ugly, ugly orange.

"What? We finished 2-14? Who cares?! James Wilder is the best running back in the league! Just you wait! We're getting Steve Young! We're getting Bo and Vinny and Broderick Thomas and Keith McCants and Charles McRae and Eric Curry! Our kicker is Donald Igwebuike!" By the early 1990s, my love of the Bucs was so deep, and so visibly beyond reason, that I willingly chose Tampa Bay when my college bud-

Acknowledgments

dies and I each put $20 in a pot and played an entire season of the video game "Tecmo Super Bowl." (I finished in second, because Tecmo's designers, for some reason, gave catlike reflexes to a little-known Buc defensive back named Wayne Haddix. He was an interception machine.)

When, in the late 1990s, the Bucs "got good" with Warren Sapp and Derrick Brooks and a handful of other stars, I was absolutely thrilled, but still found myself inexplicably nostalgic for the old Bucs. Why? Who knows? But this book is for them, for the 0-26 expansion Bucs, for Doug Williams's Bucs, and for those Bucs of the '80s and '90s who suffered through fourteen losing seasons in a row.

Second, and perhaps most important, I wish to acknowledge all of the people and interviewees who made this book possible, from former players, coaches, and administrators to reporters, politicians, boosters, colleagues, friends and family members, agents and editors, professors and researchers, Florida historians, and fans.

They are as follows: Allan Leavitt, Bob and Terrie Alwood, Betty Castor, Bill Marcum, Bob Moore, Barry Smith, Bob Huckabee, Dan Ryczek, Glenna Hancock, Ken Herock, Leonard Levy, Pat Marcuccillo, Randy Hedberg, Steve Rosenbloom, Tom Bass, Curt Mosher, Dick Crippen, Dick Greco, Duane Bradford, Gary Mormino, Hubert Mizell, Hugh Culverhouse Jr., Bill Kollar, Charley Hannah, Dave Green, Council Rudolph, Dewey Selmon, Jack Gurney, Jack Harris, John Lopez, Lee McGriff, Tom Oxley, Pat Toomay, Robert Kerstein, Mary Anderson, Ron Martz, Sandra Freedman, Terry Hanratty, Mark Cotney, Mike Boryla, Thom Stork, Dan Rooney, Linda McEwen, Buddy Martin, John Rauch Jr., Dave Pear, Pete Johnson, Dave Hargitt, Paul

Acknowledgments

Stewart, Dana Nafziger, Brandi Winans, Steve Leeper, Rich Hill, Jayne Portnoy, Travis Puterbaugh, Farley Chase, Jofie Ferrari-Adler, Jack Scovil, Thomas LeBien, Alton Peacock, Stephen C. Mitchell, Tim Rozgonyi, Jeff Sotzing, Barry Popik, Ben Zimmer, Garson O'Toole, Robert Tout, Bob Fitzgerald, Angel Oliva II, Angel Oliva III, Bob Waldrop, Binky Waldrop, Kelly Oliva, Nancy Vuic, Kara Dixon Vuic, and my beautiful son, Asher.

Thank you.

Notes

Introduction

1 Transcripts of Johnny Carson jokes provided courtesy of Carson Entertainment Group.

2 "Sack Johnny," *St. Petersburg Times*, December 17, 1977.

3 Michael Katz, "Buccaneers (0-22) See Chance to Make 'History' against Giants," *New York Times*, November 13, 1977.

4 Jack Gurney, "Bucs' Fame Grows with Every Defeat," *Sarasota Herald-Tribune*, December 10, 1977.

5 Greg Bishop, "When the Bucs Went 0 for the Season," *New York Times*, December 2, 2007.

6 Bruce Lowitt, "Bucs a Threat, Claim Saints," *Anchorage Daily News*, December 10, 1977.

7 Ron Martz, "Well, Forget about Encouraging Words," *St. Petersburg Times*, December 13, 1977.

8 Ron Martz, "For Once, McKay Gets to Dissect the Other Guy," *St. Petersburg Times*, December 14, 1977.

9 Comments made by Crippen during the Tampa Bay History Center symposium "Tampa Sports Remembered," June 29, 2011.

10 From 1942 to 1945, it should be noted, the Chicago Cardinals lost twenty-nine games in a row. But, as the NFL sees it, the World War II–era Cardinals were actually two teams. In 1942, the Cardinals lost their last six games, then in 1943 went 0-10. However, in 1944, while hundreds of NFL players were in the military, the Cardinals merged for a season with the Pitts-

burgh Steelers. Known as "Card-Pitt," that team went 0-10, then in 1945, the reconstituted Cardinals lost three more. Therefore, the Cardinals lost nineteen in a row, Card-Pitt ten.

11 James Irwin, "Top 10: Memorable NFL Losing Streaks," *Washington Examiner*, September 27, 2009.

12 "Worst Shall Be First in Stupor Bowl," *USA Today*, January 22, 2009.

13 Mike Current, *Rememberin' Life in the Trenches* (Spearfish, ND: Rhino Holdings, 2000), n.p.

14 Fred Goodall, "Winless '76 Bucs Rooting for Dolphins to Pick Up Victory," *Ocala Star-Banner*, December 14, 2007.

15 For a collection of McKay quotes, see Chris Harry, Joey Johnston, and Richard McKay, *Tales from the Bucs Sideline: A Collection of the Greatest Bucs Stories Ever Told* (Champaign, IL: Sports Publishing, 2004), 89–91.

16 Jennifer Barrs, "He's Still Called Coach at 75," *Tampa Tribune*, January 31, 1999.

17 Will Grimsley, "McKay Sticking to Helm of Bucs' Ill-Fated Ship," *Ocala Star-Banner*, December 5, 1977.

18 Tom Archdeacon, "Commentary: Buccaneers an NFL Laughingstock No More," *Dayton Daily News* (OH), January 25, 2003.

19 Ira Kaufman, "Shades of '76," *Tampa Tribune*, November 22, 2008.

20 Fred Goodall, "Those 1976 Buccaneers Know All about Losing," *Coeur d'Alene Press* (ID), December 28, 2008; Fred Goodall, "'76 Bucs Relish Being Last Team to Finish Season without a Victory," Associated Press Newswires, December 13, 2007.

21 Brad Biggs, "Bucs Know It's No Laughing Matter," *Chicago Sun-Times*, January 25, 2003.

22 Doug Williams, *Quarterblack: Shattering the NFL Myth* (Chicago: Bonus Books, 1990), 101.

23 Joey Johnston, "Those Amazing Bucs," *St. Petersburg Times,* October 2, 1997.
24 Tom Zucco, "It's Time for a Change," *St. Petersburg Times,* January 11, 1992.
25 Joe Gibbs and Ken Abraham, *Racing to Win: Establish Your Game Plan for Success* (New York: Crown, 2009), 60.

Chapter 1: The Promoter(s)

1 In 1926, however, Red Grange and the Chicago Bears played an exhibition game in Tampa against a semipro squad known as the Tampa Cardinals. See Travis Puterbaugh, "Red Grange Busted in Temple Terrace, 1/3/26," *Tampa Sports History,* December 31, 2007, http://tampasportshistory.blogspot .com/2007_12_01_archive.html.
2 Bill Marcum, interview with author, January 4, 2011.
3 "Namath Hurls 60-Yard TD in Jet Win," *Los Angeles Times,* August 14, 1965.
4 Tom McEwen, "Construction of Bucs Began 30 Years Ago," *Tampa Tribune,* August 9, 1998.
5 According to the U.S. Census Bureau, the population of Baltimore in 1900 was 508,957.
6 Gary R. Mormino, *Land of Sunshine, State of Dreams: A Social History of Modern Florida* (Gainesville: University Press of Florida, 2005), 59–60.
7 David Colburn and Lance Smith, "A Florida Perspective on the 21st Century," *Gainesville Sun,* January 24, 1999.
8 Stanley K. Smith, "Florida Population Growth: Past, Present and Future," University of Florida Bureau of Economic and Business Research, June 2005, http://www.bebr.ufl.edu/files /FloridaPop2005_0.pdf.
9 "Hillsborough Growing, Tampa Population Off," *St. Peters-*

Notes

burg Times, June 18, 1970; Robert Kerstein, *Politics of Growth in Twentieth-Century Tampa* (Gainesville: University Press of Florida, 2001), 108–12.

10 Betty Castor, interview with author, January 8, 2014.

11 "Along the Way, More New Cities, Incredible Accomplishments," themacklecompany.com, http://www.themackle company.com/femjrstorypublic/18-deltona-alongtheway .htm.

12 "Pinellas Hit Hard by U.S. Defense Cuts," *St. Petersburg Times*, August 20, 1971; "Pinellas Is First," *Evening Independent* (FL), March 17, 1970.

13 Elizabeth Whitney, "Onecontinuouscity Seen for Suncoast by 2018," *St. Petersburg Times*, March 11, 1968.

14 Travis Puterbaugh, email correspondence with author, April 8, 2014.

15 Bill Marcum, interview with author, January 4, 2011.

16 John Garrett, "Suncoast Classic Coming Up," *Sarasota Herald-Tribune*, February 6, 1968.

17 Joe O'Neill, "The Life and Times of a Super Bowl Franchise," *Tampa Tribune*, January 26, 2003.

18 Aaron R. Fodiman and Martha Margolis, "More than a Legend: Tom McEwen," *Tampa Bay Magazine*, November/December 2000, p. 76.

19 David Harris, *The League: The Rise and Decline of the NFL* (New York: Bantam Books, 1986), 16.

20 "Each Club to Get $320,000 a Year," *New York Times*, January 11, 1962.

21 Harris, *The League*, 15.

22 Arthur Daley, "Still Up in the Air," *New York Times*, April 2, 1969.

23 Bill Marcum, interview with author, January 4, 2011.

24 Charles Maher, "Culverhouse Wanted Rams, Got Tampa

Bay," *Los Angeles Times*, November 6, 1977. Other sources claim Culverhouse offered $17 million, and not $17.5 million.

25 Michael Janofsky, "The Owner Who Brought a Big Bonus to Tampa," *New York Times*, January 15, 1984. Culverhouse filed the July 1972 suit in New York City, then filed a second suit in December 1972 in Los Angeles.

26 "Bucs' Owner Takes Pass on Retirement," *Chicago Tribune*, April 15, 1985.

27 "The Sporting Blood of Hugh Culverhouse Stirs Enduring Appetite for Competition," *American Banker*, February 5, 1985, p. 16.

28 Rick Stroud, "Hugh Franklin Culverhouse, 1919–1994," *St. Petersburg Times*, August 26, 1994.

29 Quoted in Harris, *The League*, 229.

30 Denis M. Crawford, *Hugh Culverhouse and the Tampa Bay Buccaneers: How a Skinflint Genius with a Losing Team Made the Modern NFL* (Jefferson, NC: McFarland Press, 2011), 20. For more on Culverhouse's two Rams-related cases, see Crawford, chapter 1, "You Just Bought Yourself a Lawsuit!," 15–27, and Patrick Zier and Bill Clark's two-part series, "Questions Surround Bucs Ownership: How Did Culverhouse Get the Team?" *The Ledger* (FL), February 1–2, 1976.

31 Bill Marcum, interview with author, January 4, 2011. The four-city meeting with Jim Kensil is detailed in Joe Marshall's "The NFL's Expansion Plan Is Zero Population Growth," *Sports Illustrated*, October 23, 1972, p. 83.

32 Leonard Levy, interview with author, December 12, 2011.

33 "NFL's Growth in '75 Seen," *New York Times*, November 25, 1973.

34 Tom McEwen, "Rozelle to Tampa: Welcome to the NFL," *Tampa Tribune*, April 25, 1974.

Notes

Chapter 2: The Suns of Beaches

1 Robert M. Collins, *Transforming America: Politics and Culture During the Reagan Years* (New York: Columbia University Press, 2013), 7.

2 Mary Campbell, "Led Zeppelin on $3-million Tour," *Rome Daily News* (GA), June 8, 1973.

3 "'Distressed' Tag Pinned on Bay Area," *St. Petersburg Times*, March 15, 1975.

4 Clayton Reed, "Tourism Brighter Despite 1974 Data," *St. Petersburg Times*, February 22, 1975.

5 "'Distressed' Tag Pinned on Bay Area."

6 Kevin Phillips and Albert E. Sindlinger, "Major Market Consumer Confidence," *Bryan Times* (OH), April 23, 1975.

7 "Is Tampa's Air Worst?" *Sarasota Herald-Tribune*, July 30, 1974.

8 Jim Curtis, "More Pollutants for Us to Breathe," *Sarasota Herald-Tribune*, December 12, 1976.

9 Thomas Becnel, "Where to Go, What to Do in Tampa During RNC," *Gainesville Sun*, August 24, 2012; Jim Curtis, "Radiation in Tampa River Linked with Mining Plant," *Sarasota Herald-Tribune*, December 14, 1982.

10 "What Happens If We Do Nothing," *St. Petersburg Times*, May 10, 1972.

11 "Red Tide and Pollution Killing Millions of Gulf Fish," *Sarasota Herald-Tribune*, July 29, 1971.

12 "Big League Opportunity," *St. Petersburg Times*, April 26, 1974.

13 Tom McEwen, "McCloskey Gets Franchise," *Tampa Tribune*, October 31, 1974.

14 David Harris, *The League: The Rise and Decline of the NFL* (New York: Bantam Books, 1986), 232.

Notes

15 Tom McEwen, "Breakfast Bonus," *Tampa Tribune*, December 7, 1974; Tom McEwen, "Brunch with Hugh a Classy Affair," *Tampa Tribune*, December 8, 1974.

16 Leonard Levy, interview with author, December 12, 2011.

17 Harris, *The League*, 232.

18 McEwen, "Brunch with Hugh a Classy Affair."

19 Tom McEwen, "Tampa's NFL Franchise: $4 Million Down," *Tampa Tribune*, December 8, 1974.

20 Ibid.

21 Alan Lassila, "Hicks Got Surprise Welcome to NFL Team's Committee," *Sarasota Herald-Tribune*, February 12, 1975.

22 Leonard Levy, interview with author, December 12, 2011.

23 Bill Marcum, interview with author, January 4, 2011.

24 Pete Dougherty, "Former Green Bay Packers GM Ron Wolf Learned About Scouting from Oakland Raiders Owner Al Davis," *Green Bay Press-Gazette*, October 11, 2011.

25 Peter Richmond, *Badasses: The Legend of Snake, Foo, Dr. Death, and John Madden's Oakland Raiders* (New York: Harper, 2010), 139–40.

26 Jack Gurney, "I Wish I Could Bring the Raiders—Wolf," *Sarasota Herald-Tribune*, May 1, 1975.

27 Ron Wolf and Paul Attner, *The Packer Way: Nine Stepping Stones to Building a Winning Organization* (New York: Macmillan, 1999), 10.

28 Tom Bass, interview with author, December 28, 2010.

29 Alvin Dominique, "NFL History: The Road to Free Agency," bleacherreport.com, April 17, 2008, http://bleacherreport.com/articles/18183-nfl-history-the-road-to-free-agency.

30 Gary Meyers, "Expansion Teams Start Slowly—Tough Times Ahead, but Cap, Free Agents Help," *Seattle Times*, August 6, 1995.

31 Tom Bass, interview with author, December 28, 2010.

32 Bob Ruf, "Bucs' Leroy [sic] Selmon: A Very Human No. 1, Million Dollar Baby," *Sarasota Herald-Tribune*, April 18, 1976.

33 Joe Henderson, "Selmon Product of Where He Came From," *Tampa Tribune*, September 11, 2011.

34 Hubert Mizell, "Bucs: Sympathy and Slim Pickings," *St. Petersburg Times*, November 7, 1975.

35 Statistics compiled by Tony Villiotti, "Let the Draft Holidays Begin," Post.com, April 29, 2015, http://www.nationalfootballpost.com/let-the-draft-holidays-begin/.

36 Mizell, "Bucs: Sympathy and Slim Pickings."

37 Hubert Mizell, "Culverhouse: I've Never Met Ara," *St. Petersburg Times*, January 2, 1975.

38 James J. Doyle, "Trojans Select Pro Assistant as Mentor," *Ellensburg Daily Record* (WA), November 11, 1975.

39 John McKay and Jim Parry, *McKay: A Coach's Story* (New York: Atheneum, 1974), 37.

40 Ibid., 74.

41 Chris Field, "No Surprises," AFAFalcons.com, December 17, 2002, http://airforce.scout.com/2/82496.html.

42 Jeff Prugh, "Coaches Laugh, Cry over Conflict in NCAA Rules," *Lewiston Morning Tribune* (ID), February 18, 1973.

43 Michael Bradley, *Big Games* (Dulles, VA: Potomac Books, 2006), 144.

44 Steven Travers, *The USC Trojans: College Football's All-Time Greatest Dynasty* (Lanham, MD: Taylor Trade, 2010), 64.

45 Dan Jenkins, "That's Not Thunder You Hear, It's USC," *Sports Illustrated*, November 27, 1972, p. 34; Joey Johnston, "McKay Left a Legacy of Success, Sarcasm," *Tampa Tribune*, June 16, 2010.

46 Jeff Prugh, "McKay Will Leave USC for Tampa Job," *Los Angeles Times*, October 31, 1975.

47 John Underwood, "Three Hour Difference," *Sports Illustrated*,

August 23, 1976, p. 17; Patrick Zier, "Bucs Return to the Business at Hand," *The Ledger* (FL), December 25, 1979.

48 "McKay to Pilot N.F.L.'s Tampa," *New York Times*, November 1, 1975.

49 John Smith, "Did You Hear the One About . . . ?" *Evening Independent* (FL), December 5, 1975.

50 Patrick Zier, "Tampa's Bucs Unveil McKay," *The Ledger* (FL), December 5, 1975.

51 Doug Doughty, "UVA Gave Shula a Start 50 Years Ago," *Roanoke Times*, February 19, 2008.

52 "Football Dropped at Tampa," *Milwaukee Journal*, February 28, 1975.

53 Joe Jares, "In a Kingdome by the Sea," *Sports Illustrated*, April 19, 1976, p. 85.

54 "Florida's Steve Spurrier Wins Heisman by a Landslide," *Spartanburg Herald* (SC), November 23, 1966.

55 Sheila Moran, "Spurrier Breaks In, Helps Upset Colts," *Tuscaloosa News* (AL), October 20, 1969.

56 Bill Chastain, *The Steve Spurrier Story: From Heisman to Head Ball Coach* (Lanham, MD: Taylor Trade, 2002), 86.

57 Patrick Zier, "Spurrier Home to Wear Buc Uniform," *The Ledger* (FL), April 6, 1976.

58 Tom Bass, interview with author, December 28, 2010.

59 "Swift Said He Is Retiring," *The Ledger* (FL), March 31, 1976.

60 "McKay Satisfied with Draft Picks," *Sarasota Herald-Tribune*, April 1, 1976.

61 Sam McManis, "Panthers, Jaguars Enjoy Success Right Away with Help from NFL," *Contra Costa Times* (CA), January 11, 1997.

62 Ken Herock, interview with author, January 12, 2012.

63 Jim Selman, "Bucs Complete Operation Success," *Tampa Tribune*, April 10, 1976.

Chapter 3: Ten Weeks of Two-a-Days

1 Pat Toomay, interview with author, January 11, 2011.

2 Barry Smith, interview with author, April 25, 2013.

3 Jim Brockman, "Bucs Get Upgrade to Luxury," *Bradenton Herald*, August 22, 2006.

4 Pat Marcuccillo, interview with author, December 20, 2010.

5 Tom Bass, interview with author, December 28, 2010.

6 Jim Selman, "Buc Trimming Task Sends Two Packing," *Tampa Tribune*, July 9, 1976.

7 Larry Guest, "Pro Football's Executioner," *Sentinel Star* (FL), September 3, 1976.

8 "Buccaneers Log," *Tampa Tribune*, July 10, 1976; "McKay Hopes Multiple Offense Confuses Foes," *Sarasota Journal*, July 14, 1976.

9 Tom McEwen, "When the Turk Knocks, It's Goodbye," *Tampa Tribune*, July 14, 1976; Guest, "Pro Football's Executioner."

10 John Meyer, "The Turk at Work," *Evening Independent* (FL), July 21, 1976.

11 McEwen, "When the Turk Knocks, It's Goodbye."

12 "McKay Calls Win 'Most Significant,'" *Spokesman-Review* (WA), September 25, 1979; "Better Players Needed Says Tampa's McKay," *Victoria Advocate* (TX), August 3, 1977.

13 Bob Huckabee, interview with author, December 29, 2010.

14 Pat Marcuccillo, interview with author, December 20, 2010.

15 Greg Hansen, "Seahawks, Bucs Built on Contrasts," *Evening Independent* (FL), October 15,1976.

16 "Tampa Swamped by Kickers," *Lewiston Morning Tribune* (ME), April 23, 1976.

17 "Tampa Bay Buccaneers Still in There Kicking," *Morning Record* (CT), April 23, 1976.

Notes

18 "Aging Kicking Specialist with Tampa," *Lodi News-Sentinel* (CA), May 28, 1976.

19 Jim Austin, "Kick," *Evening Independent* (FL), July 9, 1976.

20 Scott Fowler, "Bucs' Futility Record Hard to Match," *Charlotte Observer*, September 28,1995.

21 The number of Buccaneer players released in the preseason was tabulated from the "1976 Project" at Bucpower.com and from newspaper articles. See http://www.bucpower.com /76project-players.html.

22 Pat Toomay, interview with author, January 11, 2011.

23 Jack Gurney, "McKay Not Impressed with First Practice Session," *Sarasota Herald-Tribune*, July 7, 1976.

24 Mike Current, *Rememberin' Life in the Trenches* (Spearfish, SD: Rhino Holdings, 2000), n.p.

25 Jay Lawrence, "Bucs Guard Gordon Still Growing," *Sentinel Star* (FL), August 13, 1976.

26 David Whitley, "With Win, Bucs Can Exorcise Ghosts," *Orlando Sentinel*, January 19, 2003.

27 Bob Chick, "Ira," *Evening Independent* (FL), September 28, 1976.

28 Jim Selman, "Injuries No Joke to Hurting Bucs," *Tampa Tribune*, July 12, 1976.

29 Jack Gurney, "McKay Satisfied with Bucs' Scrimmage Showing," *Sarasota Herald-Tribune*, July 25, 1976.

30 "Rampaging Fans, Rain Shorten All-Star Game," *Register-Guard* (OR), July 24, 1976.

31 "Defense: Out with the Old, In with the New," *The Ledger* (FL), September 8, 1977.

32 Tom McEwen, "Abe at Peace after Long, Fulfilling Life," *Tampa Tribune*, September 24, 1997.

33 Jeff Pearlman, *Sweetness: The Enigmatic Life of Walter Payton* (New York: Gotham, 2011), 142.

Notes

34 Bob Markus, *I'll Play These* (Bloomington, IN: Xlibris, 2011), 138.

35 John Smith, "He Grins and Bears the Past," *Evening Independent* (FL), January 31, 1976.

36 Tom McEwen, "Honestly, Abe Causes Headaches," *Tampa Tribune*, July 7, 1976.

37 John Lopez, interview with author, January 24, 2011.

38 Rick Stroud, "Legends of Lee Roy," *St. Petersburg Times*, July 23, 1995.

39 Ron Martz, "Pear Gives Bucs a Big Lift," *St. Petersburg Times*, July 27, 1976.

40 Pat Yasinskas, "Pearadox: Free-spirited Family Man," *Tampa Tribune*, August 27, 1995.

41 Jack Harris, interview with author, January 20, 2011.

42 Dan Ryczek, interview with author, December 17, 2011.

43 Martz, "Pear Gives Bucs a Big Lift."

44 Jack Gurney, "Ferocious Pear Ripens as Team Leader," *Sarasota Herald-Tribune*, September 17, 1977.

45 Yasinskas, "Pearadox: Free-spirited Family Man."

46 Dave Newhouse, "Long Forgotten Raiders Coach Honored in Hall," *San Mateo County Times* (CA), August 14, 2004.

47 Alan Schmadtke, "The Worst Team Ever," *Orlando Sentinel*, January 21, 2003.

48 Joey Johnston, "Spurrier Laments Loss of 'Wonderful Friend' McEwen," *Tampa Tribune*, June 5, 2011.

49 Bill Chastain, *The Steve Spurrier Story* (Lanham, MD: Taylor Trade, 2002), 91.

50 Bill Marcum, email correspondence with author, June 12, 2012.

51 John Crittenden, "Throw to the Damned 'X,'" *Miami News*, April 20, 1977.

52 Chastain, *The Steve Spurrier Story*, 90.

Notes

53 Patrick Zier, "Offensive Tackle Reavis Retires," *The Ledger* (FL), August 3, 1982.

54 Dan Ryczek, interview with author, December 17, 2011.

55 Martin Fennelly, "We Can Now Laugh at the Dark Ages of the Bucs' Past," *Tampa Tribune*, January 23, 2000.

56 Ron Martz, "McKay: Injuries Won't Activate Panic Button," *St. Petersburg Times*, July 28, 1976.

57 Pat Toomay, "A Debilitating Case of Bucs Fever," ESPN Page 2, http://espn.go.com/page2/s/toomay/ 011227.html.

58 Tom Bass, interview with author, December 28, 2010.

59 Pat Marcuccillo, interview with author, December 20, 2010.

60 Bill Buchalter, "McKay Happy to Be Home . . . But Against the Rams?" *Sentinel Star* (FL), August 1, 1976.

61 Milt Gross, "Bills' Hero Half Irish, Half Jewish," *Miami News*, October 31, 1966.

62 "Go Down Kicking," *Pittsburg Post-Gazette*, January 28, 1991.

63 Frank Pupello, "Booth 'White Shoes' Lusteg," *Frank Pupello—21 Stinkin' Years*, July 20, 2010, http://go330mph .wordpress.com/2010/07/20/booth-white-shoes-lusteg/.

64 "The Locker Rooms," *Los Angeles Times*, August 1, 1976.

65 For video of McKay's sideline comments during the Los Angeles game, see "Films Encore: John McKay Wired," NFL .com, http://www.nfl.com/videos/tampa-bay-buccaneers /0ap2000000046822/Films-Encore-John-McKay-wired.

66 Hubert Mizell, "The 'Twix': NFL's Top Secret Lifeline," *St. Petersburg Times*, August 5, 1976.

67 John Meyer, "Emotion Plays for Bucs," *Evening Independent* (FL), August 16, 1976.

68 Leslie Timms, "A Very Low Point," *Spartanburg Herald* (SC), August 16, 1976.

69 Tom McEwen, "Could It Be a New McKay Dynasty?" *Tampa Tribune*, August 16, 1976.

Notes

70 Ibid.

71 Hubert Mizell, "Stadium Authority, Bucs Agree to Lease," *St. Petersburg Times*, April 18, 1975.

72 "Money: Pro Football's Real Muscle," *Florida Trend*, June 1976, p. 41.

73 Ken Blankenship, "Pelé, Griese, Back-to-back?" *St. Petersburg Times*, August 10, 1976.

74 "State Declares 'NFL Day' for Bucs Debut," *Tampa Tribune*, August 21, 1976; "Water Parade Precedes Buc-Dolphin Battle," *Tampa Tribune*, August 21, 1976.

75 Tom McEwen, "NFL's Top Crowd Cheered Our Bucs," *Tampa Tribune*, August 22, 1976.

76 John Crittenden, "Full Speed in Reverse," *Miami News*, August 23, 1976.

77 Alan Lassila, "Spirited Bucs Way Ahead of Schedule," *Sarasota Journal*, August 23, 1976.

78 Jerry Greene, "Give Bucs 'Moral Victory'; Dolphins Full of Praise," *Sentinel Star* (FL), August 22, 1976.

79 Don Pierson, "Bears Edge Tampa Bay," *Chicago Tribune*, August 29, 1976.

80 Hubert Mizell, "To Coach McKay: Let Fans Have Their Say," *St. Petersburg Times*, September 7, 1976.

81 Martin Fennelly, "Remember 'Tight Man,'" *Tampa Tribune*, December 18, 2007.

82 Bill Buchalter, "Go Gators: Reaves Starts vs. Spurrier," *Sentinel Star* (FL), September 3, 1976.

83 Ron Martz, "Often Wrong *Playboy* Puts Bucs at 2-12," *St. Petersburg Times*, July 13, 1976; Jim Selman, "Bucs' Slate: It Won't Be Any Picnic," *Tampa Tribune*, July 25, 1976.

Notes

Chapter 4: The Aft Deck of the *Lusitania*

1 Roger Kahn, "Aboard the *Lusitania* in Tampa Bay," *Time*, November 22, 1977, p. 55.

2 John Lopez, interview with author, January 24, 2011.

3 Bill Brubaker, "Honeymoon Ends Quickly for McKay in Tampa Bay," *Miami News*, July 26, 1977.

4 Hubert Mizell, "McKay Show a $60,000-a-Year Sideline," *St. Petersburg Times*, August 24, 1976; Ron Martz, "McKay's Half Hour: The Show That Refuses to Die," *St. Petersburg Times*, July 10, 1979.

5 Pete Johnson, interview with author, March 6, 2013.

6 Tim McDonald, "Portrait of McKay: Conflicting Emotions," *Evening Independent* (FL), November 6, 1984.

7 Jack Gurney, "We're Better—McKay," *Sarasota Herald-Tribune*, August 5, 1977.

8 Dave Green, interview with author, March 7, 2013.

9 Bud Crussell, "Gibron Asks for Time to Build Winner," *Ocala Star-Banner*, October 6, 1977.

10 Hubert Mizell, interview with author, January 13, 2011.

11 One version of the story, this one involving a three-year plan, appears in Alan Lassila, "McKay Tells Players to 'Keep the Faith,'" *Sarasota Journal*, September 21, 1976.

12 "McKay Not Worried About Job," *Ocala Star-Banner*, November 3, 1977.

13 Jennifer Barrs, "He's Still Called Coach at 75," *Tampa Tribune*, January 31, 1999.

14 Hugh Culverhouse Jr., interview with author, March 22, 2013.

15 Bill Marcum, interview with author, January 4, 2011.

16 Quote taken from the response section of the online arti-

cle "The Greatness of Hugh Culverhouse," joebucsfan.com, http://www.joebucsfan.com/?p=49765.

17 Ray Kennedy and Nancy Williamson, "Money: The Monster Threatening Sports," *Sports Illustrated*, July 17, 1978, p. 34; "Redskins in the Red," *Chicago Tribune*, September 24, 1976.

18 "Money: Pro Football's Real Muscle," *Florida Trend*, June 1976, p. 37.

19 Ray Kennedy and Nancy Williamson, "Who Makes What," *Sports Illustrated*, July 24, 1978, pp. 42–43; "Redskins Lead League in Payroll," *Observer-Reporter* (PA), November 18, 1977.

20 Hugh Culverhouse Jr., email correspondence with author, March 26, 2013.

21 "People Call Culverhouse a Pennypincher," *Sarasota Herald-Tribune*, July 23, 1977.

22 Bill Marcum, interview with author, January 4, 2011.

23 John Lopez, interview with author, January 24, 2011.

24 Tom Oxley, interview with author, January 8, 2011.

25 Ibid.; story also appeared in Mike Tierney, "A Golf Shot; an Injured Gull—a Happy Ending," *St. Petersburg Times*, May 28, 1977.

26 Bill Marcum, interview with author, January 4, 2011.

27 Hubert Mizell, interview with author, January 13, 2011.

28 Hugh Culverhouse Jr., interview with author, March 22, 2013.

29 Patrick Zier, "Being a Bucs Fan Makes It Easy for Culverhouse to Blackout Games," *The Ledger* (FL), December 2, 1979.

30 "TV Blackout Again Ruled Legal Ploy," *St. Petersburg Times*, December 24, 1972.

31 Ron Martz, "Sellout! Bucs Make TV," *St. Petersburg Times*, September 29, 1978.

32 Alan Lassila, "Team Offense Needs Maturity," *Sarasota Journal*, September 13, 1976.

33 Terry Hanratty, interview with author, April 3, 2013.

Notes

34 Alan Lassila, "Bay Bucs Debut Very Painful," *Sarasota Journal*, September 13, 1976.

35 Greg Hansen, "A Hang Dog Debut," *Evening Independent* (FL), September 13, 1976.

36 Dewey Selmon, interview with author, March 6, 2013.

37 Dave Green, interview with author, March 7, 2013.

38 Jack Gurney, "Oilers Ruin Bucs' NFL Debut 20–0," *Sarasota Herald-Tribune*, September 13, 1976; Lassila, "Team Offense Needs Maturity."

39 Ron Martz, "Gen McKay of the Bucs: We Shall Return," *St. Petersburg Times*, September 14, 1976.

40 Ray Holliman, "Bucs: The Trouble's in the Front Line," *St. Petersburg Times*, September 20, 1976.

41 Joe Valerino, "Bucs' Defense Impressive," *The Ledger* (FL), September 20, 1976; Jim Achenbach, "Chargers' Prothro Says Bucs Lack Offensive Speed," *Sarasota Herald-Tribune*, September 20, 1976.

42 Bill Buchalter, "McGriff, McKay: So Similar . . . Yet Different," *Sentinel Star* (FL), August 12, 1976.

43 Lee McGriff, interview with author, February 4, 2013.

44 Larry Guest, "No Elaboration Necessary About Tampa Non-Offense," *Sentinel Star* (FL), September 20, 1976.

45 Jack Harris, interview with author, January 20, 2011.

46 Ron Martz, "McKay Accentuates Positive (Such As It Is)," *St. Petersburg Times*, September 12, 1976; Patrick Zier, "Bucs' Line Woes Show in One Play," *The Ledger* (FL), September 21, 1976.

47 Tom McEwen, "The Juice," *Tampa Tribune*, September 24, 1976.

48 Dave Green, interview with author, March 7, 2013.

49 Patrick Zier, "Buccaneers Get Close but Stumble," *The Ledger* (FL), September 27, 1976.

Notes

50 Ron Martz, "Bucs Stop O.J., Bills Stop Bucs," *St. Petersburg Times*, September 27, 1976.

51 Ron Martz, "Baltimore Chops Up Bay Bucs," *St. Petersburg Times*, October 4, 1976.

52 Patrick Zier, "Lee Roy Anxious to Make Contact," *The Ledger* (FL), July 18, 1979; Alan Lassila, "Lee Roy an Impatient Spectator," *Sarasota Journal*, October 13, 1976.

53 "Injuries Have Hit Tampa Bay Hard," *The Ledger* (FL), October 5, 1976.

54 Pat Toomay, "A Debilitating Case of Bucs Fever," ESPN Page 2, http://espn.go.com/page2/s/toomay/ 011227.html.

55 John Lopez, interview with author, January 24, 2011.

56 Toomay, "A Debilitating Case of Bucs Fever."

57 Bob Huckabee, interview with author, December 29, 2010.

58 Hubert Mizell, interview with author, March 13, 2011.

59 John A. Rauch, email correspondence with author, June 19, 2012.

60 Barry Smith, interview with author, April 25, 2013.

61 Tom Bass, interview with author, December 28, 2010.

62 Gary Ledman, "Low Profiles, High Payoffs," *Evening Independent* (FL), July 24, 1979.

63 Tom Edrington, "McKay Says Bucs Ready for Seahawks Tomorrow," *Tampa Tribune*, October 16, 1976.

64 Tom McEwen, "Bucs vs. Seattle: Sometimes the Future Is Now," *Tampa Tribune*, October 17, 1976.

65 Tom McEwen, "Officials Left Fans on 'Hold,'" *Tampa Tribune*, October 18, 1976.

66 Ray Holliman, "Major Breakthrough for Curtis—and Seahawks," *St. Petersburg Times*, October 18, 1976.

67 Richard Lemanski, "Moore Cries Innocence on Holding Calls," *The Ledger* (FL), October 18, 1976.

Notes

68   "Who's That Booing Steve Spurrier?" *Miami News*, March 9, 1977.

69   Terry Hanratty, interview with author, April 1, 2013.

70   Tom Ford, "A Disgrace to All Dolphins," *Tampa Tribune*, October 25, 1976.

71   Patrick Zier, "Bucs Take Giant 'Step Backward,'" *The Ledger* (FL), November 1, 1976.

72   Hubert Mizell, "McKay: We're Working on 0-14," *St. Petersburg Times*, November 1, 1976.

73   Zier, "Bucs Take Giant 'Step Backward.'"

74   Gary Shelton, "From Ball Boy to West Coast Hero," *St. Petersburg Times*, January 29, 2006.

75   Mike Current, *Rememberin' Life in the Trenches* (Spearfish, SD: Rhino Holdings, 2000), n.p.

76   Guest did a two-part series on Tampa Bay's troubles. See Larry Guest, "Trouble on the Bay," *Sentinel Star* (FL), February 13, 1977, and "John Jr.'s Role Helped Destroy Buc Morale," *Sentinel Star* (FL), February 14, 1977.

77   Greg Hansen, "This Time Fans Aren't Idiots, Writers Are," *Evening Independent*, October 11, 1977.

78   Charley Hannah, interview with author, March 3, 1977.

79   Pat Marcuccillo, interview with author, December 20, 2010.

80   John Mossman, "Bucs' First Denver Trip Irked McKay," *Sarasota Herald-Tribune*, December 25, 1993.

81   Roger Kahn, "Aboard the *Lusitania* in Tampa Bay," *Time*, November 22, 1977, pp. 54–55.

82   "Pitt's Dorsett 'Incredible" Says Army Coach," *Observer-Reporter* (PA), October 20, 1975.

83   Dave Renbarger, "Ricky Bell Spurns Spotlight," *Michigan Daily*, December 12, 1976.

84   "Ricky a Bell Ringer for Southern Cal," *Tuscaloosa News* (AL), October 13, 1976.

Notes

85 Patrick Zier, "Dream Backfield," *The Ledger* (FL), January 1, 1982; Tom McEwen, "Bucs Want Bell, Not Dorsett Because . . ." *Tampa Tribune*, November 20, 1976.

86 Al Sokol, "Anthony Davis: Glamorous Life in Toronto Not So Glamorous," *The Ledger* (FL), November 5, 1976.

87 Ron Martz, "Bucs Land Davis for Next Season," *St. Petersburg Times*, November 17, 1976.

88 Bob Moore, interview with author, May 9, 2014.

89 Jack Gurney, "Bucs Just About Ready to Quit," *Sarasota Herald-Tribune*, December 15, 1976.

90 Jack Gurney, interview with author, March 11, 2013.

91 Bob Moore, interview with author, May 9, 2014.

92 "The List: Best NFL Defense of All-Time," ESPN.com, http://espn.go.com/page2/s/list/bestNFLdefense.html.

93 "Steelers Battle Friend and Root for Old Rival," *Miami News*, November 30, 1976.

94 Glenn Sheeley, "Terry Facing a Rat-a-Tat-Tat," *Pittsburgh Press*, November 28, 1976.

95 Glenn Sheeley, "Is the Rat Trapped Behind Offensive Line?" *Pittsburgh Press*, November 28, 1976.

96 Patrick Zier, "Bucs Are Massacred at Three Rivers," *The Ledger* (FL), December 6, 1976.

97 Patrick Zier, "Bucs' Jordan Remembers First Steeler Blitz," *The Ledger* (FL), November 7, 1980.

98 Rich Emert, "Don't Feel Sorry for Bucs; John McKay," *Beaver County Times* (PA), December 6, 1976.

99 Toomay, "A Debilitating Case of Bucs Fever."

100 Dave Green, interview with author, March 7, 2013.

Notes

Chapter 5: Go for O!

1 Thom Stork, interview with author, June 4, 2014.
2 Warren Sapp with David Fisher, *Sapp Attack: My Story* (New York: Thomas Dunne Books, 2012), 76.
3 "Press Release from the Office of Senator William Proxmire, 4 November 1977," Carnegie Mellon University Digital Collections, http://digitalcollections.library.cmu.edu/awweb/awarchive ?type=file&item=580408.
4 Jack Gurney, "Bucs Fame Grows with Every Defeat," *Sarasota Herald-Tribune*, December 10, 1977.
5 Jon Nordheimer, "Tampa Loves Its New Fame, If Not the Traffic," *New York Times*, November 13, 1976.
6 Paul Trigaux, "Tampa Bay's Identity Crisis: Maybe It's Time to Fix It," *St. Petersburg Times*, August 16, 2011.
7 Michael Sasso, "Leaders Work to Establish Bay Area's 'Brand' for RNC," *Tampa Tribune*, April 14, 2012.
8 "Readers' Interest Perked Up by Bucs, Gators, Seminoles," *Tampa Tribune*, December 10, 1977.
9 John Clancy, "The Losingest Team in Football," *Oui*, October 1977, p. 134.
10 Jack Harris, interview with author, May 1, 2014.
11 Sandra Freedman, interview with author, January 7, 2014.
12 Dick Greco, interview with author, January 7, 2014.
13 Pat Toomay, interview with author, January 11, 2011.
14 Pat Toomay, "From the Ridiculous to the Sublime," ESPN Page 2, http://espn.go.com/page2/s/toomay/020903.html.
15 Pat Toomay, interview with author, January 11, 2011.
16 Hubert Mizell, interview with author, March 13, 2011.
17 Dana Nafziger, interview with author, June 12, 2014.
18 "Carlton Will Be 'Restored,' 'Rejuvenated,'" *Boca Raton News*, August 9, 1977.

Notes

19 Greg Hansen, "I Was Out of Place," *Evening Independent* (FL), April 14, 1977.

20 Jim Joanos, "Remembering the 'Magic Dragon,'" nolefan.org, March 2006, http://www.nolefan.org/garnet/garnet46.html.

21 Tom Callahan, *The GM: A Football Life, a Final Season, and a Last Laugh* (New York: Random House, 2007), 221.

22 James R. King, "NFC's Boryla Unexpected Pro Bowl Hero," *Beaver County Times* (PA), January 27, 1976.

23 Jack Gurney, "Boryla Spurns 'Skins Offer," *Sarasota Herald-Tribune*, July 13, 1977.

24 Ron Martz, "As Expected, Bucs Tap Bell," *St. Petersburg Times*, May 4, 1977.

25 Hubert Mizell, "It's Somewhat Frightening Playing for an 0-14 Team," *St. Petersburg Times*, May 4, 1977.

26 Greg Hansen, "It's Ricky Bell All the Way," *Evening Independent* (FL), April 30, 1977.

27 Dan Ryczek, interview with author, December 17, 2011.

28 Patrick Zier, "Bucs' Line Lacks Unity, Says Winans," *The Ledger* (FL), November 29, 1977.

29 George Vecsey, "Tom Bass: Poet and Coach," *New York Times*, September 4, 1983.

30 Mike Tierney, "Bass Is Slowly Lifting Chargers from NFL's Cellar," *St. Petersburg Times*, January 15, 1983.

31 Jack Gurney, "Dewey Meets Challenge at New Position," *Sarasota Herald-Tribune*, August 3, 1977.

32 Tom Bass, interview with author, December 28, 2010.

33 Greg Hansen, "The Trojan Buccaneers," *Evening Independent* (FL), May 4, 1977.

34 Tom McEwen, "Johnson and His Big White Car," *Tampa Tribune*, August 27, 1977.

35 Tom Bass, interview with author, December 28, 2010.

Notes

36 Jim Selman, "Reynolds to Mongolia (Tampa) or Not?" *Tampa Tribune*, August 22, 1977.

37 Greg Hansen, "Lewis: Bucs' Hit Man," *Evening Independent* (FL), December 6, 1977.

38 Hubert Mizell, "The Randy Hedberg Story," *St. Petersburg Times*, September 16, 1977.

39 "Tampa Bay Bucs Have Last Laugh on Colts," *Daytona Beach Morning Journal*, September 12, 1977.

40 Tom McEwen, "Why Not?" *Tampa Tribune*, September 14, 1977; Ron Martz, "Bucs' Hedberg Becomes Sudden Hero," *St. Petersburg Times*, September 13, 1977.

41 Mizell, "The Randy Hedberg Story."

42 Alan Lassila, "Hedberg Says Own Errors Caused Bucs Poor Show," *Sarasota Journal*, September 19, 1977.

43 Mark Cotney, interview with author, June 15, 2014.

44 Hubert Mizell, "Bucs Offense: Sack but No Sock," *St. Petersburg Times*, October 10, 1977.

45 Zier, "Bucs' Line Lacks Unity, Says Winans."

46 "Tampa's McKay Is Frustrated," *Spartanburg Herald* (SC), October 12, 1977.

47 Mizell, "Bucs Offense: Sack but No Sock."

48 "Fan Suggests Classified Ad for Bucs," *Evening Independent* (FL), October 14, 1977.

49 "Ledger Readers Share Their Views on the Bucs," *The Ledger* (FL), December 25, 1977.

50 "Some Advice for the Bucs," *Evening Independent* (FL), November 11, 1977.

51 Alan Lassila, "Bucs Say Adios to A.D., Consider Grambling Quarterback," *Sarasota Journal*, May 1, 1978.

52 Patrick Zier, "Bucs' Bell Does It All Well," *The Ledger* (FL), October 23, 1978.

Notes

53 Alan Greenburg, "Bell Matures with Bucs," *Victoria Advocate* (Canada), January 4, 1980.

54 Glenna Hancock, interview with author, March 31, 2013.

55 Mike Current, *Rememberin' Life in the Trenches* (Spearfish, SD: Rhino Holdings, 2000), n.p.

56 Lee McGriff, interview with author, February 4, 2013.

57 Patrick Zier, "Like Him, Hate Him, He Remains McKay," *The Ledger* (FL), September 8, 1977.

58 Ron Martz, interview with author, March 9, 2013.

59 Mark Cotney, interview with author, June 15, 2014.

60 Charley Hannah, interview with author, March 3, 2013.

61 Tom McEwen, "Culverhouse Backs Wolf, McKay," *Tampa Tribune*, November 3, 1977.

62 "Culverhouse Boosts Ownership," *Daytona Beach Morning Journal*, January 4, 1979.

63 Pat Leisner, "Culverhouse: Buccaneer Owner Counselor to Corporation and McKay," *Morning Journal* (FL), December 31, 1981.

64 Ron Wolf and Paul Attner, *The Packer Way: Nine Stepping Stones to Building a Winning Organization* (New York: Macmillan, 1999), 10–11.

65 Glenna Hancock, interview with author, March 31, 2013.

66 Jack Gurney, "McKay, Wolf Expect to Stay, Defend Management of the Bucs," *Sarasota Herald-Tribune*, November 30, 1977.

67 Bill Brubaker, "Winless Tampa Bay Loses Another," *Miami News*, July 12, 1977.

68 Hubert Mizell, "An Afternoon Nap with the Zero Gang," *St. Petersburg Times*, November 28, 1977.

69 Ron Martz, "Bucs Reach New Low in 17–0 Loss," *St. Petersburg Times*, November 28, 1977.

70 Jack Gurney, "Bucs Continue to Skid 17–0," *Sarasota Herald-Tribune*, November 28, 1977.

Notes

71 Tim McDonald, "Portrait of McKay: Conflicting Emotions," *Evening Independent* (FL), November 6, 1984.

72 Tom McEwen, "The Invisible, Fickle Fan," *Tampa Tribune*, October 27, 1977.

73 Skip Bayless, "What's Really Going On in Tampa Bay?" *Los Angeles Times*, November 5, 1977.

74 Rick Abrams, "Musings on Absurdity: What If the Bucs Won?" *St. Petersburg Times*, November 16, 1977.

75 Jack Harris, interview with author, May 1, 2014.

76 Jack Gurney, interview with author, March 11, 2013.

77 Dave Green, interview with author, March 7, 2013.

78 Ron Martz, "Sluggish Bears Overcome Bucs 10–0," *St. Petersburg Times*, December 5, 1977.

79 Greg Hansen, "Bears Were Treated—to Bumps, Bruises," *Evening Independent* (FL), December 5, 1977.

80 Dewey Selmon, interview with author, March 6, 2013.

81 "Saints Wary of Bucs," *Ocala Star-Banner*, December 11, 1977.

82 "Tampa Bay at New Orleans," *The Ledger* (FL), December 10, 1977.

83 Hubert Mizell, "At Long Last, the Taste of Caviar," *St. Petersburg Times*, December 12, 1977.

84 Tom Bass, interview with author, December 28, 2010.

85 Jack Gurney, "Repercussions of Bucs' Win Are Widespread," *Sarasota Herald-Tribune*, December 13, 1977.

86 Ron Martz, "Bucs Halt Futile Odyssey 33–14," *St. Petersburg Times*, December 12, 1977.

87 Ron Martz, "Case for the Defense: 6 Steals, 3 TDs," *St. Petersburg Times*, December 12, 1977.

88 Patrick Zier, "Victory Provides Fun," *The Ledger* (FL), December 12, 1977.

89 Ibid.

90 "Buccaneers Humiliate Saints," *Ocala Star-Banner*, December 12, 1977; Martz, "Bucs Halt Futile Odyssey 33–14."

Notes

91 Jack Harris, interview with author, May 1, 2014.

92 "'Fandemonium' Reigns in Tampa," *Tampa Tribune*, December 12, 1977.

93 Pat Marcuccillo, interview with author, December 20, 2010.

94 Greg Hansen, "And Did They Celebrate," *Evening Independent* (FL), December 12, 1977.

95 "Hey, Hey, Hey, the Bucs Won," *Tampa Tribune*, December 13, 1977.

96 "The Bucs Won," *St. Petersburg Times*, December 13, 1977.

97 "Bucs Unify Us," *Evening Independent* (FL), December 20, 1977.

98 "Two for Tampa," *Daytona Beach Morning Journal*, December 19, 1977; Ron Martz, "Grand Finale: 17–7 Home Victory over Cards," *St. Petersburg Times*, September 19, 1977.

Chapter 6: We Is the Champions!

1 In 1968, the Oakland Raiders selected Tennessee A&I quarterback Eldridge Dickey in the first round of the combined NFL-AFL draft, but since the Raiders also chose Alabama quarterback Ken Stabler in the second round, it can be argued that Dickey had been drafted not as a quarterback but as an "athlete." Dickey was immediately converted to receiver and never played a down for the Raiders at quarterback.

2 For an impressively researched list of African-American quarterbacks who have played in the NFL, see Greg Howard, "The Big Book of Black Quarterbacks," Deadspin.com, http://deadspin.com/the-big-book-of-black-quarterbacks-1517763742.

3 Hubert Mizell, "Long-Awaited Day for Grambling," *St. Petersburg Times*, May 3, 1978.

4 Dan Sewell, "Growing Up: Williams Gives Tampa Bay a Leader," *Boca Raton News*, September 28, 1978.

230

Notes

5 Roger Mills, "Gruden Is Quick to Honor History," *St. Petersburg Times*, June 15, 2002.

6 Hubert Mizell, "Grambling Gun Drills Chiefs," *St. Petersburg Times*, October 9, 1978.

7 "Tampa Rioters Torch Spanish Area Homes," *Palm Beach Post*, June 13, 1967.

8 "Tampa's Lack of Negroes on Boards Criticized," *Sarasota Herald-Tribune*, March 3, 1968; Bill Heltzel, "Housing Discrimination: In This Area 'It's Significant Enough to Be Alarmed Over,'" *Evening Independent* (FL), July 24, 1979.

9 Sheila Mullane, "Sakkis Says Dixie Hollins Students to Behave or Else," *Evening Independent* (FL), March 6, 1976; "Florida Still Scarred by Klan's Burning Crosses," *Evening Independent* (FL), August 11, 1981.

10 Doug Williams with Bruce Hunter, *Quarterblack: Shattering the NFL Myth* (Chicago: Bonus Books, 1990), 94.

11 Dave Krieger, "Williams Still Remembers Where He's From," *Chicago Tribune*, September 2, 1978; Williams, *Quarterblack*, 93.

12 Williams, *Quarterblack*, 93.

13 Jack Gurney, "Bucs Have Edge in Fan Support Today," *Sarasota Herald-Tribune*, January 6, 1980.

14 Patrick Zier, "Giles Valuable Commodity for Bucs' Offense," *The Ledger* (FL), September 27, 1979.

15 "Offense: Improvement Is Essential," *The Ledger* (FL), September 7, 1978.

16 Patrick Zier, "Williams Difference for the Bucs," *The Ledger* (FL), October 9, 1978.

17 Jack Gurney, "Williams Passes and Runs Over Bears," *Sarasota Herald-Tribune*, October 23, 1978.

18 Stu Schneider, "In One Word, Bucs' Season Was Frustrating," *The Ledger* (FL), December 19, 1978.

Notes

19 Hubert Mizell, "Bucs Prove They're Real as Rain," *St. Petersburg Times*, September 24, 1979.

20 Ibid.

21 Harold Bubil, "Honest John Pulls No Punches," *Sarasota Journal*, November 28, 1979; Gary Ledman, "Blocked," *Evening Independent* (FL), November 26, 1979; Hubert Mizell, "McKay Hot, Pops Off, Cools, Apologizes," *St. Petersburg Times*, November 27, 1979.

22 Bob Graham, "Fans' Barbs Make McKay's Eyes Red," *Tampa Tribune*, November 26, 1979.

23 Bob Verdi, "Harried Bucs, Williams Try to Relax . . . Desperately," *Chicago Tribune*, December 13, 1979.

24 Tom McEwen, "The Buccaneers Are Chokeneers," *Tampa Tribune*, December 10, 1979.

25 "McKay Launches Tirade," *Victoria Advocate* (TX), December 12, 1979; Jack Gurney, "Williams Still McKay's Man," *Sarasota Herald-Tribune*, December 12, 1979.

26 Alan Lassila, "The Hole Gets Deeper," *Sarasota Journal*, December 10, 1979.

27 Jack Gurney, "Bucs Get Kick Out of First Title," *Sarasota Herald-Tribune*, December 17, 1979.

28 Bob Chick, "Giles Caught in Flood of Emotion," *Evening Independent* (FL), December 17, 1979.

29 Jack Gurney, "Bucs Dance to Division Title," *Sarasota Herald-Tribune*, December 17, 1979.

30 Byron Rosen, "NFL Union Tips Its Hat to Its Own at Banquet," *Washington Post*, April 20, 1980.

31 Lee McGriff, interview with author, February 4, 2013.

32 Joe Marshall, "Turnover in Tampa Bay," *Sports Illustrated*, January 7, 1980, p. 14.

33 Harold Bubil, "One Step Away . . . But Bucs Must Keep Their Intensity," *Sarasota Journal*, December 31, 1979.

34 Dan Reeves, "Buc Defense Played with Uncharacteristic Emotion," *The Ledger* (FL), December 30, 1979.

35 Michael Katz, "For Bucs, the Spread Is Not the Point," *New York Times*, January 4, 1980.

36 Michael Katz, "Bell Gains 142, Scores Twice," *New York Times*, December 30, 1979.

37 "Sports Interest Hostages," *Milwaukee Sentinel*, December 26, 1979.

38 Jack Gurney, "Bucs Have Rams Where They Want Them . . . at Home," *Sarasota Herald-Tribune*, December 31, 1979.

39 Thomas Boswell, "McKay Walking on Water," *Washington Post*, January 4, 1980; "Buc Mania Nearly Costs Lives," *Palm Beach Post*, January 3, 1980.

40 Donna Newsome, "They're Armed for the Long Wait," *Tampa Tribune*, January 1, 1980.

41 Jack Ellison, "Bucs' Fight Song Hits Top of Chart in Tampa Bay Area," *Tampa Tribune*, January 6, 1980.

42 Jim Beamguard, "Buccaneer Fever Sweeps Tampa Bay," *Tampa Tribune*, January 6, 1980.

43 Joey Johnston, "Those Amazing Bucs," *St. Petersburg Times*, October 2, 1997.

44 Dave Kindred, "Williams Watches Disintegration from Sideline," *Washington Post*, January 7, 1980.

45 John Crittenden, "Rams Make Buccaneers True Believers," *Miami News*, January 7, 1980.

46 Mark Goodman, "Tampa's John McKay: Behind Football's Biggest Turnaround," *Rome News-Tribune* (GA), September 7, 1980.

47 Jerry Greene, "Former Buc Ricky Bell Dies," *The Ledger* (FL), November 29, 1984.

48 Jeff Pearlman, "Two Carries, Six Yards," sbnation.com, August 20, 2013, http://www.sbnation.com/longform/2013

/8/20/4636066/ricky-bell-profile-san-diego-chargers-tampa
-bay-buccaneers.

49 Chris Dufresne, "The Last Days of Ricky Bell," *Los Angeles Times*, March 4, 1985.

50 "Ricky Bell Dies of Cardiac Arrest at Age 29," *Pittsburgh Post-Gazette*, November 29, 1984.

51 Joey Johnston, "A Lasting Legacy," *Tampa Tribune*, November 26, 2004.

52 Ibid.

53 Tom McDonald, "Emergence of New Weapons May Take Pressure off Williams," *Evening Independent* (FL), September 3, 1982.

54 Williams, *Quarterblack*, 107; Doug Lasswell, "Bucs Playing Waiting Game with Williams," *Sarasota Herald-Tribune*, July 16, 1983.

55 Mike Flanagan, "Doug Made Choice Between Future, Fame," *Evening Independent* (FL), February 11, 1984.

56 Mike Thomas, "Passing the Bucs," *Orlando Sentinel*, December 31, 1995.

57 "Payton Provides Spark as Bears Handle Bucs," *Schenectady Gazette* (NY), November 10, 1986.

58 Patrick Zier, "Buccaneers Are Also Losing at Turnstiles," *The Ledger* (FL), December 26, 1985.

59 Paul D. Staudohar, *Playing for Dollars: Labor Relations and the Sports Business* (Ithaca, NY: Cornell University Press, 1996), 59.

60 Patrick Zier, "Owners Appear to Be Holding All the Cards," *Herald-Journal* (SC), September 27, 1987.

61 "Bucs' Bucks," *The Ledger* (FL), July 9, 1992.

62 Michael Janofsky, "Rookies Get Less in NFL Cost Cuts," *New York Times*, September 18, 1985.

63 Charley Hannah, interview with author, March 3, 2013.

64 Patrick Zier, "Tampa Bay Buccaneers Showing Signs of Confusion," *The Ledger* (FL), April 17, 1977.

65 Don Banks, "The Most Botched NFL Draft Pick Ever," *Sports Illustrated*, n.d., http://www.si.com/longform/nfl-draft-82/index.html.

66 Greg Hansen, "McKay Says He Had No Part in Wolf's Leaving," *Evening Independent* (FL), February 22, 1978.

67 Patrick Zier, "Culverhouse Doing Things Backwards," *The Ledger* (FL), January 3, 1992.

68 Mike Bianchi, "Bucs: No Bargains in This Basement," *Gainesville Sun*, September 18, 1991.

69 Peter King, "Terrible Tampa Bay," *Sports Illustrated*, September 27, 1993, p. 48.

70 Jerry Greene, "Farrell's Revelation: I Want Out of Tampa Bay," *Orlando Sentinel*, December 3, 1986.

71 Charlie Denn, "Tampa Bay Makes Right Moves to End History of NFL Futility," *Daily Press* (VA), October 19, 1989.

72 Tim Leone, "Williams' Return Exorcises Ghosts of the Past," *Sarasota Herald-Tribune*, September 7, 1992.

73 "Bucs Stay in Tampa with Big Price Tag," *Milwaukee Journal*, January 17, 1995.

74 Ira Kaufman, "First Bucs Coach McKay Dies, 1923–2001," *Tampa Tribune*, June 11, 2001.

75 Frank Litsky, "NFL Expansion Surprise: Jacksonville Jaguars," *New York Times*, December 1, 1993.

76 "Jaguars, Panthers Will Get Extra Picks," *Gainesville Sun*, September 29, 1994.

77 "NFL Salary Cap Increased by $2.5 Million," *Philadelphia Inquirer*, March 23, 1995.

78 Paul Domowitch, "They May Walk Before They Crawl," *Daily News* (PA), January 28, 1995.

79 Don Pierson, "Oh, for a Winner," *Chicago Tribune*, October 5,

1995; Vito Stellino, "Breaking the Mold," *Baltimore Sun*, January 10, 1997.

80 John Romano, "Timing Is Everything," *St. Petersburg Times*, December 20, 1996.

81 John Helyar, "Free Agency Scores for Jags, Panthers," *Globe and Mail* (Canada), January 10, 1997.

82 Romano, "Timing Is Everything"; Matthew Kredell, "McKay Finds the Way for Tampa Bay," *Inland Valley Daily Bulletin* (CA), January 24, 2003.

83 Gary Shelton, "Hoisting New Colors," *St. Petersburg Times*, April 10, 1997.

84 Tom Balog, "Dungy Bids Farewell," *Sarasota Herald-Tribune*, January 16, 2002.

85 David Whitley, "Mega-bucs!" *Orlando Sentinel*, January 27, 2003.

86 Bruce Lowitt, "Culverhouse Gift Is Payback for the Past," *St. Petersburg Times*, April 20, 2002.

87 Jeff Testerman, "Finally, Absolution Comes to a Tearful Culverhouse Heir," *St. Petersburg Times*, April 20, 2002.

Epilogue: From the Yucks to the Bucs and Back Again . . .

1 Jason La Canfora, "Moneyball, NFL Style," NFL.com, June 26, 2009, http://blogs.nfl.com/2009/06/26/moneyball-nfl-style/.

2 Gregg Rosenthal, "Team-by-Team Salary Cap Numbers, If There Were a Salary Cap," profootballtalk.nbcsports.com, http://profootballtalk.nbcsports.com/2010/09/19/team-by-team-salary-cap-numbers-if-there-were-a-salary-cap/.

3 Rick Stroud, "Pain Is His Constant Companion," *Tampa Bay Times*, April 8, 2015; Will Hobson, "Strings Attached," *Tampa Bay Times*, November 30, 2014; Timothy Burke, "Report: Buc-

caneers Employ Indentured Servants as Concessions Workers," Deadspin.com, November 30, 2014, http://deadspin
.com/report-buccaneers-employ-indentured-servants-as
-conces-1664733321.

4 Howard Altman and Joey Johnson, "Lightning Strike Injures
at Least 7," *Tampa Tribune*, December 22, 2014; Fred Goodall, "Bucs' C. J. Wilson Placed on Reserved/Retired List," *Fair-
mont Bugle* (NC), July 25, 2015.

5 Kenny Stein, "From the Yucks to the Bucs and Back Again:
How Tampa Bay Lost Its Way," bleacherreport.com, October
28, 2009, http://bleacherreport.com/articles/280301-from-
the-yucks-to-the-bucs-and-back-again-how-tampa-bay-lost
-its-way.

6 Wayne Stewart and Roger Kahn, *The Gigantic Book of Baseball
Quotations* (New York: Skyhorse, 2007), 72, 433.

7 Russell Schneider, "Browns Notes," *Plain Dealer* (OH), November 22, 1979.

8 Jerry Kirshenbaum, ed., "Scorecard," *Sports Illustrated*, October 13, 1980, p. 32.

9 John Clayton, "Tampa's McKay Never at a Loss for Words,"
Pittsburg Press, November 5, 1980; Barry Lorge, "Music Re-
veals Chargers' Malaise," *San Diego Union*, November 9, 1981.

10 "Half-Holiday," *Daily Chronicle* (OR), October 4, 1894; Hub-
bard Keavy, "Hollywood Chatter," *Daily Illinois State Journal*,
January 31, 1936. The author wishes to thank the talented
linguists Barry Popik, Ben Zimmer, and Garson O'Toole for
their help in learning the origins of the execution quote.
See Barry Popik's blogpost entry, "What do you think of the
musician's execution?"/"I'm in favor of it," barrypopik.com,
September 3, 2015, http://www.barrypopik.com/index.php
/new_york_city/entry/what_do_you_think_of_the_musicians
_execution_im_in_favor_of_it/.

Notes

11 Carian Thus, "Why We Love When Losers Win and Heroes Fail," unitedacademics.com, January 28, 2013, http://www .united-academics.org/magazine/underdog/the-paradox -explained-why-we-love-when-losers-win-and-heroes-fall/.

12 Ken Pomponio, "Any Given Season: Parity Alive and Well in the NFL," TheSportsPost.com, July 23, 2014, http://thesportspost .com/nfl-parity-super-bowl-championships/.

13 Elliot Hannon, "You, Average American Viewer, Have 189 TV Channels. Here's How Many You Actually Watch," Slate .com, May 6, 2014, http://www.slate.com/blogs/the_slatest /2014/05/06/nielsen_survey_finds_record_number_of_tv _channels_but_we_re_not_watching.html.

14 "Carson Signs New Contract" *Dispatch* (NC), March 29, 1974; Matt Yoder, "A Closer Look at ESPN's Ratings," awfulannouncing.com, July 24, 2013, http://awfulannouncing .com/2013/a-closer-look-at-espn-s-ratings.html.

15 Laurence Leamer, *King of the Night: The Life of Johnny Carson* (New York: HarperCollins, 2001), 15.

16 Tom Jones, "Unacceptable Bucs Loss Raises Doubts About Leadership," *Tampa Bay Times*, September 13, 2015.

17 Greg Auman, "Giles Sees Much of Doug Williams in Jameis Winston," *Tampa Bay Times*, May 13, 2015.

About the Author

Jason Vuic is the author of *The Yugo: The Rise and Fall of the Worst Car in History* and *The Sarajevo Olympics: A History of the 1984 Winter Games*. He has appeared on NPR's *Weekend Edition* and APM's *Marketplace*, on *Fox and Friends in the Morning*, on CBC's *The Current*, and on C-SPAN's *Book TV*. Raised in Punta Gorda, Florida, he lives in Fort Worth, Texas.

Visit www.jasonvuic.com.